What Could Possibly GO WRONG?

Also by Leland E. Burch
Greer, SC – *The Center of the Universe*

What Could Possibly GO WRONG?

by Leland E Burch

ISBN-10: 1499655541
ISBN-13: 9781499655544

Library of Congress Control Number: 2014909790
CreateSpace Independent Publishing Platform
North Charleston, South Carolina

Dedication

Margaret Griffin Burch

This collection of "Off the Record" columns is dedicated to my wife, Margaret Griffin Burch, without whom my career as Editor of *The Greer Citizen* would not have been possible.

I owe my wife everything, especially for her unflinching courage in the face of many adversities, for her support and encouragement in my life's calling, and for "turning the other cheek" when I frequently poked fun at her in these columns.

While I was putting in 50 to 60-hour work weeks that routinely included at least three nights at the office, Margaret was at home doing most of the raising of our four sons. In addition to those responsibilities, she taught music to help supplement our income. But that's not all.

When it became obvious that one of our sons, who had been diagnosed with a learning disability, was not receiving an adequate education in public schools, my wife took up his cause. She eventually sought the help of Congressman Carroll Campbell who suggested that the best way to ensure that children received adequate educational opportunities was to serve on the school board. Margaret took that advice to heart and ran for the District 18 school board seat, which she won in a spirited campaign in 1982. During her 20 years of service on the school board, Margaret became the first female chairman of the board. She overcame much opposition and adversity to obtain several new school facilities for our community including Greer High, Greer Middle, Chandler Creek Elementary and Woodland Elementary.

Even today, my wife remains an ardent supporter of public education. Margaret played a key role in the establishment of the Greater Greer Education Foundation that raises funds for scholarships and local classroom grants. She has served as chairman of the board since the beginning in 2008.

Acknowledgements

This book would not be possible without the assistance and encouragement of numerous individuals.

I want to express deep appreciation to my brother, Walter M. Burch, who labored for many years as General Manager of *The Greer Citizen*. He helped the newspaper succeed financially, and that, in turn, provided a platform for my Off the Record columns that compose this book.

I am also indebted to Julie H. Holcombe and Gloria Fair for retyping numerous columns that were written before the era of backing up our daily work on discs. Their efforts not only saved me untold hours slaving over the keyboard, but also ferreted out numerous spelling and grammatical errors that tend to creep into my texts.

Speaking of errors popping up, I am extremely grateful to Bobbi Burns and Marilyn Hendrix for proof reading the book. Their efforts made it respectable.

Award-winning photographer Eddie Burch made several of the photos that appear in the book and the cover.

The late Suzanne Greene provided the hand-drawn illustrations featured in the book. A renowned Greer artist, Greene was a constant encourager and an inspiration that spurred me on to complete this book, the second in a series of three.

Finally, I greatly appreciate the technical information and invaluable advice given by two acclaimed authors with Greer roots, Bill Piergiovanni and Mickey Beckham.

Table of Contents

What Could Possibly Go Wrong?
Life of the Party – Jan. 7, 1987 1
The Pause that Refreshes – Feb. 17, 1999 4
The Flight from Hell – Mar. 26, 2008 7
Coming Home to Roost – May 28, 2003 10
Another Big, Bad Idea – Oct. 20, 2004 12
I'm Thankful It Wasn't Any Worse – Nov. 10, 2005 15
Death by Gillette – Mar. 19, 2003 18
The Party Animal – Apr. 7, 2004 20
She Has Bad Luck Every Day – Apr. 11, 1993 22

Life Is Like That
Modern Inventions Confusing – Sept. 18, 2002 25
Mothers Teach Us a Lot – May 9, 2001 28
Never Admit Anything – Aug. 29, 2001 30

Headline News
WWJD Question Goes Unanswered – Mar. 5, 2003 33
Barbershop Sign Missing – March, 2014 36
Playboy Controversy Ripe for County Council – Apr. 2, 1997 39
The Color of the Day – July 31, 2002 41
Be Prepared – Feb. 26, 2003 43
I'd Make Sure the South Wins Next Time – Apr. 19, 2011 ... 46
Dear Shannon: The Citadel Needs You More – May 10, 1995 49

Cell Phones
I Still Can't Hear You – Feb. 9, 2005 51
The Passing of an Old Friend – May 21, 2009 54
Can You Hear Me Now? – Jan. 20, 2010 57

Let's Go Out to Eat

The Wreck of the Burch Bank Account – Aug. 4, 1993 61

Catch of the Day – July 6, 1994 64

A Microwave for Your Head – Feb. 12, 1997 66

Half Baked – Aug. 17, 2005 68

Lard of the Month

Lard of the Month – Nov. 28, 2006 71

New Diet Has Me Pumped – Feb. 18, 2004 74

The Trans Fats Police – Jan. 17, 2007 77

Dinner Table Etiquette

The Chicken and Peas Circuit – Mar. 24, 2004 79

Cafeteria Ed – Oct. 14, 1987 81

The Inlaws

The Five-hour Birthday Party – Jan. 29, 1997 83

Nuptials in Never Never Land – Oct. 19, 2005 86

Mr. Nobody, George Camp – Nov. 11, 2009 88

The Frozen Chosen

Que Sera, Sera – June 1, 2005 91

The Spiritual Gift – Nov. 19, 2003 94

Making Someone Happy – Nov. 4, 1987 96

The Invincible Wayne Cole – Nov. 4, 2009 98

Keys to the Kingdom – Aug. 16, 1989 101

The New Preacher Showed Up – Sept. 11, 1996 103

Keys to the Kingdom II – Mar. 12, 2003 105

Providentially Hindered – Jan. 8, 1997 108

Everyone May Live Happily Ever After – Mar. 5, 2008 110

The Downside of Home Ownership

Showerhead from Hell – Apr. 13, 2005 113

We May Knock Out the Walls – Mar. 10, 1993 115

Customer Non-Service – Sept. 27, 2006 117

The Night Visitor – Jan. 13, 1993 120

Newspaper Publishing

Management Is Not My Strong Suit – Sept, 22, 1999 123

The Cure for Insomnia – Aug. 31, 1998 126

Repetitive Motion Threat – Apr. 14, 1999 128

One Wild Ride – Dec. 16, 1987 130

We Need Truth in Absenteeism – Feb. 15, 1995 132

The Sky Is Falling – Oct. 29, 2003 134

Out of the Twilight Zone – Nov. 15, 2006 137

What Is an Editor Emeritus Anyway? – July 2, 2008 140

The Good Old Days

Remember the Good Old Days? – July 19, 1992 143

Why Is That?

More Smug Than Ever – Jan. 15, 2011 147

Put Your Congressman to Work – Mar. 5, 2005 150

Compulsive Hoarding – Apr. 14, 2010 153

Old Hackers

Beach Bloomers Blunder – Apr. 18, 2007 157

Old Grump, Times Four – Mar. 19, 2009 160

Going and Going – Apr. 19, 2006 164

Hot Wheels

You Never Forget Your First Car 167

Get That License – Oct. 18, 1989 170

Red Neck Test Driver – Dec. 15, 1999 172

Better Than a Yugo – June 6, 1990 175

An Adventure in Motoring – May 29, 1991 177

Curmudgeon in a Ragtop – Nov. 13, 2002... 180

Bargain Hunting
Mall Shoppers Similar to Marines – Dec. 16, 1992............................. 183
Bigger Than a Bread Box – Nov. 17, 2010... 185
Learn Your Vegetables – June 9, 1993... 188
New Expert on Women's Clothing – Mar. 31, 2004............................. 190
Shoppers Anonymous – Nov. 30, 1994.. 193
Geezer Super Heroes – Jan. 10, 2007 195
Lurching Toward Christmas – Dec. 11, 2008...................................... 198

Living Healthy
The Health Test – Apr. 15, 1989... 201
Clinton Has Lost the Red Neck Vote – Aug. 16, 1995........................ 203
Getting Fit – June 15, 2009... 205
Shaping Up – Jan. 9, 2008 208

Let Me Show You My Scar
Broken Back – Feb. 10, 2012 211
I Can Top That – Feb. 17, 2012 214
There's No Place to Sit in Chair Yoga – March, 2012......................... 216
Answered Prayers – June 23, 2010.. 218
New Year's Diet Lasted Only One Day – Jan. 10, 2001....................... 221
Stamping Out Foot Disease – Sept. 25, 2008...................................... 223
The Killer Toe – Aug. 28, 1996 226

Headed to Surgery
The Eyelid Opener – May 14, 2014.. 229
The Atomic Appendix – Dec. 4, 1996... 233
Another Form of Terrorism – Nov. 14, 2001 235
Your Call Is Important to us – Feb. 20, 2008.. 238

What's Wrong With Our Schools

    School Requires a Big Load – Aug. 7, 2002 241

    What's Wrong with Our Schools – Sept. 20, 1995 245

    Grading Our Schools – Nov. 12, 2003 247

    The Parents Entrance Exam – Aug. 20, 1991 249

    Homework for Parents – Feb. 18, 1987 252

On the Horn

    Answering Machine Speaking – Oct. 15, 1997 255

    It's Here Again – The Phone Book – Oct. 8, 1997 258

Costly Excursions

    Remind Me Not to Go Skiing Again – Jan. 3, 2003 261

    Travel Series Cancelled – July 11, 2007 264

    Fasten Your Seat Belts – Dec. 5, 2001 267

The Joys of Time Sharing

    Locked Out (part 1) – Apr. 17, 2008 271

    Locked Out (part 2) – Spr. 24, 2008 274

    Mr. Home Handyman – Nov. 18, 2009 276

Long Waits Always

    The DMV – Where Time Stands Still 279

    Old Folks Don't Have Time to Wait – Nov. 15, 1995 282

    Always Long Waits, Always 284

The Sporting Life

    How Do You Shoot a Fish? – Sept. 21, 1994 287

    Wake Me Up When It's Over – June 30, 2010 289

    Cured of Braves Fever – May 13, 1992 291

    Blimps Deserve Equal Time – Sept. 13, 1989 293

The Easter Bunny

    What I Like About Easter Is…– Mar. 31, 1999 295

    The Easter Bunny – Apr. 14, 2004 297

Happy New Year

    The Year of the Oops! – Dec. 29, 2010.. 301

    Better Resolutions – Jan. 2, 2002 304

Foreword

What Could Possibly Go Wrong? Nearly anything as it turns out—because truth is really stranger than fiction. This is a collection of humorous but true "Off the Record" columns that I wrote over a period of 26 years when I was Editor of *The Greer Citizen* newspaper. When life handed me lemons, I made lemonade by writing about them.

My father, the late Edd A. Burch, originated "Off the Record" in 1936 when he became Editor of *The Dalton* (GA) *Citizen*. His columns focused on local people, community activities, occasional reminisces of growing up on the farm, and with many jokes mixed in to give readers smiles. After purchasing *The Greer Citizen* in 1942, he continued writing the column until his death in 1985.

That's when I stepped up to write the column. I soon learned that readers enjoyed humor that I would inject, and my version of "Off the Record" took off in that direction. The great majority of my columns were aimed at drawing laughs to brighten readers' days, so I was always on the lookout for humorous incidents that occurred in the lives of acquaintances and especially my family. I suppose that I succeeded, at least in a small way, because the columns won numerous awards in S.C. Press Association competitions over the years.

Many readers encouraged me to publish these columns in a book. As it turned out, I have a series of three books because there are too many columns that I considered "fit to reprint" to be contained a single volume. I hope you enjoy them.

What Could Possibly Go Wrong?

Life of the Party--Jan. 7, 1987

There's nothing like a little excitement to liven up a party. Learning that lesson the hard way during the holiday season has greatly expanded my horizons. Now I am in great demand as a partygoer who can instantly change a dreary gathering into an awesome and memorable experience.

My life changed completely the night I arrived at the home of Greenville County School District Superintendent Dr. Roy Truby, looking forward to a sumptuous Yuletide buffet. Once inside, I made the mistake of sticking close to Joe Dill. We stood in a corner, keeping our distance from Greenville's society leaders for fear of exposing ourselves as a couple of red necks. Besides, I figured Dill was the only other person at the party who spoke the same language, Greereze.

I was uncertain about the variety of strange looking food choices since there were no hot dogs, burgers or French fries on the buffet table. But I noted that Dill's heaping plate appeared to contain a large sample of everything on the spread.

"I recently went off my diet," Dill explained between mouthfuls. Then he motioned me to come over behind his easy chair. Raising his plate for illumination from the light of a nearby lamp, Dill began pointing out various layers in his mountain of delicacies. "Now this is chicken, I'm pretty sure, even though it doesn't look like chicken" he was saying, while spearing a cream-covered object with his fork. "There's really no way to disguise chicken....hummmm......I smell something burning," Dill noted between munches.

"Surely it's not burned," I responded.

"No, I mean something's on fire!" Dill said, raising his voice.

"You're right, Joe! It's me!" I yelped, suddenly sensing an extremely hot spot in the middle of my back. Yes, I was in flames, right there in the home of the Superintendent and surrounded by dozens of dignitaries.

Like all Georgia crackers do, I apparently had backed up to the flames to feel the warmth. This flame happened to be a bookshelf candle that I had failed to notice, and it had burned a softball-size hole in the back of my brand new suit coat.

Dill said he was considering throwing me down and rolling me up in the rug to extinguish the flames, but to do that, he would have had to put down his plate. While Dill was mulling what action to take, I managed to extinguish the blaze myself by wiggling out of the blazing coat and stomping out the flames with no additional harm other than a red face.

The fun was only beginning, however. In an instant, I had become the center of attention, taking the limelight away from my wife who had recently become the first-ever female to be elected chair of the school board.

Two lawyers serving on the board, Melvin Younts and Duke McCall, spent the next hour arguing loudly over which one would represent me in a lawsuit over the hazardous candle. But I quickly decided that a lawsuit would be unnecessary, because I was already miles ahead. I had gone from a wallflower to a new career as a professional partygoer. And when the word gets around, I can command a handsome fee for attending parties.

The Pause that Refreshes--Feb. 17, 1999

Occasionally, I hear people describing a "heavenly" experience. By contrast, I believe the Man Upstairs sometimes sends the opposite—a taste of hell—just to keep us straight. I had such an experience last Tuesday night.

I was running late and dressed hurriedly for the annual gathering of big wigs at the Greer Economic Development summit. As I walked into the banquet hall of the posh Greenville-Spartanburg Airport Marriott Hotel, I had a sense that something odd was going on with my feet. I glanced down and was horrified to see that in my haste to get dressed, I was still wearing a brown loafer from work on one foot and a dressy black Sunday wing tip shoe on the other. Instantly, I realized this could be one of my most ever embarrassing moments. It could rank alongside the occasion in my high school days when I was on a date with a girl that I desperately wanted to impress, and I dropped the collection plate during the Sunday evening service at the First Baptist Church.

I quickly glanced around to see if anyone was laughing at my confused attire. But apparently no one had noticed. Instead, the thirsty throng was anxiously pressing toward the bar for libations. As I backed through the horde to a table in the corner and stuck my legs under the cloth to hide my feet, I made a mental note to congratulate Peter McCord on his promotional skills. The economic development guru had passed out coupons for free cocktails to draw a crowd.

The meal was sumptuous, and McCord outdid himself by using only three minutes to recount the year's successes of luring more than $600 million in new development.

When Furman President David Shi took the microphone, I felt a call of nature. By the time Dr. Shi had launched into a seventh joke about The Citadel, SC's coastal reformatory made famous by Shannon Faulkner, my bladder was stretched tighter than a drum. Two Diet

4

Cokes during the social hour, three glasses of iced tea during the meal, and a couple of after-dinner coffees were rushing through my plumbing like a Smoky Mountain waterfall.

The ever-intensifying pain reminded me of the last time I delivered a kidney stone. But I dared not get up and walk out in front of the community's upper crust. Wearing two different shoes, not to mention the likelihood of making a splash that would never be lived down, was an unacceptable risk. I could go from being merely a harmless Grumpy Old Man to a Geezer Needing a Sitter in the blink of an eye. Never again would I be allowed to approach the Ryan's dessert bar without a chaperone.

My legs were interlocked like a pair of pretzels, on guard against an accident. I stretched backward to lengthen my body in hopes of holding on for a few more minutes. I started to speculate if one's bladder makes a noise like a balloon when it bursts.

Economic development is not an emotional subject, but tears came to my eyes as Dr. Shi thundered on. I think he suggested Greer should build a high tech industrial park with an accompanying college campus to produce computer nerds, but I couldn't tell from my notes. I could no longer focus on my handwriting because my eyeballs were floating. If a fire had broken out, I could have doused it in seconds.

Even though my plight was the opposite of a nomad dying of thirst in the desert, I began to experience a mirage. I had visions of urinals dancing above the speaker's head. As Dr. Shi plunged into a description of a Furman study program in Jamaica, my chattering teeth were playing random tunes like wind chimes. I was horizontal in my chair, fervently appealing to the Greek God of the Latrine to levitate me to the men's room. And, failing that, I was wondering how to best sound a warning for everyone to roll up his pants because there was about to be a flood.

When Dr. Shi sat down, no one saw me leave, for I was a blur. I left burn marks on the carpet as I rocketed across the ballroom.

5

The welcome news was discovering one empty stall in the men's room. The other news was that it takes quite a while to empty a 64-ounce container of soda through a straw. To pass the time, I explained in detail to fellow sufferer Larry Wilson in the next stall how an outhouse could be installed under the outdoor coat racks that he had erected at the State Auto building.

The Flight from Hell--Mar. 26, 2008

Driving to the Greenville-Spartanburg Airport through a blanket of fog as thick as pea soup should have given me a clue that something was amiss. My wife had spent the past week visiting her sister in Reno, NV, and I was on the way to meet her when her flight arrived at 11 p.m. Saturday.

Ever the optimist, I parked in the short-term (5.3 cents per minute) lot, and soon located an info board that indicated my wife's Confounded Air Lines plane had already landed, well ahead of schedule. But there was no sign of my wife. Nor any other passengers, for that matter. Dozens of other meeters and greeters were milling around, asking questions that no one could answer.

Eventually, Bob, a friendly GSP policeman mingling in the crowd, deduced that the Confounded Air Lines clerk must have posted the flight as having arrived by mistake, then locked the office and went home thinking the day's work was finished. Bob explained that the radar display board was showing tiny blue airplanes labeled with flight numbers still circling the airport, waiting for an opening in the fog in order to land.

Then we heard a loud swoosh, and my wife's blue plane turned red. "What happened!?!" I demanded.

"I don't know. I've never seen anything like that," Bob replied. "But red means the plane is leaving."

Several blue planes eventually landed, but my wife's red plane just kept going, even beyond Asheville 60 miles to the north. Meanwhile the parking lot meter continued to click off 5.3 cents per minute.

At the stroke of midnight, my cell phone rang. It was my wife explaining that her plane had landed in Knoxville, TN, where it would be refueled. Then the flight would return to GSP in an hour.

"Did you see what happened?" she asked.

"No, we couldn't see anything," I said.

"Our airplane came in sideways, across the runway lights. Thank goodness the pilot pulled it straight up at the last second or else we would have hit the terminal. Everyone was terrified, but we were spared because two preachers are on board!" she exclaimed.

I pointed out that even though the Wright Brothers may have built the plane, it should be capable of making an instrument landing.

"Oh, no. The pilot said he could not see the instruments because of the fog," she explained.

Another hour's worth of 5.3 cents per minute later, my phone rang again. "We're still on the ground in Knoxville," my wife said. "The pilot can't talk to GSP because the FAA air traffic controllers closed the tower and went home."

I looked out the window and saw the stars. "Tell the pilot the fog has lifted. He can come back," I advised.

"I'm not telling the pilot anything," she said.

Bob eventually reappeared and answered more questions, explaining that the FAA tower in Atlanta controls GSP flights after 11:30 p.m. "The pilot should have no problem landing here. In case the plane is not returning, however, you should wait in front of the Confounded station ticket counter. If the baggage handlers leave, you will know it's not coming back," he advised.

"We're still in the plane," my wife grumped, calling again at 12:30 a.m.

"Don't give up," I said even as the parking lot meter continued to gnaw away at my life savings. "Congress recently passed a law prohibiting passengers from sitting in a plane on the runway for more than two hours."

At 1:30 a.m., the baggage handlers stumbled over my chair in a rush for the door. My phone rang seconds later. "I know, I know," I said. "The plane is not coming back."

"Yes, but they are going to put us up in a hotel. We will fly in tomorrow," my wife replied.

After shelling out $18 to get out of the parking lot, I arrived home at 2 a.m. when another call came. "Guess what?" my wife said. "There are no vacant hotel rooms in Knoxville. Every room has been taken by rednecks in town for the NASCAR race at Bristol. We are going to have to sleep on the floor in the airport lobby."

I finally made it to bed with hopes of resting up before renewing combat with the birds of the unfriendly skies. At 3:30 a.m., however, the phone rang again. "Do you mind going on line and getting the customer service number for Confounded Air Lines?" my wife asked. "We want to file a complaint because they found hotel rooms for the flight crew, and the airport has locked the restrooms."

At 8:30 a.m. she called again to say "the airline gave us a $6 voucher to eat breakfast at the Hyatt next door, but the meal cost $10."

I was leaving for GSP at 11 a.m. when another call came. "We are in the plane again, but the flight crew isn't here," my wife said. "Apparently no one told them the time we were supposed to depart."

At 12 noon, still another call. "The flight crew showed up, but the airplane's computer will not function. So we are just sitting here," she said.

The two preachers were first off the Confounded jet when it finally landed at GSP at 2:30 p.m. "This has been a flight from the underworld," declared one minister.

"Why don't you just call it like it is—the flight from h...!" the other countered.

"A flight that is 16 hours late makes the airport look bad," I complained to GSP Executive Director Gary Jackson on Monday.

"Figure it this way," Jackson explained. "When you average that flight with the last 100 on-time arrivals, it makes all of them only 16 minutes late."

Coming Home to Roost--May 28, 2003

Until recently, I had not known the meaning of the old saying, "when the chickens come home to roost."

I confess to knowing next to nothing about chickens in general. I have spent a lifetime avoiding chickens, especially at the dinner table. I think I acquired an aversion to chickens because I was fed large doses of chicken soup and broiled hens, like every day, while I was a sickly toddler. Chicken and castor oil were the remedies that got me through many childhood ailments, allegedly caused by a bad set of tonsils.

When I was growing up, my dad owned a few chickens that he kept in a wooden hen house in our back yard. The roosters made a lot of noise, and I kept my distance. You can't play with a chicken like a puppy.

As a light-headed young adult, I once brought home a load of fresh chicken manure for my rose garden in my 1972 Plymouth station wagon. Afterwards, the car rusted from the inside out.

I do know about Chicken Littles. They are with us always, even still scratching to find weapons of mass construction in Iraq.

The other day I was turned onto a rare, perhaps historic discovery—an intelligent chicken. That bird is the centerpiece of one of the most amazing stories I ever heard.

According to Pam Dill, a young boy named Alex owned a chicken that he no longer wanted. He decided to use the tried and true approach employed by people who have too many cats. Alex put the unwanted bird in his truck, took it to Landrum and let it out in hopes the chicken would wander into a good home.

The next day, the chicken was back, strutting around Alex's back yard after having accomplished a feat that would make a homing pigeon proud.

Alex was not about to be outwitted by a chicken. When Pam's son, Cory, happened to stop by, Alex seized upon a new opportunity. He stuck the bird in the back of Dill's pickup truck.

When he arrived home, Dill spotted the chicken and ushered it out of the truck, hoping the bird would head back to Alex's house. Tired of walking, however, the chicken decided to wait until the next morning to hitch a ride. The bird hopped onto the back axle when Dill's truck pulled out of the driveway the next day. Instead of going to Alex's residence, however, Dill headed to Greenville where he worked as a courier for a law firm.

Dill spotted the chicken when he arrived at the prestigious McBee Avenue office. The bird hopped out from under the truck and walked into the street where it was hit by a passing car.

Dill thought that was the end of the hitchhiking chicken. But when he reached home at the end of the day, the bird fluttered out from under the truck, having left considerable evidence of where it had ridden.

The chicken then marched under Pam Dill's van and refused to move. She had to push it out with a board, making sure it did not hitch a ride with her. "I was going to prayer meeting, and the Baptist Church is no place for a chicken," she declared. When she returned home, the bird was perched on the kitchen windowsill, looking inside.

Since the chicken has taken up residence with the Dill family, they are considering arranging a guest appearance for it on the Tonight Show. Afterward, they can put the bird on exhibit and charge admission.

Another Big, Bad Idea--Oct. 20, 2004

Like the popular television commercial claims "what happens in Las Vegas, stays in Las Vegas," I was sworn to secrecy following a recent visit to Lake Murray. "Don't worry," I promised my friend Bill Hendrix. "I will keep it strictly Off the Record."

Breaking in Hendrix's new potato gun began as a 'Survivor'-type adventure but with a cast of elderly folks. Almost immediately, it evolved into something comparable to one of Sen. Jim DeMint's Big Bad Ideas.

Hendrix had received a potato gun as a birthday gift to defend his castle in battles with the inhabitants of Metts' Island, just across the inlet on the lake. Most of the battles have been fought with rotten eggs and water pistols, but the war had escalated recently when Hendrix fell and broke his arm while chasing the invaders back to their pontoon craft.

As fate would have it, Hendrix's wife Marilyn talked about the potato gun from the moment we arrived in the morning until we took it out for test firing that night.

Of course I had lectured my kids a million times "never play with guns." But, at my age, there's not much else to play with. Besides, I figured it was okay since President George W. Bush had lifted the ban on assault weapons, and his approval rating shot up to 99% among the NRA membership. Then too, no potato guns were found in Saddam Hussein's arsenal of weapons that sparked the Iraq War, the reason being because the ammo cannot be grown in the desert.

It was Saturday night, and we were acting like a bunch of drunks who had gotten liquored up for the weekend—which probably would have been much more profitable. My wife offered the sobering reminder that "Marilyn always goads us into doing something dangerous, and then she skips out." I checked and sure enough, there was

Marilyn perched on the porch, as far away from the lake as one could get and still observe the action.

The minor technicality is that I know nothing about guns, having shied away from loud noises since I was a child. Now that I can barely hear a loud noise, I took a great interest in Hendrix's new toy.

I had never seen a potato gun before. This weapon of mass destruction was made from a couple of pieces of large PVC plumbing pipe welded together. It has a push-button trigger that fires a spark to ignite the gunpowder. The gunpowder is women's hair spray. A big puff is sprayed into the chamber and a plastic cap then screwed on before firing.

One must ram a potato down the barrel with a broom handle, an act reminiscent of loading a Civil War cannon. This is an extremely tedious method of engaging in combat, especially since the potatoes must be selected with great care, Sweet potatoes will not do because they are too sticky. Idaho potato skins are too thick. The preferred projectile is a hard white potato, just slightly larger in diameter than the barrel.

As we were loading the cannon, I remembered that my mother would not approve of wasting potatoes in this manner "while children are starving in China." But, I dismissed the thought because there are no starving children in China these days since their parents have taken most of our well-paying textile jobs.

Hendrix stepped up to take the first shot, intending to move a flock of geese from the dock area for an early flight south for the winter. The potato soared into the air and splashed harmlessly among the geese. But the noise sent the birds into a panic, quickly removing the only target (other than Metts' Island) from our range.

When it came her turn, Nancy Welch aimed the gun straight up and fired. We lost sight of the potato, but all sorts of things fell from the trees—leaves, pine cones, twigs, a bird nest and even a possum rained down for what seemed like ten minutes.

At last, the gun was ready for the acid test—a missile launch toward Metts' Island. Although she had never touched a gun in her life, my extraordinarily prissy wife stepped up to do the honors. Hendrix forced an especially large potato into the gun barrel. The spud proved to be too large. My wife aimed and fired. Instead of launching the huge potato, the charge blew out the trigger, scorching her hand in the process.

She took off running for the house where Marilyn was bent over with laughter. "Where's the refrigerator!?!" my wife demanded. Hendrix thought she was looking for a yellow pages magnet with a lawyer's phone number.

"No!" she exclaimed. "I need ice cubes for my hand!"

I'm Thankful It Wasn't Any Worse--Nov. 30, 2005

Because our Sunday school teacher's wife is in the hospital, I have been pressed into service to teach the class this month, a situation that has resulted in sharply declining attendance. At this rate, I will be talking to the wall about the book of James in another week or so.

This little New Testament book never made a bestseller list, perhaps because it dishes out many truths about life, including some that are hard to swallow. James exhorts us to be thankful when troubles come along, for these trials make us stronger. Although I should have attained Super Hero status for my troubles, I would be more thankful simply not to endure any more trials. Yet they seem to crop up all the time.

Take Thanksgiving, for instance. My mother-in-law took a turn for the worse in the nursing home, so my wife decided to spend the night by her bedside on Thanksgiving Eve. Then my wife, who hates cats, didn't get any sleep in the recliner for fear that one of the home's pet cats would wander into the room and jump in her lap.

Since my wife had no time to cook, we ended up at my brother-in-law Gary Griffin's home for Thanksgiving dinner. Thankfully, the meal was a great improvement over last year's Thanksgiving outing at a restaurant—that is until the feast came down to the last surviving piece of pumpkin pie. Which happened to be near enough for me to catch the aroma and within arm's reach of Gary's father-in-law, Bill Harrill.

"Leland, don't write about me eating two pieces of pie," warned Mr. Harrill as he devoured the mouth-watering treat.

"You know I wouldn't do a thing like that," I responded.

My brother, Walter, awoke on Thanksgiving morning to find that one of his offspring had left the refrigerator door open all night. "The turkey and my $75 honey baked ham were room temperature by the

15

time we found out," Walter said. Big tears filled his eyes as Walter explained what happened next.

"Everyone was afraid the meat might have spoiled, and the guests who were coming tonight would sue if they got food poisoning. So I brought the ham and turkey downtown and put them in the dumpster," (where they obviously were in elite company among the leftovers from the nearby upscale Gerard's Restaurant).

"But Walter," I said, "surely nothing was wrong with the ham. Those things are prepared with so many preservatives they could sit at room temperature for a month." That remark brought forth even bigger tears.

My mother-in-law took a turn for the better, so my wife spent Friday and Saturday preparing to host our church fellowship group for supper. I ended up going to the supermarket three times for orange juice to make punch. The first time, I got orange juice with pulp— which simply would not do because our guests must have filtered juice. Then, one of our sons drank half of a carton of the pulpless juice after my second run to the store. We locked the refrigerator after the third trip.

I spent most of Saturday afternoon raking leaves and sweeping the front walk and driveway. That night, nobody parked in the driveway. My wife said I didn't plan well enough—I should have swept the road instead.

After the crowd admired my wife's decorating prowess to the politically correct degree and enjoyed the food, eight of the men adjourned to watch a football game, huddled around the 10-inch television set in our sunroom. (We had ordered a larger TV, but with the way our luck is running, it is still on the boat from China.)

A short time later, someone mentioned doing the dishes, and the entire crowd made a mad dash for the door.

"They didn't stay very long. That was a surprise," my wife remarked later.

"Oh, it's because the football game is at halftime, and they wanted to get home before the second half began," I explained. "I'm sure it had nothing to do with washing dishes."

As I was drying serving bowls and being thankful that the long holiday weekend wasn't any worse—well it was. A few minutes later, one of our sons came in and announced that his vehicle had lost a chance encounter with a tree. Trees always win. I'm certain that lesson must be contained in II James if the book is ever found among the Dead Sea Scrolls.

Death by Gillette--March 19, 2003

One of the big events in our lives is attending the annual Verne Smith Humanitarian Awards Banquet, which honors outstanding citizens for helping disabled people who cannot help themselves. Not only do we get to rub elbows with some of the state's big wigs, but the banquet is free.

We were running late when the time came to get ready for the event, and I was anxious to be among the first in line. Too anxious. I was shaving faster than usual, not peering closely into the mirror either, because I don't like the looks of a bag of wrinkles with a double chin staring back at me—when oops! I sliced my face just under my lower lip.

After all these years, I finally got the gist of my dad's expression "bleeding like a stuck pig" as I watched a red sea roll down my chin. I knew right then we wouldn't get a seat near the head table.

A sub-chapter of Murphy's Law decrees, "the size of a shaving cut is in direct proportion to the importance of the upcoming event." I've seen people with less gruesome-appearing injuries than mine receive a helicopter ride to the emergency room. If the Bloodmobile had been handy, I could have hopped aboard and become an instant Hall of Fame donor.

Not having that option, I grabbed a couple of ice cubes and applied them to the cut. Instead of freeze-drying the wound, I ended up with cold blood.

Miraculously, I stayed on my feet, managing to overcome a life-long history of being unable to cope with the sight of blood. (When I was a teenager, I ripped a gash in my thumb on a nail in a peach basket at Taylors Peach Shed. I headed toward the office to get a Band Aid but passed out cold after taking a couple of steps.)

Obviously, we were going to be "fashionably late" even if my last resort at stopping the bleeding was successful. That was to apply a styptic stick the size of a baseball bat. It shriveled my face like a prune—not a pleasing experience.

While this ordeal was taking place, I did not receive a single expression of sympathy from my wife. I guess she just couldn't relate to my predicament. A run in her panty hose is the only disaster that ever seems to befall her while preparing for a momentous occasion. But I was thankful that she did not dial attorney Ronnie Bruce to start proceedings in a wrongful death suit against Gillette.

When the bleeding finally stopped, I realized I wouldn't be able to eat for fear of reopening the cut. That was not a bad thing, especially if I could even manage to miss several meals in a row, I would be able to squeeze into some of the trousers in my closet.

When we were served, it was the first time I have ever been grateful that my plate was piled high with links of the food chain that I avoid at all costs. I whispered to my wife that she would just have to eat a few bites from my plate, as if she was pregnant and eating for two. She did not think that was funny, so I simply sat there and glared at the untouched food.

After a bit, a big shot with the State Department of Disabilities in Columbia leaned over and inquired if I was OK. "Oh, yes," I replied. "I'm just on a special diet and not allowed to eat Chicken Michelin, broccoli or cauliflower."

But the cherry pie for dessert did not go begging. I gobbled it down, taking a chance that if I began bleeding, people would think I merely had bad manners, allowing the pie to dribble down onto my necktie.

The Party Animal--April 7, 2004

When I heard the news that the movie "Man on Fire" is being released to theaters everywhere on April 23, I knew the secret will soon be out. I might as well go ahead and confess about going down in flames so I can avoid the embarrassing questions later on.

It all began a few years back when my wife and I were invited to a holiday season drop-in at the home of the Superintendent of Greenville County Schools, and I accidently set my brand new suit on fire.

After the word got out, that was the last time we were invited to a party until recently when we joined a church fellowship group; no one is excluded, not even party animals.

And so, on a recent Saturday night I found myself in the home of Nancy Welch, sneaking from the dining room to the kitchen for a second helping of key lime pie. That's when my fixation on candles, which had been in remission for years, raised its ugly head. I couldn't help but notice the world's largest candle on the living room coffee table. The candle was fashioned in the shape of a huge lamp, complete with a wax shade, and I thought to myself that if it continued burning, the result would be the biggest mess you ever saw.

Not only had I been hearing about hotels (like Welch's) without sprinkler systems on the TV 11 o'clock panic-attack news, but the curiosity of a nosy newspaper reporter also got the best of me. So I leaned over for a closer look. I observed that a metal cup with a wick was tipped over, about to fall out of the lamp. I reached inside the shade to straighten the cup, and it popped out, spewing a glob of hot wax across Welch's beautiful new black carpet.

Although the wax created an interesting pattern on the otherwise plain carpet, I had the feeling that Welch would not be happy. I immediately got down on my hands and knees and began picking at the wax. Just then Carolyn Coleman entered the room. Coleman, who was visiting to see if the group was even stranger than advertised before joining, remarked, "I didn't know Presbyterians faced east when they are praying."

"We don't, and I'm not praying!" I hissed. "I spilled this stupid wax on the carpet, and I'm trying to get it up."

"Quick. Get some ice. We'll freeze the wax, and get it up!" Coleman exclaimed. So we ran to the kitchen for a bucket of ice cubes and began rubbing them on the carpet. The wax didn't budge, but the ice gave the rug a frosty sheen.

"What are you two doing down on the floor?" asked Nancy's husband, Bob Harrison, who wandered into the room.

"We're trying to get this wax off the carpet before Nancy finds out," I explained.

Bob offered to vacuum it up. When the vacuum cleaner roared to life, Nancy herself dashed into the living room demanding, "What's this noise all about?"

"Oh, that," I said. "Bob is demonstrating the Oreck vacuum. I think he already has orders for two of them."

Of course, I had to confess to my latest social blunder when the Oreck failed to pick up a single drop of tallow.

"Not only have we been kicked out of the fellowship group," my wife fumed on the way home, "but when word of this gets out, we will be prohibited from setting foot in every china shop in the state."

She has Bad Luck Every Day - April 11, 1993

Another Friday the 13th is coming our way this week. But that's no problem for my wife. She has bad luck every day.

Take last Tuesday for instance. That was August 3. She started the day by rushing to an important meeting of the Strategic Planning Committee and BMW Manufacturing Co. executives.

According to the agenda, five people were to give a presentation totaling 20 minutes. But Ron McKinney got his wires crossed and gave a one-person presentation for 50 minutes. McKinney pontificated on the history of highways, beginning with the dark ages when a cave man invented the wheel and had to make a wider path after it rolled over someone. By the time McKinney got to BMW, their plant manager was in a coma—and things were going from bad to worse for my wife.

She was now late for her Bible class. And when she got to the class, at a church in Greenville, my wife tripped over a doorstop in the middle of the hallway. (If she had arrived on time, the door would have been open). Anyway, she cut a flip and made the mistake of attempting a one-arm landing.

She didn't go into shock right away. Even stayed for the Bible class. But afterward, when my wife got back into her mobile telephone (most people refer to them as cars), she was unable to turn the ignition switch with her right hand.

"I had this accident," she announced when I arrived home for lunch two hours later. "I can't lift my arm."

Immediately, I realized she wouldn't be able to operate the can opener. So I dialed Burger King and reserved a table for supper.

Then my wife decided to get an x-ray, and went to the hospital. But they wouldn't make an x-ray because she hadn't been referred by a doctor, even though the Burch family has seems to have a doctor behind every bush. So she drove to Greenville, got permission for the x-rays and returned to Allen Bennett Hospital in Greer. Once she had the x-rays, my wife drove back to Greenville to get the results. By the time she had learned the bad news and straggled home wearing a cast, it was dark and her gas tank was empty.

"It only hurts when I laugh," she warned, "so don't write anything in the paper about my broken arm."

That was last week. Besides, I always try to find the good that comes from life's misfortunes, and my wife's broken arm has delivered at last three blessings. First, she has learned how to operate the microwave with her left hand. Second, she will not be able to write a check for at least six weeks. And third, our ambulance chasing attorney has promised to get us a big settlement for a "reasonable" fee.

Meanwhile, I keep reminding my wife that if she had only taken my advice and played football in the yard with the boys when they were growing up, she would have known how to fall. Even golfers like myself fall down and take it in stride. I also advised her to postpone returning to the rigors of attending Bible Class at least until she completes a course in Karate school or 60 days of eight lifting at the Greer Athletic Club.

Until then, don't send cards, send money.

Life Is Like That

Modern Inventions Confusing--Sept. 18, 2002

I fear the reason that we old folks live in a muddled state of confusion is because time has passed us by.

Whoever said, "you can't teach an old dog new tricks" knew what he was talking about. I have already concluded that I will never be the owner of a satellite dish because I do not possess the brainpower to learn a new set of triple digit TV channels. I still have not recovered from the last time Charter Cable scrambled the two-digit channel line-up, and that was three years ago.

Anyone who has purchased a pair of scissors recently knows that the seemingly simple task of cutting a piece of paper has become an unsought adventure. Not only do today's scissors handles come in an array of shapes and colors, they also are being made with increasingly smaller finger holes. I can no longer get my thumb and fingers in the new scissors handles—just my fingertips. And that makes cutting extremely difficult. At least, being the boss, I can order others on the staff to do the trimming.

The same set of issues applies to the ordinary task of brushing my teeth. It is increasingly difficult to cope with the modern toothbrushes. The confounded things are no longer straightforward. Today's toothbrushes are "ergonomically designed"—apparently in an effort to prevent carpel tunnel syndrome among people who insist on brushing ten or more times a day.

The newest toothbrush handles are no longer straight but have more curves than a mountain road. That would be okay if they are not also shaped like an hourglass—fat at the top and bottom, but thin in the middle. Because of the new architectural flairs, modern toothbrushes will not fit in the toothbrush holder over our bathroom sink.

Since there is no place to park our newest toothbrushes, they don't get used. I have a whole drawer full of them—not because I set out to start a toothbrush collection, but because I am given a new one every time I visit the Painless Dentist. The assortment of toothbrushes serves only as a reminder of how many cavities I have had filled.

Twenty First Century toothbrush handles are also longer than ever, almost stretching into the tidy bowl brush category. If I still had my tonsils, I could scrub them with the newest toothbrushes.

Since I don't have to dig that far, I am forced to stand farther away from the bathroom mirror to prevent breaking it with a long-handled toothbrush. This is not as simple as it sounds. My eyeglasses are fitted to focus the exact distance from my nose to my hands so I can see what I am holding. Thus, when I stand back, things start to get fuzzy, and I have to feel my way around. Cleaning my teeth with the new style brushes has become a hit-and-miss activity.

I can remember when the only decision you had to make in selecting a toothbrush was the color. Today's toothbrush handles come in purple, silver, slime green, hot pink and other shades that match kids sneakers.

The new brushes also have multi-colored bristles. When the bristles begin to change color over time, it is said to indicate that you should rush to the dentist to get another toothbrush. But at my age, I can't remember what color the bristles were yesterday. Therefore, I can't be certain if the colors are different today. In fact, the bristles fell out of my old toothbrush before I even considered using a new one.

I do recall that the Department of Homeland Security has warned if your toothbrush is orange, you should be on high alert for a terrorist in the bathroom.

Mothers Teach Us a Lot - May 9, 2001

I had the world's greatest Mom, and I'll bet you did too. Everyone I know thinks his mother was the best. And that is one reason why we will celebrate Mother's Day this Sunday.

Sarah M. Burch, bless her heart, devoted her life to trying to raise me in the proper way. The jury is still out on whether or not she succeeded, but I think I am finally beginning to make good use of some of the lessons she taught me. Like not to say anything at all if I could not make a "nice" remark. I was sternly admonished about this when a great aunt gave me a box of handkerchiefs for my birthday instead of the fire truck I was hoping dearly to receive. I could not bring myself to say, "Thank you for this wonderful present." So I said nothing. Some of my relatives never knew I could talk.

My mother taught me logic: "Because I said so, that's why" was her answer whenever I questioned the plans for my day's activities.

My mother taught me about religion: "You better pray that stuff will come out of the carpet" on the occasion when I "oiled" my tricycle in the living room. I had emptied an entire bottle of that most dreaded remedy for any ailment, castor oil, over the three-wheeler. It never squeaked again, though.

My mother introduced me to the science of osmosis: "Close your mouth and eat your supper."

My mother taught me stamina: "You will sit there until you eat all that fried okra." I did not get up from the table for over an hour, and only then after I had cleaned my plate by emptying the okra into my pockets.

My mother taught me about envy: "There are millions of unfortunate children in this world who go to bed hungry every night." I wished they could have the okra, broccoli, spinach and other horrid green vegetables on my plate.

My mother taught me about contortionism: "Will you just look at the dirt on the back of your neck!", she often exclaimed right after I got out of the bathtub.

My mother taught me about the weather: "Your room looks like it has been hit by a tornado." She invented tornado drills long before the Weather Bureau got around to it.

My mother taught me foresight: "Make sure you always wear clean underwear, in case you are in a wreck."

My mother tried to teach me behavior modification: "Stop acting like your father!"

My mother taught me how to solve physics problems: "If I yelled because I saw a transfer truck coming toward you, would you listen then?"

My mother taught my brother and me how to appreciate a job well done: "If you're going to kill each other, do it outside in the yard. I just finished cleaning!"

My mother taught me about irony: "Just keep on laughing, and I'll give you something to cry about."

Oops! I nearly forgot that my mother also tried to teach me about hypocrisy: "If I've told you once, I've told you a million times—don't exaggerate!!!"

Never Admit Anything--Aug. 29, 2001

On more than one occasion when sitting down to a meal, I heard the late Dr. Warren Snoddy declare, "If everyone will knock over their milk, we can get started."

I was reminded of that just the other night when I overturned a large glass of iced tea on the kitchen counter. My kitchen experience is limited to prying open cartons of ice cream, and it showed when I attempted to make a sandwich. I can still see the replay in slow motion in my mind: turning quickly in a small space, my elbow struck the glass, and I was unable to react quickly enough to prevent it from tipping over and sending tea everywhere, like a Myrtle Beach high tide rolling in.

The consequences of such a seemingly insignificant accident are monumental.

You quickly discover there is more liquid on the floor than was ever in the glass. And the longer a spill stays, the worse it gets. So I sprang into action to clean it up as quickly as possible, using an entire roll of paper towels (which, fortunately, I had bought on sale). The puddle was so large that I checked twice to make sure no sharks were swimming around in it.

Meanwhile, the tea was encircling my wife's array of dozens of Tupperware containers that house every cooking ingredient known to mankind. Each one had to be lifted individually in order to remove the sticky residue. By the time the kitchen was restored to some semblance of order, I needed crisis counseling.

Men don't like to admit failure, especially me. Even worse, overturning a glass of tea could get my name entered into the FBI Profile of Kitchen Klutzes if it became known. Besides, this mishap really wasn't my fault. I reasoned that if it were not for all of my wife's stuff on the counter, I would have had enough space to make a sandwich without causing a catastrophe.

So I used one of my lifelines to phone a friend, Denby Davenport, now a semi-retired attorney in Greenville. "Denby, should I tell my wife about spilling a glass of tea?" I asked, soliciting free advice.

"I don't think you should ever confess to doing anything wrong," Davenport said. "Any woman who is offended only gets mad, or worse, she gets even. And if you don't admit to anything, she will never know for sure that you did something."

I knew Denby must be right. No need to own up and give my wife another setback in her lifelong mission to improve my table manners.

When she arrived home a few minutes later and asked, "What was that you were putting into the garbage can? Was it ice cubes?" I silently kicked myself for thinking the ice would melt before she returned. I should have ground up the cubes in the dispose-all.

I finally answered, in Denby fashion, "I have made a lot of mistakes in my life. But out of respect for our family, and because of a special request of the Lipton Tea Company, I cannot go into the details at this time."

But my wife was far from satisfied, and immediately launched into her imitation of Nite Line News celebrity Connie Chunk, "In that case, do you know what happened to all of the iced tea?" she demanded to know.

"Well, I was very close to the tea, probably too close. But I can tell you, I didn't drink it," was my final answer.

"If we had gone out to eat, like I suggested, this wouldn't have happened," she said, continuing the inquisition.

"If you had fixed supper, like I suggested, it wouldn't have happened either," I countered.

"That does it!" she exclaimed. "Now that we have that long term care insurance policy, I'm going to have you committed to the nursing home"….at which I grabbed for the hotline to my attorney friend. "Denby!" I screeched. "I took your advice, and now I'm being packed off to the nursing home."

"Well," he replied, "what more did you expect? You got all the advice you paid for."

Headline News

WWJD Question Goes Unanswered--March 5, 2003

Today's headlines: **War with Iraq. The Economy in the Dumps. North Korea Building an H Bomb.**

As if we didn't have enough things to worry about, the nation's collective conscience is also being taken to task for driving SUVs. We have become saddled with the WWJD question: "What Would Jesus Drive?" The well-meaning intention behind this question is to shame us for driving gas guzzlers, assuming everyone could agree that Jesus would drive a very fuel-efficient vehicle, like a Volkswagen bug, instead of an SUV.

I believe it is presumptuous to assume that our little minds know what Jesus would do in every situation. His contemporaries of 2,000 years ago were constantly amazed because Jesus always did the unpredictable. Since that is only my opinion, however, I assembled a panel of the community's wisest citizens to tackle the WWJD question. Here's what they decided:

Jesus rode a donkey into Jerusalem amid great rejoicing on the occasion that Christians now celebrate as Palm Sunday. There wasn't a more humbling ride in Biblical times than a donkey. Does that mean Jesus would drive a Yugo in the Christmas Parade?

Someone interjected that while a Hummer is probably unlikely, Jesus should be in a car with a sunroof for quick ascension at the next Pentecost.

Since Jesus charged His followers to "feed my sheep," would He roll down Wade Hampton Blvd. in an 18-wheeler with the Bi-Lo supermarket bull emblazoned on the side?

Jesus was purposely obscure for most of His 33 years on earth, so it may be safe to assume that He would not be driving a car with a big number on the door like a NASCAR racer.

I know we may be treading on dangerous ground, but an argument could be made for Jesus driving a Honda, based on the Bible verse that states: "they were in one Accord."

A theory was advanced that Jesus would not be driving at all because He could not spare the time for waiting in line at the DMV to get a license.

Jesus was known to appear out of thin air with no known means of transportation. Obviously, He really doesn't need a ride.

That being settled, my anonymous committee moved on to the next question: "What Would Jesus Eat?" We know that He fed the multitude of 5,000 with only five loaves of bread and two fishes. Someone declared that Long John Silver's could qualify as a sanctified eatery.

Honey-covered locust was the popular fast food served in '03 BC, but that isn't on the menu in any Greer restaurant. If Jesus were to appear at Burger King, it would probably set off a demonstration of animal rights activists. And sausage biscuits are out, because He cast out demons and sentenced them to reside in a herd of pigs.

The panel thought Manna is the best answer to the food question.

That brought my research team to: "What Would Jesus Drink?" A panelist wonders if Jesus would appear in a TV commercial wearing one of those white mustaches as the result of drinking milk.

Another declared that Jesus would prefer diet Coke because fewer calories, like using less gasoline, are better.

Of course, Jesus turned water into wine at a wedding feast, and that opened up another can of worms, which we did not pursue.

One person, however, did wish to speculate about "What Would Jesus Wear?" Would He sit in the stands wearing a Cheese Head hat at a Green Bay Packers football game? Would He be wearing blue jeans with tools hanging from His belt to ply the trade of a carpenter? If so, He would not be able to get through security screening at an airport.

As you can see, we didn't get any farther with the WWJD question than the sages who have been trying for ages to answers such deep questions as "If a tree falls in the forest, does it make a sound if no one is there to hear it?"

Therefore, I decided that it is okay to continue driving my SUV. But just in case, I'm hanging one of those "God is my co-pilot" license plates on the front bumper.

Barbershop Sign Missing - March, 2014

The large sign above the entrance to Bullock's Barbershop went missing on a foggy night in the month of February 2014.

It isn't like nothing had ever vanished in Greer, S.C. There are cherished memories of the long gone parking meters, taxi cabs, GARP, Strategic Planning Committee, Chili Cook-off, Kiwanis Pancake Supper, Lincoln High School, The Leader Department Store, Lewis' Drive-In, The Grand Theatre, and the list goes on.

Yet it is difficult to overstate the magnitude of the sign theft, which is comparable to Jacob stealing Essau's birthright. As one of the most notable events in the history of Greer, the sign heist sparked a new level of hype across a wide spectrum of the news media: television stations interrupted programs to announce bulletins, newspapers printed special editions, Web publications emitted countless tweets. The vanished sign even got thousands of 'likes' on Facebook. What's more, it is the only incident that ever lured Greer Police Chief Dan Reynolds away from the golf course in the middle of a round.

Bullock's sign was a cornerstone of the community's heritage, because it marked the exact location of the center of "The Center of the Universe," as is so thoroughly documented in Leland Burch's best selling page-turner by the same name, *Greer, S.C. – The Center of the Universe*. Bullock's Barbershop is where everything (at least gossip, rumors and the like) begins and ends. With not even so much as a bronze marker on Trade Street now, future Greer residents may never be able to locate the center.

The stolen sign was obviously priceless. Certainly barber Mike Bullock could not possibly obtain another one of that size, 25 feet long and two feet high, for the same amount, $10, which he had invested in the original sign.

Greer Police Detectives, who have been working 24-7 to crack the case, have little to go on. Bullock apparently did not know the sign was missing until he drove down Trade Street to have a look around following a snowstorm that shut down the town. Bullock happened to glance up at the front of his shop and observed the sign was missing. "Normally, I always park in back of the building and come in the back door," he explained later.

When Bullock met with investigators outside the shop, an employee of a nearby business firm barged into the conversation to report that the sign had been gone for several weeks. He thought Bullock was having the sign repainted since it was beginning to show its age with traces of rust, peeling paint, etc.

Swiping the sign must have been difficult since it was attached to the front of the building high above the sidewalk. It was much too large to be carted off undetected in the back of a pickup truck. So, how could the sign simply vanish into thin air with no witnesses, no fingerprints? And, why didn't the attached department store security tag set off an alarm when the sign walked out Greer's front door?

Many theories have been espoused to fill the vacuum left by the lack of evidence. The most popular is the conspiracy theory: A rival tribe is striving to relocate the center of the universe to Sugar Tit where it was before Manning Greer gave passing trains permission to dump manure at the Trade Street crossing.

Hijacking: The sign is being held as ransom, to be exchanged for freeing hostages who must reside against their will in Georgia.

Aliens: A flying saucer hovered over Trade Street while a creature descended to the top of the barbershop, tied a rope to the sign and lifted it off for a souvenir that will fetch a fortune on the planet Neptune.

Mechanical failure: The bolts attaching the sign rusted and fell off. High winds during a recent thunderstorm blew the sign into the stratosphere where it traveled thousands of miles before coming to rest in the middle of the Atlantic Ocean.

Confiscation: America's "po but proud" competition team commandeered the sign to be used as a bobsled in the Winter Olympics.

My own theory: The sign melted as the result of hot air emanating from the barbershop. The molten tin dribbled down the side of the building and into the storm drain. This narrows the suspect list to several thousand males who get haircuts at the shop, especially those who visit Bullock's every single day: Ronnie Bruce, Javan Collins, Tommy Williams, and Ken Emory.

I feel entitled to collect the reward being offered: A one-day pass to Wal-Mart to observe an associate actually lowering prices.

Playboy Controversy Ripe for County Council
--April 2, 1997

At my age, I figured nothing in the world could shock me. Wrong! I was absolutely flabbergasted the other day when a copy of *Playboy* magazine was discovered in the Greenville County Library, a hallowed institution surrounded by downtown churches.

This situation has diverted my attention from such cosmic issues as global warming and depletion of the ozone layer. People are asking my opinion about this latest crisis.

First, it has become crystal clear why record numbers are signing up for literacy classes at the library. And I may at last get some bang for the bucks I have invested in Friends of the Library membership dues. At the very least, I have learned that I should visit the library occasionally just to see what is going on.

Apparently *Playboy* magazines have been in the library for years, but not displayed out in the open. The magazines are surely in mint condition because nobody knew the Playmates were available for viewing. If the word had gotten out, crowds of panting men would have been elbowing each other for positions in front of the library magazine shelves, just as they do in Barnes & Noble and other trendy bookstores.

We have been informed that *Playboy* is kept behind the librarians' desk—in a plain brown wrapper, I suppose. I imagine it would be terribly embarrassing to ask one of the spinsters, wrapped in a long sleeve sweater with her hair rolled in a bun, to hand over the hard core stuff in exchange for your library card.

It may have been a coincidence, but as soon as speculation arose that the library would cancel its subscription to *Playboy*, a truckload of cable TV converter boxes was stolen. Whoever gets their hands on one of those boxes can watch *Playboy* around the clock in their own home without having to fight the crowds at the library.

In its defense, the library issued a statement contending that *Playboy* contains well-written, literary-type articles. Yeah, right. If that's the case, maybe someone should thumb through each issue with a pair of scissors and snip out the photos of naked women. The centerfold could be labeled "for medical purposes only" and set aside to help old men score higher on their monthly blood pressure checks at the library.

I'm confident the Greenville County Council will jump in and resolve the *Playboy* controversy. Judging by the success of last year's resolution condemning gays and lesbians, County Council probably cannot resist the temptation to go for an encore and condemn Playmates.

It is doubtful that County Council could get away with a law banning *Playboy* magazine since they were unable to outlaw topless bars. That would be unconstitutional. But they could pass an ordinance banning horny men. Once that element is removed from society, along with rapidly-disappearing gays, it might be scary to look around and see who is left.

Meanwhile, I have decided that the *Playboy* controversy gives credibility to the recently deceased Heavens Gate cult. One of the benefits of the Marshall Applegate's ordination by castration is that none of the cult members were ever again tempted to gander at *Playboy*! They were able to stay focused on departing for the spaceship in the tail of the Hale-Bopp Comet.

The Color of the Day--July 31, 2002

It's good that I learned about colors in kindergarten so I can decide whether or not to get out of bed in the mornings.

We are living in a color-coded world. It didn't happen all at once, but has been gradually sneaking up on us, like a snake in the grass.

DHEC now issues daily bulletins to warn us, by color, about the ozone levels in the air. If it is a Red Day, you should not go outside. Orange and Yellow Days are risky, but Green is okay.

I recently headed out the door to enjoy a Green Ozone Day on the golf course only to catch a Red warning issued by the federal Department of Homeland Security. The government has five different colors to designate the various alert levels for the possibility of a terrorist attack.

If the state of South Carolina declares a Red Flag Day you cannot start a fire—anywhere. Whenever the Forestry Services posts the Green Flag, I would grill hamburgers if only my wife had not given our gas grill to Goodwill. The grill was taking up space in the basement, and it did not have a light that determined when the meat was done (Green) or not (Red).

Whenever I turn on the television to CNBC's *Power Lunch from Wall Street* to check on my IRA mutual fund, I get an instant attack of indigestion if the stock market arrows are in Red. That means I must consider canceling our reservations at the nursing home. If the arrows are Green, I know there is a chance I may be able to retire before reaching the age of 75.

A Green flag starts every NASCAR race. Sometimes, a Red flag comes out to stop a race so there can be a Green-White-Checkered flags finish, a situation that I have yet to figure out.

When you are behind the wheel, the Red traffic light means stop, Green is for go and Yellow could bring a ticket if you don't slam on the breaks. I knew about that even before kindergarten because my dad had a habit of talking to Red lights when he became impatient to get moving.

You would think the U.S. Postal Service would be in touch with the world's red-green color scheme. Not so. Whenever the Green light is on in the lobby of the Greer Post Office, it means the mail is NOT yet in the boxes. That is to be interpreted as Green—go back home. Even after the three cents hike in the price of a postage stamp, the Post Office cannot afford to change the Green bulb to a Red one that, according to my logic, would mean no mail is available. In fact, there are all sorts of other possible uses for having a Red light in the Post Office, like the Junk Mail is ready to be picked up. Or there is a 30-minute wait from this point in line until your turn comes at the window. Or the Snail is on vacation today.

There are no warning flags at the DMV office—just a board flashing numbers.

A fax from Columbia arrived at the newspaper office on Friday afternoon stating that the DMV would offer only "limited service" during the upcoming holiday week at the end of the year. I wasn't surprised, for that either meant business as usual or it was a really bad joke. So I rushed to the DMV office because my vehicle tag was expiring. It was 15 minutes before closing time, and I found myself 100 numbers down in the Red line in the wait to get a sticker for my license plate.

I could not help but notice that a woman sitting next to me was frantically punching numbers on her cell phone. Finally connecting with a relative the woman said, "leave the Greenville office and hurry to Greer to get your tag renewed." I can't imagine the number of people that must have been waiting at the Greenville DMV office. The woman said, "turn left at the Red light and look for a parking lot full of cars. I think we can get out of here in time for the 9 o'clock movie."

Be Prepared--February 26, 2003

Open my toolbox and you will find only one item: a roll of duct tape.

Like a good Scout, I was prepared in February, 2003, when the Office of Homeland Security ordered all citizens to put in a supply of duct tape as the first line of defense against chemical and biological attacks.

My only concern is why The Pentagon took so long to get around to broadcasting the virtues of duct tape—something I have known all along. After all, it has been years since this technological breakthrough replaced rubber bands, paste, string and chewing gum as the household adhesive of choice. I can only assume that duct tape has such numerous wartime applications that it was classified top secret by the CIA.

War seems inevitable since Saddam Hussein refused CBS anchor Dan Rather's suggestion to comply with UN Resolution #12,884 by revealing where Iraq's supply of duct tape is hidden. If launched on a missile, a roll of duct tape becomes a nuisance of messy destruction by sticking enemy forces to their tracks.

I applaud the government, though, for postponing the duct tape panic as long as possible. In the week since Secretary of Homeland Security Director Tom Ridge's decree, not only has the State Legislature introduced a bill to eliminate the sales tax on duct tape, many people have started hoarding the stuff. I was reminded of our ancestors who buried jars filled with sugar in their back yards and stashed gasoline ration stamps in safe deposit boxes during World War II.

Among its millions of uses, duct tape is an indispensable tool in the world of motor sports. Known to NASCAR crew chiefs as "200 miles-an-hour tape," it is used to strap fenders and hoods back into place on cars that have been nearly demolished in crashes. Race teams have acquired duct tape in assorted colors to match their cars' paint schemes.

Unfortunately, silver is the only color duct tape available to the average citizen. But this is not necessarily a drawback. When the handle fell off our new refrigerator from outer space, I duct-taped it back in place, and my wife has never noticed.

She did object, however, when I duct-taped the gold bumper of her car after it was ripped apart by a high curb in a parking lot. I did not get defensive because it proved to be less expensive to install a new bumper than have the car painted to match the duct tape.

I have actually taped ducts with duct tape. I even made a Gutter Helmet out of duct tape.

For years, librarian Joada Hiatt used duct tape to hold the books together in the old Davenport Library.

I find the sticky side of duct tape comes in handy, too. I use it to remove lint from my navy blue suit. And if my computer falls off my desk and shatters on the floor, I will use duct tape to bail it back together.

Duct tape is an excellent dieting resource. Simply wrap a frozen hamburger with duct tape before thawing it in the microwave, and it will severely restrict the number of calories that you can ingest.

I will be armed to the teeth with duct tape when war breaks out. I will wrap it around my house and create Fort Burch. Inside, I will be wearing a bulletproof vest of duct tape. I have even set aside an extra roll for binding up Iraqi spies who might surrender at my doorstep.

And if the terrorists infiltrate the Internet and cause my computer to crash, I will use a Sharpie marker to write coded messages on the back of duct tape and send them to my friends.

I'd Make Sure the South Wins Next Time--April 19, 2011

Here's a news flash. The U.S. Postal Service is issuing a new series of postage stamps commemorating the 150th anniversary of the Civil War. These are so-called "Forever" stamps, so you can use them to mail letters forever without having to buy more postage. This also means that the arguments about why the Civil War was fought and who started it can continue forever.

We can anticipate more war re-enactments featuring middle age men with such large bellies that they cannot march off to the battlefield without becoming winded. That's quite a contrast with the original Civil War participants who were as skinny as splinters after having nearly starved to death while marching hundreds of miles and living off the land. Someone should import starved Ethiopians to be the re-enactors. But wait—that would be considered slavery, which, according to most historians, is why the war was fought.

When I was growing up, no one had heard of a Civil War reenactment. In fact, even after many decades, my ancestors were still enraged over the South losing the "War of Northern Aggression." They felt cheated by fate—the untimely death of Stonewall Jackson and uninformed decisions that doomed the Confederacy to defeat. It was like a football team that lost because of a fumble, poor coaching or incompetent officiating. Worst of all, we were left with no bragging rights to counteract Yankee arrogance. We could only point to our moral victory for having held our own despite being heavily outnumbered, outspent and outgunned.

My mother repeated the Civil War tales that her grandfather had told her as a child, and I wish I could remember them. Unfortunately, I was focused on the first new invention of my generation, television, with such enlightening programming as Howdy Doody. Anyway, my great-grandfather, Robert Hammond "Foddy" Baker was shot in the head in a battle in Virginia and lived to tell about it. At least he had that as an excuse for being somewhat daft, but his descendants don't have an excuse. "Foddy" Baker was one of thousands of Confederate soldiers who walked home after the war ended.

Even 150 years later, we have never forgiven General Tecumseh Sherman for his march of devastation through the South. Sherman's troops actually burned Columbia, although at the time most natives thought it was just another mid-summer scorcher in the hottest place this side of Hades.

I don't plan to ever watch a Civil War re-enactment because I figure it's like seeing a movie after you have read the book. Like when the great ship sinks in the film "Titanic," I know how the Civil War turned out.

Don't look for me among the re-enactors, either. For my family's honor, I refuse to participate in losing the war a second time. If the re-enactments were left up to me, the South would win this time.

Such an outcome would do wonders for the nation. I would have General Stonewall Jackson lead the Confederates on a victory march through the North. The Rebels could torch such wastelands as Detroit, Cleveland and Jersey City, thereby saving billions of tax dollars being poured into urban renewal.

Many other issues would be resolved. There would be no controversy about if, when, and where to fly the Confederate Flag. The flag could be worn on T-shirts, caps, thongs, etc., and motorists could sport the stars and bars on license tags and bumper stickers without inciting a riot.

Victory by the boys in Gray would give us a new national flower: Kudzu. Not to mention a new national health food: Moon Pies. Grits would replace French Fries on McDonald's menus, and moonshine would replace Bud Lite as the national beverage. Art galleries would exchange gnarled metal sculptures for rusted cars sitting on cement blocks and pink flamingos perched in white sidewall tire planters.

Instead of baseball, apple pie and Chevrolet, the national culture would consist of NASCAR, cornbread and coon dogs under the front porch. Chickens would be considered household pets, and a professional wrestler would be named Chief Justice of the Supreme Court.

The Southern version of the post-war carpetbaggers invasion would be a million man march across the Mason-Dixon line. Slow talking Dixiecrats would take over every town council in New England and begin dispensing free advice, like: "Y'all ain't doing this right. Down South, we always do it this way."

Dear Shannon: The Citadel Needs You More
--May 10, 1995

I sometimes catch myself thinking if I'm not incredibly stupid, then I must be coming down with Alzheimer's. Surely I missed something along life's way because things keep coming up that just don't make sense. Take Friday when the lead story on the front page of the daily newspaper announced that the S.C. State Senate had voted to give $3.4 million to Converse College to install a new military curriculum in order to prevent Shannon Faulkner from becoming the first female ever to enroll at The Citadel.

I noted with pride that Greer's Sen. Verne Smith voted against the proposition. That means at least one rational person remains in the legislature.

Only five months earlier, citizens voted out dozens of incumbents for iodic excesses like this effort to save the males at The Citadel. They were replaced by a new wave of politicians who also promised to cut the budget and eliminate property taxes. It is obvious that the only change in Columbia was the names.

It hasn't been that long ago that you could have bought The Citadel—lock, stock and barrel—for $3.4 million and thrown away the key. Now the Corps of Cadets, terrorized by one 18-year-old female, is quaking behind the fortress-like walls and begging to be rescued by the legislature.

The state spends $6,000 annually on each cadet who attends The Citadel. At that rate, my accountant friend Paul Lister figures it would be cheaper to send every cadet to Converse and leave The Citadel to Shannon by herself. In fact, a dozen Shannon Faulkners could probably replace our entire armed forces. Then we really could do away with taxes. We would never have to fear terrorists again either.

If Wofford or Furman were smart, they would give Faulkner a football scholarship. Perhaps that would lead to a rare win on the gridiron.

At any rate, it would be cheaper to bribe Faulkner to simply go away than to send her to Converse. She could retire to the Bahamas on less than $3.4 million. And the state could save the $1.4 million annually that it will spend to maintain a military training program at Converse.

I find it difficult to believe that Converse wants Faulkner or $3.4 million to establish a military curriculum. In this era of Women's Lib, females have become militant without having to attend classes on the subject. Besides, the Converse girls probably would spend the state revenue windfall to hire maids to make the beds and clean their dorm rooms.

I'll bet Converse would not amount to much of a military school anyway. When it comes to physical fitness, Converse girls don't like to carry more than one silver platter at a time. Their only experience at hand-to-hand combat is grabbing for the same phone.

In the old days, girls were taught how to attack with rolling pins. Those items have been replaced by bread making machines that require premeditation and teamwork for launching.

At Converse, the heat of battle means learning how to boil water in Home Economics 101. You won't find many Converse girls volunteering to spend the night in a tent or dig a latrine. The nearest they could come to closing ranks would be parking their BMWs bumper-to-bumper.

So Shannon, please stay at The Citadel where you belong. If the boys can deal with your presence, it will make men out of them—eventually.

Cell Phones

I Still Can't Hear You--Feb. 9, 2005

During the past week, hundreds? of readers inquired about my new cell phone.

Well, as of last Wednesday, I had not received a single voice mail, even though I had paid through the nose for service. A helpful technician, who fielded my complaint when I called the "Lowering the Bar" service provider, determined that I had erased part of the 25 digit voice mail number programmed into my phone. Apparently it happened when I spent a day pushing buttons and working my way through all 150 of my phone's features beyond simply making and receiving calls. The technician talked me through 83 steps required to reprogram my voice mail.

And then nothing happened for two more days. About lunchtime Friday, I pulled out this world's largest pocket watch to check the hour and noticed that the clock had disappeared from the window of my phone. In its place was an announcement: "You have three missed calls."

That was startling since my phone had never rung. Hurriedly, I punched the ten digits required to check my voice mail. The first message, sent at 9:05 a.m., stated: "This is Nurse Feelgood at Tanglewood Middle School. Pernicious isn't feeling well. Can you come and pick her up?"

A second message, recorded at 9:40 a.m., followed: "This is Nurse Feelgood again. Pernicious has a headache and is feeling worse. Please pick her up in the school health room immediately."

The time of the third message was 10:10 a.m. It stated: "For the last time, this is Nurse Feelgood, and Pernicious is crying, raising he.., and disturbing the entire Tanglewood health room. If you don't get over here and pick her up right now, I am going to call your parole officer and turn you in, you low-life *&#@&*%#@ of a parent."

Two days later, I heard my new cell phone ring for the first time. It was a man calling long distance, wanting to speak to Moe. "I'm sorry," I informed the caller. "Moe has had his parole revoked by a school nurse, and they gave me his phone number because no one could reach him in prison using the Lowering the Bar network."

Some may think I am complaining about my cell phone. Actually I am very thankful that it only receives calls when the wind is blowing from a certain direction. That has prevented embarrassments such as occurred on Sunday. One of the world's loudest cell phones burst forth like an air horn at a funeral during the closing prayer of the morning worship service at the sedate First Presbyterian Church. It was about 12:10 p.m., and the caller may have assumed that the service would be over at that time. Obviously the caller wasn't a member because our church services last well past noon since Presbyterians need more religion than most.

Right there, on the fourth row from the pulpit, it occurred to me that in Biblical times this incident would have ranked alongside the burning bush—an alarming event followed by a voice bursting forth from an inanimate object.

By the time the phone erupted a second time, everyone in the congregation was wide-awake. One would have thought that the owner would have answered or at least cut the phone off. I sat upright, smugly secure in the knowledge that my phone wasn't the one ringing.

This particular noisy cell phone was buried inside a woman's purse, one of those crate-like affairs the size of a piece of luggage. She was frantically digging through the bag but could not put her hands on the phone. It was hidden under too much other stuff.

She pulled out a billfold; a pair of socks; a CPW religious calendar; a make-up kit complete with comb, brush, mirror, lipstick, etc.; a stack of greeting cards; a tuna fish sandwich; three candy bars; breath mints; an I-Pod; hand lotion; spray perfume; and a couple of unmentionable items.

As I watched the debris flying out of that purse, a light bulb came on inside my brain. At last I understood why Greer Police Department investigators always file incident reports that state: "the purse snatcher struggled to steal the woman's purse." Those things must weigh a ton!

Eventually, the woman dug out the cell phone and shut it off. The phone responded by emitting a loud gurgling sound, similar to the last three seconds of a toilet flush.

"If that was Jesus calling, maybe He left a message." said Dr. Kyle hopefully, after making it through the pastoral prayer without losing his composure.

The Passing of an Old Friend--May 21, 2009

Shortness of breath, tightness in the chest, pain shooting down the left arm—all warning signs of a heart attack and impending death. This hasn't happened to me—yet. But something nearly as bad occurred the other day when my cell phone suffered a coronary. The phone flashed a warning message "unauthorized charger" on its screen whenever I attempted to recharge the battery. The same message appeared when I plugged it into the three other Motorola chargers, which we can't seem to do without, in our home and cars.

My phone was obviously dying as the bars had dwindled to none. Not stopping to consider that I somehow had survived for many years without a cell phone, I rushed to the phone store emergency room.

After squeezing into the only available parking space, I entered the lobby packed with people. Obviously this was the 'friends and family' network as seen in TV commercials. They were milling around and waiting, like families gathered in a hospital emergency room.

And just like the hospital, you have to check in at the phone store—answer a bunch of questions on a computer touch screen. Really dumb questions like, "Why are you here?" "Do you want to buy a phone?" "Pay a bill?" "Get a life?"

My issue was not among the options listed on the screen. And neither was shoplifting, which prompted me to wonder why all display phones are bolted to the wall. Eventually I typed, "My phone is dying" on the screen.

The computer replied: "Your name will be called when a technician is available."

Some 45 minutes later, I was summoned to the service counter. "My phone is giving me a death message," I explained. "It's two years old, and just like every other device that we can't do without, our microwave ovens, copiers, etc., it seems to be expiring the very day after the warranty has run out."

"I've seen other phones with this same problem. Yours is a goner," pronounced the tech while conducting an autopsy on the phone.

"Can't you like put it on life support, just to see what happens?" I asked, fighting back tears. "It has all of my friends' phone numbers stored inside, numbers that I have never bothered to learn."

"Well, you are due for a new phone, you know," the tech countered in a consoling voice while reviewing my two-year-old contract. "You and your wife both can get new Strawberry Storm phones for free. It's only an additional $60 a month with a 10-year contract or an early termination fee of $6,000."

"How long does it take to learn how to use the Strawberry Storm touch screen?" I inquired.

"Actually, it's a pretty steep learning curve, probably about nine months in your case," he admitted.

"But, but…couples can have a baby in that length of time," I protested.

"Well, at your age a baby's not going to happen," the tech replied.

"Look, I'm here only because I need phone for talking," I declared. "I don't want a phone that will force me to get a second job to pay monthly bills. I don't talk into computers, so I don't want a phone that surfs the web, sends Emails, or gives driving directions. And if I wanted to listen to music, I'd buy an I-pod. The only special feature I want is for my phone not ring on the golf course, in the middle of my backswing."

"We have only one old fashioned model that's just a phone," he said. "It's $29.95, but that doesn't include the funeral expenses for your dead phone."

"Oh, I do want my phone to have a proper funeral," I said. "I'd like a traditional ceremony with someone delivering an emotional eulogy. I want the old Motorola to be remembered for how brave it was, how it boldly disconnected wrong numbers and spam calls, how it patiently endured all the useless gossip, how it once fell in a mud

55

puddle but faithfully kept on working like the Energizer Bunny. There wouldn't be a dry eye in the place."

"Then there is arranging for the burial," the tech continued. "You just can't dump a cell phone in the landfill because of all the new environmental regulations."

"What are the options?" I asked.

"Some dead cell phones go into the Alexander Graham Bell mausoleum along with their predecessors including bag phones, rotary dials and Dixie Cups with strings," he explained. "On the other hand, you could donate your phone's innards to our transplant program and have the shell cremated."

"I think I'll go that route," I said. "This phone has been such an important part of my life that I will scatter the ashes on top of my desk where they will never be disturbed."

Can You Hear Me Now?--Jan. 20, 2010

The score is: Cell Phones 1-Leland & Wife 0, and time's running out in the Super Bowl of Communication. Either we spend another day in the Horizon store swapping our new phones or resign ourselves to keeping them for two years, which at our age is probably for life.

Selecting a cell phone is like buying underwear. It's very personal, after all, because phones sometimes are carried in places that only an airport full-body scanner can detect.

When our old phones died the day after the warranties expired, I thought replacing them would be simple, like way back when the only decision to make was picking a new decorator color, beige or green, to replace the old black rotary dial model. When we couldn't get through the door at the Horizon store before having to sign in at a computer, I should have known it wasn't going to be simple.

The computer asked why we were there. Since I wasn't wearing a ski mask and carrying a shotgun, and since I wasn't delivering emergency relief aid to customers who had been waiting for days, it should be obvious that I only wanted a phone. While waiting, we browsed along walls filled with a baffling array of phones that confused us even more than we are ordinarily.

"What features do you want in a phone?" asked the clerk when we were finally summoned to the sales counter.

"I just want to make calls," I said.

"Do you want a GPS application?" he continued.

"No," I said. "I'm not lost."

"We have phones that play music," the clerk mentioned.

"I already have a radio," I replied. "And I don't need a phone for playing games, either."

"Okay, okay. Do you want a touch screen phone?" asked the clerk.

"Absolutely not!" I screeched. "My big fat fingers would hit two or three icons at a time, and I would never be able to make a call."

When the clerk handed me an 'idiot-proof' Hamstrung Hubris, I noticed other shoppers were snickering. One whispered that I reminded her of her grandfather. "Actually," her companion mumbled, "he's more like my two-year-old."

The clerk then sold me a $29.95 plastic carrying case that made my new phone protrude from my waist like a ballooning hernia. If I attempted to take it on an airplane, screeners would think I'm wearing a hand grenade.

When her turn came, my wife announced, "I want an I-Phone because my sister has one."

"We don't have I-Phones," the clerk hissed and then pulled out a half dozen imitations. "Our phones are free if you make Horizon the beneficiary in your Will," he explained.

"How long will it take me to learn how to use this phone?" she asked.

"For you, no more than four to six weeks," he answered.

My wife left with a Victrola Hemorrhoid—so named, I later decided, because it is a "pain in the a…!"

Glancing at my watch, I noted we had been in the store for four hours, during which time the price of gas had gone up three times at the BP station. "Do you have a cot?" I asked. "I've missed my afternoon nap."

"No," the clerk said. "Now you have to select your calling plan. You can list up to five friends for free," he said.

"But I don't have that many friends," I protested.

"All right," he said. "What emergency numbers do you want on your phone?" I had him plug in 911, AARP and the Soup Kitchen.

Three days later, we were out driving when my side began throbbing like an appendicitis attack. It was my phone, but since I could not see the tiny screen without my specs, I had no idea who was calling. "Hello," I said.

"Hello! Can you hear me?" the caller inquired.

"That's a familiar voice," I thought. "Yes I can hear you." I said.

"Well you should. I'm sitting right here beside you."

I looked over and my wife was calling. She had finally figured out how to make a call. Then she asked me to call her phone. It rang and nothing happened.

"I still don't know how to answer it," she lamented.

The next afternoon, we were back at the phone store. "Mr. and Mrs. Burch please report to the assisted living counter," the computer eventually announced. There we spotted Kim Keller. "I can't use my new phone. What kind do you recommend?" my wife asked Keller.

"Oh, you should get a Crackberry Thunderstorm," Keller said. "You can punch everything on the touch screen and nothing happens."

"I would like that," my wife said. "Every time I touch this phone it goes haywire."

Five days later we were back at the store to swap the Thunderstorm because, as Keller had said, nothing happens when you touch the keypad. My wife now has an idiot-proof phone with real keys just like mine. And the Horizon check-in computer has proclaimed us "customers of the year."

Let's Go Out to Eat

The Wreck of the Burch Bank Account – Aug. 4, 1993

A week ago Sunday was the only day it rained during July. The only reason it rained that day was because the Burch family left town on vacation. It always rains when we take a vacation, and that's why crowds were lining the highways, cheering and applauding as we drove by.

Naturally the Burch luck ran out as soon as we hit the coast. The rain stopped, and the heat wave that lasted the rest of the week shattered all records. It was the only time I have been at the beach when it was too hot to go swimming.

We entertained ourselves by sitting in front of the air conditioner and prayed that it wouldn't quit.

We only ventured out to find something to eat, and that has become a full-time chore with wall-to-wall tourists lining the streets of Charleston. It requires a major battle plan to capture something other than a hamburger or pizza. As soon as you finish lunch, you have to advance to another line to get supper.

One day Elsie 'Mimi' Griffin, the matriarch of the clan, spent nearly two hours camping in the bar of Hymie's Grill on Meeting Street. The proprietor had allowed us inside to wait for dinner. 'Mimi' hunkered down under a glaring neon Bud Light sign, nibbling boiled peanuts and glancing nervously at the window in case a member of her Friendly Neighbors Sunday School Class of the Greer First Baptist Church happened to pass by.

Then I remembered that Margaret Carlisle had suggested a place by the strange name of *The Wreck of the Richard and Charlene*. I figured we had nothing to lose. After all, we once had an employee named Charlene who had a wreck, and we have a Richard who some say is a large accident waiting to happen.

The first problem was finding this restaurant. (It's at the end of a dirt road leading out to Shem Creek.) The second problem is that you don't know when you have found the place. There is no sign on the building, which is an old freezer plant. It looks like a place you shouldn't go unarmed.

Brave souls who venture inside discover that on a scale of one to ten, the food is a ten. The shrimp seem to have jumped from the water onto the grill—and that's not far from the truth. Shrimp boats unload each afternoon only 50 feet from the kitchen steps.

The atmosphere is....well, off the scale. Part of the restaurant is housed in a screened-in tent, if you can imagine such a contraption. There are also tables outside offering a view of the shrimp fleet as well as an indoor kitchen-dining room. The Wreck has no air conditioning (nor heat in the winter), but overhead fans keep a breeze going.

Diners are seated in late model Kmart plastic lawn chairs circling table tops on mini step-ladders. The décor consists of a 12-panel mirrored window suspended from the roof.

But we were hooked. So we returned to meet the owner, Fred Scott, who is a Mt. Pleasant lawyer trying to escape the legal profession. Fred explained that he bought the property hoping to build a condo by the creek. But he couldn't get it rezoned so he opened a restaurant to teach the city council a thing or two.

That sounds like Ronnie Bruce, my kind of lawyer. We returned the next day to hear the rest of the Fred's story. He said the *Richard and Charlene* was a real ship that was blown onto his dock during

Hurricane Hugo. Months later, after the remains of the ship had been hauled away in pieces, the restaurant was named in its memory.

You have probably guessed by now that the prices are non-gouging—a rarity for such food. So we went back a fourth time, even had to stay an extra day to complete the Wreck of the Burch Bank Account.

Catch of the Day--July 6, 1994

While opening the morning mail, I came across a letter from my bank. It said: "Congratulations. You have just made the final installment payment on your 1993 vacation loan. If you would like to borrow again this summer, please call 1-800- ..... while our budget buster rates are still in effect."

That prompted me to make a mid-year resolution not to go to the beach this summer. That way, I may not have to borrow money again until next July, depending on which relative's name I draw for exchanging Christmas presents.

Besides, I have spent years trying to find a decent place to eat at the beach. When I finally find one, it has been overrun by Yankees, almost like what took place during Sherman's March to the Sea some 130 years earlier.

Last summer, thanks to Margaret Carlisle, I discovered a really out-of-the way place by the unlikely name of *The Wreck of the Richard and Charlene*. This café had everything I was looking for: great food and low prices. A bonus is the atmosphere, which reminds you of the days before such modern conveniences as indoor plumbing and air conditioning.

Then I made the mistake of writing about *The Wreck* in this column. I figured it would be OK for Greer people to visit *The Wreck* because we are not pushy or obnoxious. We can also tolerate the Kmart décor, and we can even understand the language spoken by the waitresses.

Unfortunately, as often happens with many things we print first, the article was pirated by another newspaper. This time, it was "The New York Times" that plagiarized our discovery and wrote a story about *The Wreck*.

"You wouldn't believe what has happened to *The Wreck* since then," John Carlisle telephoned to say as soon as he returned from Charleston the other day. "*The Wreck* is crawling with Yankees. Now you have to stand in line to wait for a table. They're even demanding that Fred (Scott, the owner) put up a mosquito net over the picnic tables on the deck."

"That's not all," Carlisle continued. "In self defense, Fred has gone up on his prices." This means if I went to the beach, I'd be back in the same old rut: spending an entire week looking for a decent place to eat with low prices.

One of the greatest hazards of the beach is that the places that served the best food last year are putting out the worst fare this summer. Yet hordes of tourists are standing in line on the sidewalks under every neon sign.

My typical approach is to find the shortest line. When we finally get a table, my wife always asks the waitress for a recommendation. Usually, the higher the price, the better the recommendation. Once, however, a waitress actually admitted, "all of our seafood is about alike." And being brutally honest, she added, "It's all frozen."

At that point, one of my kids ordered spaghetti, which happened to be the cheapest entree on the menu. There was also the "Catch of the Day," with no price. So, while the rest of the family ordered fried shrimp platters at $9.95 apiece, I ordered the "Catch of the Day" in hopes it would be decent—but less expensive.

When the shrimp platters arrived, I saw right away this entree would not pose a problem for those who are lacking in math skills. The number of shrimp on the plates could be counted on the fingers of one hand.

When the "Catch of the Day" arrived, I ran to a phone to call my optometrist for an appointment. Either my eyes were going bad or the Catch of the Day was so small I could hardly see it.

What's worse, when the check arrived with the price, it turned out that the "Catch of the Day" actually was my wallet which had been fished neatly out of my hip pocket.

A Microwave for Your Head--Feb. 12, 1997

Have you ever been tempted to stick your head in a microwave oven? Don't. One of the side effects is death. I've heard gory tales about pets that exploded when someone attempted to dry them off in microwave ovens.

But if you think a microwave-like treatment just might cure your ear wax buildup or unclog the arteries in your brain, then I have just the place for you. We discovered it when the oldest grandchild came to celebrate his sixth birthday with us.

"Why don't we go out to the cafeteria, like on my birthday," my wife suggested. "Oh, no," I said (and I have been kicking myself ever since). "It's Cameron's birthday. We'll take him wherever he wants to celebrate."

Cameron wanted to have his birthday party at Chunky Cheeseburger. This enterprise is based on a new concept to separate you from your money. They hook you by throwing in a large pizza when you buy $35 worth of tokens that the kids can spend for 30-second whirls on a riding toy or playing video games.

I made this discovery after standing in line a half hour just to get in the door. Once inside, it was too late. You couldn't back out because the sidewalk was blocked by the line of 200 people behind you, waiting like lambs being led to the slaughter. You couldn't even discuss the merits of the limited menu choices (plain or pepperoni) with anyone in your party because of the horrendous noise that approached the threshold of pain.

Nothing else comes close to the noise level in Chunky Cheeseburger—not even the weave room in a textile mill. At least 500 kids were yelling and screaming at once for turns on the riding machines that were vibrating and shaking the building, making the Greer drag strip seem like a library reading room.

While waiting for our order of pizza, I had to put an infant top with a spout on my cup of diet Coke to keep from spilling it over everything.

When the pizza did not show up in an hour, I went to the door of the kitchen and pounded on it until someone eventually appeared. The man said he would check on our pizza. He returned ten minutes later and informed me they had lost our order.

But not to worry, he said. They would have us a pizza out in 30 minutes. And to make the time go faster, he promised to send us some bread sticks (pizza crusts with no cheese) to munch on.

Meanwhile, I had to buy another $20 worth of tokens because the kids were not about to sit still for a half hour while awaiting the pizza. It's a good thing they didn't wait for the bread sticks either because they arrived 15 minutes after the long lost pizza finally showed up.

The place did provide a salad bar for old people, like me, who have concluded that the box containing your pizza is healthier than the contents. I would have enjoyed a salad, but I was too busy trying to prevent the grandkids from proving that the place is not indestructible. And refereeing. Like all three wanted to drive the same truck at the same time, but it had only one steering wheel.

"I sure hope I don't run into anybody I know," I mumbled to myself while pulling my head down inside my coat like a turtle. Too late. Standing in line behind me at the gyrating tractor was Ron Johnson, a member of our church.

"Are you having fun yet!?!" yelled Johnson who had only one kid to keep tabs on.

"Yes!" I shouted. "The same kind of fun as when I had my last root canal."

When the pizza finally arrived, I couldn't stop my hands from shaking long enough to eat.

"Bop, why do you keep sucking on those mints?" Cameron asked.

"I haven't wanted a cigarette for 10 years, but I would just about kill for one right now," I explained as we staggered out the door.

Half Baked--Aug. 17, 2005

Like a "farmer's tan" is a dead giveaway of someone engaged in agriculture, an expanding waistline is ample evidence of my next career—that of a culinary critic. At least that is what I will be claiming when I deduct last weekend's tab on my income tax return.

We spent three days and two nights at a Five Star bed and breakfast in the mountains. Actually the resort gets more stars than five. Several guests, when handed their bills at checkout, screeched, "My stars!"

The genteel inn served more than breakfast. Lunch and dinner (or supper as I prefer) were also included. Our mission was to consume $400 worth of food in 48 hours in an upscale version of the burrito-eating contest held recently in downtown Greer. We lurched from one meal to the next, like being on an ocean cruise without the side effect of seasickness.

As soon as we arrived, even before unpacking, we rushed straight for the super buffet. In less than two minutes, I had a pile of fried green tomatoes and other goodies on my plate. Before digging in, I dusted everything with a layer of salt because I am as addicted to salt as the alcoholic who gulps a Bloody Mary before breakfast.

After salting away for a couple of minutes, however, I realized nothing was happening. Checking the saltshaker, I could see that the holes in the cap were totally clogged. After all, it rains every evening, as well as most mornings and nights, in the Great Smokies. Since there is no air conditioning in the dining room, the saltshakers suck the moisture right out of the air.

Venturing on with no salt, one small bite revealed that the food is boringly bland. As I suspected, salt doesn't pour in the kitchen either, or else they had put all of us Geezers (about 90 percent of the crowd) on a no-salt diet, which medical experts claim is good for your health.

But my response is that I am good for salt, because I'm keeping the salt mines in business. My body is already 90 percent salt and 10 percent water.

I didn't melt down my credit card filling the gas tank for a no-salt weekend excursion. I merely proceeded to unscrew the cap of my salt-shaker, and immediately a waiter pops up and asks, "What's wrong? The salt won't come out?"

Now I am doubly irritated because my number one pet peeve is stupid questions. I replied "No! Actually I am a DHEC inspector, and these non-working saltshakers will lower your restaurant's A rating at least one grade."

Eventually, the waiter produced a saltshaker in operating condition.

At last, I was set to dig into a mouth-watering slice of tomato the size of a hubcap. Wrong! Either my dinner knife wouldn't cut hot butter or else this tomato was bullet proof. It had not been peeled, and the skin was as tough as a U.S. Army flack jacket. While making several stabs at the tomato, it skidded off my plate like a kid shooting from a water slide. The tomato wheeled across my new slacks, leaving a trail of Vidalia onion salad dressing stain the size of a tire tread.

Observing my distress, the waiter rushed over with an ice cream sundae, lathered in chocolate syrup. I was delighted to go for the good stuff and skip the rest of the food pyramid.

Then the waiter offered: "Enjoy!" Which is another pet peeve, because it sounds like ordering a dog to "fetch!" If I had ordered my dog to "enjoy!" when I served him dry chow, he would have bitten me. And what if I don't "enjoy!" Do I stand in the corner or write on a blackboard?

In an effort to enjoy! I devoured two desserts (three when key lime pie was served) at each meal for the remainder of the weekend.

Dessert sparked my third pet peeve: "Are you done?" the waiter asked after another piece of pie vanished from my plate.

"No, I'm not done. I'm only half baked," I answered. "But I have finished eating because this solid wood chair is the hardest place I have sat since my third grade desk. And my arms are now too short to reach around my belly to pick up the fork."

Lard of the Month

Lard of the Month--Nov. 28, 2006

"Look, Ma! Look up there in the sky. It's a bird! No it's a plane! No it's the Goodyear Blimp!"

"I heard that, kid, all the way up here. And it's me, the old editor, that's floating with the clouds."

I got there because of Thanksgiving—the Eat Now and Pay Later Holiday. I have re-discovered that there's a limit to how much you can suck in before there's no choice but to resize in the Round and Short Department or spend 1,000 hours working out in the gym.

My wife cooked for several days before Thanksgiving. So did our sister-in-law Ruth Griffin. Together, they had prepared enough food for 50 people, but only 20 showed up. I felt duty bound to consume three helpings of turkey, dressing and macaroni pie even before Ruth had a free moment to pass a basket of homemade yeast rolls. "There are at least 1,000 calories in one of those rolls, just waiting to unite with the other fat grams throughout my body," I feared. I devoured one anyhow, just to be polite, you know.

Adding to the temptation was a huge sweet potato casserole that had been substituted for asparagus (ugh!) for the first time in 50 years at a family Thanksgiving dinner.

Eventually, I staggered toward the dessert bar where Ruth had assembled a five-layer spice cake, pumpkin pie, cookies and ice cream. She could eat it all and not gain an ounce. But not me. Of course, I sampled everything—to avoid hurting her feelings. Manners, you know.

If the legislature ever makes it illegal to overeat, like drinking to excess, I will be in trouble. I'd have to get a designated driver for exceeding the 10,000-calorie limit, or else I might see blue lights in my mirror. "You're under arrest for DUL." (driving under lard) is not what I would want to hear.

"But officer, even though I can't turn the steering wheel because it is jammed into my belly, I am supporting President George W. Bush's "no sausage biscuit left behind" initiative. And I swear that I ate only two of them." That excuse would not stand up in court if the Fat Police were armed with a Carlorielyzer.

When I tried to push back from the dinner table, I couldn't move. My arms had gotten too short. "I need a fat support group," I thought to myself. "Heck, my chair needs extra support."

I had eaten so much Thanksgiving dinner that my stomach stretched. And mixing with the hot air that I possess, it became a deadly combination. I simply floated away from the table.

I really like the view of the city from above, floating around like a gasbag. It could even help advance my career. After being named Greer's Lard of the Month, I was invited to fill in for meteorologist Christy Henderson when she goes on maternity leave since I am the size to which News Channel 7 weather watchers have become accustomed.

My hat is off to those who are pitching in to help with the post-Thanksgiving gluttony-recovery effort. Clemson fans are dining on humble pie—a low calorie dish if there ever was one. The Gamecocks are too busy crowing to eat. One USC diehard, Buzzy Stewart, is even renting himself out as a leaf blower.

Just wait until next year. I will insist that our family use only fat free Crisco in preparing the big feast.

New Diet Has Me Pumped--Feb. 18, 2004

After several weeks of waddling around with an extra spare tire, the result of over indulging at the dinner table during our recent sea cruise, I was informed by my wife, "you're going on a diet! And the first thing you have to do is to throw out all those bags of Chex snacks you brought home from the grocery store last week!"

"But, but....wait a minute." I protested. "I bought those snacks on sale. I'd hate for all the money I saved to go to waste. Besides, Chex snacks have 50 percent fewer calories than potato chips."

"Well, you aren't going to get any potato chips on this new diet, either," she declared.

"Just what will I be allowed to eat?" was my next question.

"Beans and cabbage, mostly," my wife said. "And it's oat bran for breakfast—every single day."

"Yuck!" I exclaimed. "I ate tons of oat bran years ago to reduce my cholesterol, and it didn't work. I didn't lose a single pound either," I protested, following my wife down the hall to the kitchen.

It was there I realized I had lost the argument before it got started. She was busy unpacking a huge load of groceries—every variety of dried bean and pea known to mankind, plus fixings for making three salads a day—lettuce, cucumbers, etc.—the whole nine yards. There was enough cabbage to fill a wheelbarrow.

Soon my wife was busy making black bean soup, three bean salad, tossed salad, boiled cabbage, and more.

"Pork chops would be good with this stuff," I suggested helpfully when wandering back to the kitchen an hour later. "No, the diet does not permit any meat except fish," I was informed.

"Well, at least this won't be an expensive proposition like some diet sensations, because I refuse to eat any kind of fish—unless, of course, it's shrimp," I said.

"I don't mean to complain," I said later at the dinner table, "but there is something different about these black-eyed peas."

"I can't use fatback or salt for cooking any more. All the experts say it's bad for your heart," my wife explained.

I consoled myself with the thought that I could lose 20 pounds in one week on this diet. It would be worth a week of mealtime drudgery to try to get back into my clothes rather than having to buy a new wardrobe.

I soon discovered that the Law of Unintended Consequences applied to the new diet as it applies to most well meaning, but untested initiatives. An unwanted result of a steady diet of cabbage and beans is gas—lots of it.

Not to make bathroom jokes about my predicament, but our wind chimes no longer must be hanging outdoors to ring constantly. Not only did my shoes become 'Air Jordans,' I also had to invest in a metering device, similar to those used to alert the public when the ozone level is high. The meter samples the air inside the house and flashes green, yellow or red, depending upon the amount of gas that is present. At times, the gas can get pretty intense. When the meter goes red, my wife reaches for a respirator, another medical expense that health insurance did not cover.

With so much gas, I may float away like the Goodyear Blimp. It would be a fate similar to the one that befell the late Dr. Robert Atkins, the diet guru who made millions writing helpful books for fat people. After years of passing up ice cream, cake and candy bars—all for the sake of living long enough to get into a good nursing home—Atkins slipped on an icy New York sidewalk, hit his head on the curb, and died with an empty stomach.

The newest diet reminds me of an event in history: in the aftermath of World War II when Allied forces occupied Berlin, they discovered that Adolph Hitler's scientists had invented a new explosive, more powerful than the Atom bomb. The secret formula was similar to ingredients in the cabbage and bean diet.

What is the name of this new diet book anyway?" I asked after receiving a telegram announcing that I have been selected as Gas-X customer of the month. "Oh that," my wife said. "It's called Fashioning Your Figure With Flatulence."

The Trans Fats Police--Jan. 17, 2007

Reliable inside sources, speaking on the condition of remaining anonymous, report that the Greer City Council and Greenville County Council are racing to become the first outside of New York City to ban the use of trans fats in restaurants.

If that happens, everyone will be forced to adhere to the Surgeon General's Warning: "If it tastes good, don't eat it."

Instead of sticking to the mission of finding a cure for the common cold, some over-paid medical researcher has determined that trans fats are bad for our health. That made for an instant Six O'clock TV News-on-the-Downside Fear Tracker Alert: "trans fats clog your arteries."

Ah ha! At last they have found the culprit responsible for putting so many of us in the hospital.

Wait a minute! Will anyone who knows what trans fats are, please raise your hand.

I attempted to research trans fats on the Internet and found very little—fewer than two million references. And trans fats were not listed in my most recent dictionary, the 1994 edition that was the last one printed in English before Webster converted to Spanish.

I have a sneaky suspicion that trans fats are the fancy name for fatback, an essential ingredient in Southern cooking. If fatback is banned, it will end the way of life that we have enjoyed for generations.

Health gurus contend that most of us are overweight. I say, "Compared with what?" We're about average size for the Hummers parked in our driveways.

Before banning trans fats, I hope our elected officials will consider the serious consequences of such a policy. If we slim down and become healthy, it will deal a fatal blow to the community's two new hospitals. The beds will be vacant, creating more empty big boxes than even Wal-Mart can abandon. Heart surgeons will kick back in hammocks alongside Maytag repairmen.

Removing money spent on health from circulation and squirreling it away in savings accounts will be a huge setback to the economy. And it goes without saying that every big and tall store would go out of business.

Speculation is rampant that trans-Atlantic fat will be also prohibited, meaning that all French and Italian restaurants would have to shut down. There would be nowhere to get our oil changed in five minutes or less by quaffing down a super size bag of French fries.

Enforcing a ban on trans fat is shaping up as a monumental headache. Would the city hire tasters who could sniff out a fatback-laced dish as soon as it hit the table? Would Police establish a Trans Fat SWAT Team to go after the violators?

A Trans Fat SWAT team would have to develop imbedded informants so that police could intercept delivery trucks backing up to restaurants with loads of illegal lard at 2 a.m. Pretty soon, the trans fat supply chain would go underground, like grass and moonshine. Trans fat smugglers would be driving around in cars with jacked up rear ends so that tons of salt-cured booty in the trunk would not give them away.

The law of unintended consequences would come into play by forcing police to clean up their act. Donut shops would be off limits, based on the tons of Crisco that go into each batch of the sweet treats, and the Krispy Kreme sponsorship decals would have to be removed from the fenders of our police cruisers.

That being said, I think there must be an easier way to win the war on trans fats. Perhaps Pfizer or some other major pharmaceutical company will invent a trans fat removal pill that costs ten cents to manufacture and sells for $50 at CVS. Take one and everything will come out fine in the end—except at the Western Carolina Sewer District where dynamite would be required to clear out the lines.

Lastly, the Greer Family Festival will become the Trans Fat Awareness Festival, and we all will live happily ever after.

Dinner Table Etiquette

The Chicken and Peas Circuit--March 24, 2004

"He's just like his two grandfathers," my oldest son declared. He was intervening in a family debate about where to eat out on Saturday night. None of the restaurants that we suggested suited our grandson Eli Burch, who is very picky about food.

Being just as picky as Eli, however, I breathed a sigh of relief when we wound up at an Italian restaurant. Eli ordered ravioli, stuffed with cheese, and gave it one thumb up—otherwise we would have had to stop at Burger King on the way home. I welcomed spaghetti as a break from the chicken and peas circuit—the typical meal that is served when someone calls with the invitation: "Please come to our banquet on Monday night. By the way, bring your camera."

I wish the USDA would require banquet invitations to carry a surgeon general's warning: "Caution, chicken will be served. It may be hazardous to your appetite."

I can tolerate one nugget of Calabash chicken, but two are too many. So I was thankful for having waited at the end of the line until the Soup Kitchen gave out of chicken breasts and resorted to serving country style steak at the recent annual dinner.

I had consumed a lifetime's worth of chicken meals by the time I was eight years old, the same age as Eli. Growing up as a sickly kid who attracted every germ that passed through the neighborhood,

I was constantly subjected to the time-honored remedies of chicken soup, stewed chicken, etc. The only way to escape the chicken cure was to get well—and fast.

If that wasn't revolting enough, my dad raised his own chickens. He had a large chicken coop in the back yard of our home, which would be considered in the middle of downtown Greer today. Zoning regulations prevent city residents from raising chickens nowadays, but not back then. The big birds continually pecked and scratched in the dirt, which aroused my curiosity. I once asked my mother why chickens ate sand, and she said they needed the grist to digest food. Just thinking about what the chickens ate did not make me keen on finding a drumstick on my plate.

My mother especially enjoyed fresh eggs, which my dad called "hen fruit." In fact, my dad once claimed mother ate so many eggs that she wouldn't dare look a chicken in the face. You can guess that eggs are not at the top of my list of favorite foods, either. I do make exceptions for funerals and wedding rehearsal dinners—which are judged by the quality of the deviled eggs that are served.

As far as I'm concerned, chicken is merely a filler between the appetizer and dessert. Although more research has been poured into chicken recipes than finding a cure for cancer, I can spot the bird from half a room away. Chicken is impossible to disguise in any recipe. If not considered bad manners, I'd just eat dessert first.

Banquet chicken is usually accompanied by English peas, which my dad derogatorily referred to as "chinaberries." At birth, he gave me a lifetime exemption from eating English peas. But I eventually discovered that peas are much better than the other banquet staple, broccoli, which Eli's other granddad also detests. The only kid I ever saw who loves broccoli is Carl Gibson's youngest grandson, Drayton Gibson. Grandpa Gibson says the boy will eat a ton of broccoli as long as other children aren't watching. But he won't touch the stuff when other kids are around.

Cafeteria Ed--Oct. 14, 1987

National School Lunch Week arrived with invitations to sample the fare at several area school cafeterias.

That brought back memories of my own school days at good old Central Elementary with the sharecroppers' menu. The fare consisted of cornbread and pinto beans, cornbread and cabbage, cornbread and overcooked lima beans, cornbread and turnip greens, cornbread and etc. I thought the food was terrible, but many years later I have come to realize that cornbread baking has become a lost art, not to mention the patience required to overcook limas, pintos and greens.

In this day of fast foods, students have their choice of a salad bar (in high schools), pizzas, tacos, Sloppy Joes, and other items that had not been invented when I was a kid. The only thing that hasn't changed is that kids still complain no matter what food is served in the cafeteria.

By the time a kid graduates from high school, he will have spent two full years in the cafeteria. That ought to be worth several credits, perhaps even a diploma.

Cafeteria, the only subject that no one ever fails, does teach life lessons. For example: the cafeteria is the only place in the school where a student has to stand in line and wait. Life's like that—standing in lines and waiting: to get license plates, to see the doctor, to buy a postage stamp, to get tickets to the ball game, to check out at the supermarket, not to mention being stalled at traffic lights.

Waiting in line teaches students to be creative. Amid a long line, one can discover how to pull the hair of the girl three places ahead and not get caught. Or learn how to aim a sharp pencil point at the appropriate part of another student's anatomy to draw a squeal that will silence the entire cafeteria.

Learning how to break in at the front of the line is another important cafeteria lesson. In later life, that's known as getting to the top.

Cafeteria chemistry is tying to discover what went into the spaghetti sauce. Identifying something strange on one's plate is known as cafeteria biology.

Let's not forget cafeteria athletics. Kids learn (when the teacher isn't looking) how to fire yeast rolls at a target three tables away and how to rifle English peas, like bb pellets, off the tip of a knife blade. This also instills cafeteria sportsmanship—like not ratting on the guy who just nailed you in the head with a biscuit from across the room.

Cafeteria also teaches self-defense—the art of chopping at sneaky fingers reaching for your cup of ice cream.

Most of all the cafeteria prepares one to expect those little surprises in life—like the times when someone unscrews the top of the salt shaker causing some unsuspecting kid to dump the entire contents onto his plate.

The Inlaws

The Five-hour Birthday Party--Jan. 29, 1997

Was I ever surprised! I thought it would be a snap to celebrate the annual renewal of my wife's 39th birthday on Saturday night. Instead, it turned into a five-hour ordeal.

I knew my wife would want to go out to eat. Any occasion, even Hemorrhoid Awareness Week, is enough reason for us to eat out.

And I shouldn't have been surprised when my wife invited her mother, Elsie "Mimi" Griffin, to come along. When we arrived at 6:30 p.m. to collect my mother-in-law, I mentioned that it would save a lot of time and money if she would just cook supper for us instead.

"I've forgotten how to cook," Mimi declared.

"You can't use forgetfulness as an excuse for everything," I shot back.

"Well, I'm older than you. So I can forget whatever I want to," she said, putting me in my place.

As we started out the door, my wife grabbed the phone and invited three more family members, which was fine. But the only car that the group could fit into was Mimi's 30-foot-long land yacht. The keys to the eight-year-old sedan, which had been holed up in the garage for nine months, were not in her purse. "I'm sure I remember where the keys are," said Mimi who had forgotten everything else. That led to a 30-mintue search that turned up ten sets of car keys. None fit the Cadillac.

Finally, at 8 p.m., my wife called her brother, Hayne Griffin, to ask about the keys. Hayne said he had a set and would bring them right over from downtown Greer, only a few blocks away.

Greer police would have been proud of Hayne. He did not even approach the 25 mph speed limit in the 30 minutes that took him to travel five blocks.

Already upset because she did not have the keys to the car, Mimi became furious when she had to sit in the back seat. "I can't even sit in the front seat of my own car," she complained.

Naturally, the car would not start. When I turned the key in the ignition, it activated every imaginable bell and whistle that Detroit had ever hung on a vehicle—except the engine. Even the air conditioning was trying to raise the temperature from 38 degrees to 65 and was sucking up the few volts of electricity remaining in the battery.

We finally got the engine fired by shutting off everything else.

"Where are we going?" everyone asked in unison. By then it was nearly 9 p.m., which raised the possibility that the Waffle House was the only restaurant in town still open.

My wife had cast the only vote for the Macaroni Warehouse. As usual, she won, although everyone else preferred a restaurant that actually serves macaroni.

We arrived at the Warehouse to discover there was a two-hour wait because the ATM was out of service. So we ended up at everyone else's first choice, the new J&S Cafeteria. Even so, Mimi was still unhappy. "I don't know how to get out of the back seat," she grumped.

Most of the 168 people ahead of us in line were from Greer.

"You're really getting out light tonight," whispered John Carlisle from the next table. "I had to take my wife to the Macaroni Warehouse on her birthday."

Don't tell anyone else it's my birthday," my wife threatened, "or else we will have to invite all of them next year."

And so, my wife opened her birthday present in secret. I'm not supposed to reveal what it was either. All I can say is that no one else on our block has sampled the new low fat Girl Scout Cookies.

Nuptials in Never Never Land--Oct. 19, 2005

I hope somebody pinches me soon because I am in a fairy tale dream world—a mixture of Alice in Wonderland and Cinderella.

I must have gone into a deep trance after my wife insisted that we attend the wedding of the daughter of her first cousin—whom we only see at weddings and funerals, events that are alike in most aspects except for the music. And weddings last longer. This one consumed three entire days, time that I could have spent joyfully working at the office.

As soon as we arrived on the South Carolina gold coast, we ducked in at my cousin-in-law's house to make sure all the preparations were coming along. Since we've never had to throw a wedding, we know all about how to put one on—just like old maids can tell you how to raise your children. We hadn't been there two minutes when a huge rig, the size that could have passed for a NASCAR car hauler, came rumbling up the driveway. It was the caterer's rolling kitchen for preparing the wedding reception food on site—so that it would be exceptionally fresh. The weight of the big rig ruptured the water line, sending a gusher into the air. There was no water for the bride's family until the middle of the following day—on the eve of the wedding. But it was no big deal, because nothing ever seems to happen on time in this strange land.

While the water line was being repaired, the father of the bride and three helpers spent the entire wedding eve erecting and arranging tents, tables and chairs for the reception on the huge front lawn. Actually, they did this several times to suit the official and unofficial wedding directors who kept popping in and out with different sets of orders. "This is getting to be a real burden," moaned the long-suffering father of Snow White, also know as Emmiecakes.

That night, the mother of the groom threw an oyster roast for the rehearsal dinner. The groom's father and his latest (third) wife were among the invited guests. They were 30 minutes late, but happened to be the first to arrive. (As I said, nothing happens on time.) Fortunately, we were another five minutes behind the first guests, which is the way my wife's clock operates.

All guests were instructed to park in a large cleared field and to walk in, about 500 yards down a dirt road, to a picnic shelter complete with an adult-size, three-story tree house on a bluff overlooking a river. A calypso band, low country shrimp boil, buffet spread with all sorts of food, a slide show and the whole nine yards were awaiting the guests.

The handsome prince's father was accompanying his (newest) wife down the path to the party when she, the stepmother (often described as "wicked" in fairy tales), stepped on a copperhead snake that became very agitated and bit her on the ankle. She was rushed to the emergency room 20 miles away. The last I heard, the unfortunate woman was still in the hospital, but the mother of Prince Charming had a huge smile on her face during the remainder of the weekend.

The next day, nobody slept through the wedding for fear of missing something or maybe it was because the historic church has the world's hardest wooden pews. Then it was on to the nine-hour reception. Oh yes, the food was outstanding. The caterers in the big rig really know how to cook—especially shrimp and grits.

But I could only eat so much, having extended my belt to the last notch. Unable to dance (for fear of collapsing) there was nothing to do but watch football on TV, so this was by far my all-time favorite wedding reception.

My wife's cousin has two other unmarried daughters, but their weddings could never top this one.

Mr. Nobody, George Camp -- Nov. 11, 2009

George Camp, my brother-in-law, was along for his first ever visit to the SC coast when we spent an autumn week at the Walrus Way by the Sea at Pearl's Outlet. Camp is a Connecticut Yankee, which defines an aristocratic antique. But he is not a Damn Yankee—one who comes to visit and never leaves.

Camp flew back to Hartford on Sunday after having spent the entire week hinting that he would like to be mentioned in the newspaper in my column. The advertising payoff from making print in Off the Record is unlimited. Plus it's free. Otherwise I'd have to split the proceeds with the company. And no, I cannot accept bribes—not officially anyway because there is no line on the federal income tax form 1040 for reporting a bribe.

Unfortunately, Camp is a Nobody. At least that's the name hung on him by his precocious two-year-old grandson when the kid recently made an unsuccessful stab at fitting Camp into the family album.

I patiently explained to Camp that since he is a Nobody, he would have to do something extraordinary to get his name in print. Most folks appear in my column because they are good people to whom bad things happen. Like another brother-in-law, Gary Griffin, who was once struck by a bolt of lightning. Not a cloud in the sky that day. Maybe he was being punished for playing golf on a Sunday.

I explained how Linda Nicholson shot herself in the foot. With a shotgun—all the better not to miss, my dear.

Then there are those who do something really spectacular to attract attention, like falling from on high. Bunchy Godfrey once took a plunge from a 40-foot tall stepladder.

"Be nice. You simply must put George in the column," my wife commanded rather forcefully after eavesdropping on our conversation.

"But he's a Nobody," I countered. "No one in Greer knows him. He's not even on Facebook. And, worst of all, he's a New York Yankees fan. That's why our flags are at half mast—the Yankees won the pennant again."

She reminded me that Camp's original nickname was 'First Class George' because he only flies first class. "And be grateful because George gets up every morning and makes our coffee," she added, pointing out that this is a considerable achievement in light of the fact that the coffee maker is broken.

"Yeah, but he's a typical irritating Yankee who constantly harps about things that we should do differently. Yesterday, George tried to move a deer crossing sign on the highway because he thought it was in an unsafe place for any living thing to cross the road."

"That's because George is very discerning," my wife countered. "I'd even consider him to be a gourmet."

"Yeah, right," I said, "more like a raccoon washing his food."

To prove my point, I took Camp to a red neck eatery, the Away From Home Grill. "He'll never know the difference from the other over priced places we've been," I whispered.

The Grill's atmosphere is pungent, shaped by life-size posters of the Three Stooges plastered on the walls flanked by huge TV sets, each tuned to a different channel—all the better to divert your attention from the fare. Like a quick lube shop, everything comes from the kitchen deep-fried in oil—fish, grits, baked potatoes, hush puppies, apple pies for dessert, etc.

A few minutes after our food arrived, Camp slid his fried shrimp platter over to the edge of the table where it seemed in danger of falling off. The waitress could not fail to notice, and rushed over to inquire "is something wrong with your food?"

"Yes," Camp responded, "It's inedible."

"That's another reason why George won't get in the column," I grumped to my wife afterward. "He doesn't appreciate Southern cooking."

En route to the airport on Sunday morning, we stopped for the traffic light at the intersection of artery-clogging Deep Dish Pancakes House No. 187 and another 'no beach access' alleyway. Camp bolted out of the car and dashed onto one of the glittering tourist traps that form the wall-to-wall skyline that blots out the ocean. Moments later, he emerged wearing a T-shirt that proclaimed: 'I survived the Neon Sandbox.'

The Frozen Chosen

(Presbyterians)

Que Sera, Sera -- June 1, 2005

I like to think that I am in control of my life, but a good argument can be made that it isn't so. I never wanted to go into the newspaper business, yet here I am. The only way I can explain it is to turn to religion for the answer.

The urge to write about religion strikes me about once every ten years, or as often as there is a vacancy in the chair at Bullock's Barbershop. On this rare occasion, I was inspired by Dr. Kyle Allen who boldly went where most other Presbyterian preachers fear to tread. He preached the only sermon I have heard on Predestination in 44 years as a member of the Presbyterian denomination.

I doubt that many readers of this column have lost sleep wondering what Presbyterians believe. In case you have, however, I am about to tell you.

The name Presbyterian actually describes the denomination's government, which has enough layers to drive a Libertarian crazy. We have Deacons, Elders, Presbyteries, Synods and a General Assembly that acts like the U.S. Congress.

Presbyterianism originated in Scotland. That's one reason most Presbyterians (all except a handful of the recently converted Baptists and Methodists) are notoriously thrifty.

Presbyterians do not believe in Baptism by immersion—well, our water bill is always minimal. And I have heard preachers say another trait that separates us from other denominations is that Presbyterians will acknowledge each other when shopping in the liquor store.

We realize that most folks consider Presbyterians to be stuffy. So we are making an effort to change our image with a new "contemporary" Sunday worship service where members are encouraged to wear the clothes they plan to dump in the Goodwill box on Monday morning.

Presbyterians are universally known as the "frozen chosen," which is a thinly veiled reference to both stuffiness and Predestination. Actually, the fact that Presbyterians believe in Predestination is a closely guarded secret. Predestination is a subject reserved for whispered conversations because it is extremely difficult to find any two Presbyterians who have the same understanding about this concept.

A popular notion is that Predestination means "whatever will be, will be," as in Doris Day's 1956 hit song "Que Sera, Sera." In other words, there was no way to avoid landing in the emergency room with a broken arm on Memorial Day. Although it may be relief to get such calamities behind us, Dr. Kyle declares that believing such incidents are programmed into our lives is merely fatalism.

Predestination does not mean that the world is running on autopilot. Millions of prayers are answered every day. That is the only explanation, for example, for how people miraculously recover from ordinarily fatal illnesses. On the other hand, bad things do happen to good people, and some of these tragedies cannot be explained.

The most widely held view of Predestination is that God knows what the future holds for each of us, even the everyday choices that we will make in this life. Beyond that, Predestination means that God thought of every one of us long before we were born, and ultimately we will be reunited with God in Heaven because of His grace.

If you think Predestination is a tough nut to crack, then consider Double Predestination. If there is such a thing, Double Predestination means certain people were doomed to spend eternity in Hades before they were born.

The one thing I can state with certainty about Predestination is that we don't understand the full extent of its meaning. But Presbyterians are betting the farm on the writings of the Apostle Paul.

The Spiritual Gift--Nov. 19, 2003

I was roundly chastised from the pulpit after recently publishing the minutes of our church's monthly Session meeting in the newspaper.

I contend that the only secret I revealed was the fact that none of our Elders possesses the necessary mechanical skills to properly operate a thermostat. We are like the man in the FedEx television commercial who has earned an MBA degree but doesn't know how to get a package delivered.

Ordinarily, minutes of Session meetings are carefully guarded. They are taken directly by armored courier to the Mecca of Presbyterianism, Montreat, North Carolina, where they are deposited in a vault deep in a tunnel burrowed in a mountainside of solid granite. A little old gnome, known as Yoda, sits at the entrance to the tunnel where he files away churches' Session minutes to kill time while waiting for the lost Ark of the Covenant to turn up.

It's a fact that Presbyterians are reluctant to part with anything, even a reading of the minutes. As Dr. Kyle shared with the congregation, it takes ten Presbyterians to change a light bulb—one to do the work and nine others to reminisce about how wonderful the old bulb was.

The first inkling that I was in big trouble for having "leaked" the minutes occurred when I arrived at Sunday School, just four days after having let the cat out of the bag. No sooner had I plopped down in my chair than Christy Driggers walked into our classroom and shoved a batch of papers in my hand. It was a test.

"These 160 questions will reveal your spiritual gifts, if you have any," she explained. In other words, if I didn't pass the test, I could be ex-communicated from the Session for not possessing any spiritual gifts.

The test was full of loaded true or false questions like, "Do you enjoy inviting strangers home to Sunday dinner after church?" If I ever did that, people would be paying their respects by nightfall as I lay in state at the Wood Mortuary because my wife would have killed me on the spot.

"When the group is lacking organization, do you step in and fill the gap?" another statement read. Not really.

Some questions zeroed in on musical talents, such as: "Your ability to play a musical instrument is a blessing to others." True or false. The only instrument I can play is the radio.

Also true or false: "I enjoy leading the singing at church." Actually, the regulars who sit in nearby pews have asked me to refrain from joining in the singing of hymns.

There were tons of questions about money, like: "Would you be content to accept a lower standard of living in order to give more money to the church?" Well, I'm giving ten percent of a tithe now, what more do they expect?

And, "Do you feel special when someone asks you for a handout and then doesn't bother to say thank you?" Not really. I don't remember my last handout.

There were statements about helping in other ways, such as: "My skills in repairing things benefit others." False! I have shelled out big bucks for plumbers, electricians, etc. because I can't repair anything that requires more than Elmer's Glue.

I didn't come up empty, however. I gave a resounding "yes" to the question: "When important decisions must be made, do you have all the answers?" And "When one of my friends has a problem, am I able to tell him how to resolve it?" to which I answered "true."

I also said yes to: "I always use my ability to write to let others in on things they did not know."

When Driggers added up my score she observed, "Take some comfort in the fact that you have one spiritual gift—the gift of Exhortation."

"What's that?" I asked.

"It's just a nice way of saying you have the gift of B.S.," she replied.

Making Someone Happy--Nov. 4, 1987

Ordinarily I avoid matters of religion in my columns, but I had to share the story of being awakened with a shock in church on Sunday morning. Everyone in the congregation was given a $1 bill.

Because this just the opposite of what usually takes place at church, and since no one knew of the gift in advance, there was less than an overflow crowd in attendance. Furthermore, giving a bunch of Presbyterians a dollar apiece was a great risk because that money may never see the light of day again.

But our pastor, Rev. Ray White, was serious about proving a point. He had preached a fine sermon encouraging people to develop their talents. The dollar bill was given to inspire each parishioner to put his talents to work by helping another person.

I've been worried about what to do with my dollar ever since. My first thought was to make someone else happy, so I decided to pay a bill. But I could not decide which bill to pay, and if I wanted to pay them all, I would have to borrow every dollar that other members were holding. A single dollar just doesn't go very far.

Then I remembered the sermon illustration about the king who gave a grain of rice to each of his daughters. One daughter planted that single grain of rice. By the time the king returned many years later, her grain of rice had multiplied into a plantation. She became a queen. But her sisters, who had hidden or lost their rice, took a back seat.

Since I wasn't up to planting rice, I considered investing my dollar bill in the stock market. After the recent market gyrations, there was the distinct possibility that my dollar could be worth only 50 cents in the market by next Sunday when we were to report our actions. And I would hate to confess to the congregation that I had lost my dollar.

Then it occurred to me that the best investment I could make would be to buy one of my wife's credit cards for the dollar. But she was too smart for that. Besides, she had gotten a dollar of her own at church and didn't need mine.

While the Presbyterian dollar was burning a hole in my pocket, it dawned on me that I would have to report it as income to the Internal Revenue Service. Filling out the paperwork would require an extra hour of my accountant's time. The church's $1 deal was now a very expensive proposition.

I had nearly convinced myself that the man who buried his talents had done the right thing. Until Monday morning. Our youngest son was walking out the door on the way to school when he turned and asked "where's my lunch money?"

So much for the dollar. It did make several people happy including me, my son, and the school dietician who was counting on every student to eat lunch that day.

The Invincible Wayne Cole – Nov. 4, 2009

Wayne Cole never looks for trouble. He doesn't have to. Trouble finds him.

On a recent Saturday morning, Cole was driving defensively to his office at the First Presbyterian Church where he is the associate pastor. A vehicle came flying down Taylor Road from the opposite direction, crossed the center line and hit Cole head-on. The perpetrator continued and struck a car full of kids behind Cole.

No one was injured, except Cole. And it has not been that long since Cole was driving a group of college students to a retreat at the beach when the church van was sideswiped and rolled over an embankment. Cole was the only person injured, suffering a concussion that laid him up for weeks.

Upon hearing the crash on Saturday, Greer Fire Marshal Scott Keeley ran from his house nearby to the accident scene, and inquired, "What hurts?" Cole did not hesitate: "Just about everything."

Cole's more serious injuries include five broken ribs, a broken kneecap and a shattered ankle.

Cut in the mold of Clark Kent, Cole is quiet and unassuming. So it should have been no surprise when paramedics pried Cole out of the wreckage and removed his jacket that they were greeted by a huge S emblazoned on his royal blue undershirt.

Cole's value was certainly no surprise to the church family, which reacted by circling the wagons. In Presbyterianism, that means appointing committees. At least eight committees have been established to fill in for Cole.

One committee opens Cole's mail—he has received enough "get well" cards to tip over a luggage cart. A sister committee is writing cards and letters that Cole ordinarily sends.

Another committee of 25 is scurrying about making Cole's daily hospital visits and bereavement calls.

A fourth committee threw up its hands and hired a professional to teach Cole's Disciple Bible Study classes.

The fifth committee is offering pastoral counseling in Cole's place. So far there have been no takers.

The sixth committee is engaged in round-the-clock prayer for the pastor, Snow White, who morphed into Mother Hubbard when two other staff members, Susan Tompkins and Whitney Moss, went down with the H1N1 flu.

The seventh committee is guarding Cole's hospital room to prevent visitors from interrupting his rest. An eighth committee has established two Web sites devoted to providing minute-by-minute updates on Cole's daily progress. Here's a sample that I downloaded from a typical morning, Tuesday, Oct. 27th:

2 a.m. – Nurse wakes Cole to inquire how he's feeling.

3 a.m. – Nurse wakes Cole to install new bag of IV fluid.

4 a.m. – Nurse wakes Cole to take his temperature.

5 a.m. – Orderly wakes Cole for his daily sponge bath with Bradford Pear blossom-scented anti-bacterial soap.

6:30 a.m. – Nurse wakes Cole to take his egg order for breakfast: poached or hard-boiled.

7:30 a.m. – Breakfast tray arrives with a single rock-like egg, dry toast and unsweetened hot tea.

7:45 a.m. – Cole dozes off to catch up on sleep.

8:15 a.m. – Doctor wakes Cole to check on his multiple injuries.

9:15 a.m. – Physical therapist wakes Cole and rolls him out of bed to exercise.

9:45 a.m. – Cole buzzes nurse for pain medication

10:02 a.m. – Phone wakes Cole from a drug-induced slumber. Caller instructs Cole to have his wife, Suzie, report to the Smith Library at 11:30 a.m. in bullet-proof vest and combat boots to take part in a SWAT Team round-up to reclaim overdue books.

10:30 a.m. – Cole opts out of bedpan program.

11:30 a.m. – Greer Country Club calls to inform Cole that they have found a dozen golf balls with his name on them—in the woods.

12 noon – Cole buzzes nurse to enforce no visitors rule during *As the World Turns*.

12:30 p.m. – Orderly delivers lunch of slime green Jello, milk, two crackers and chicken soup, the only known cure for injured feelings.

12:35 p.m. – Cole buzzes nurse to report feeling nauseous.

The silver lining is that Cole's car, the only Honda capable of qualifying for Cash for Clunkers with it's mildew-shade paint job, was totaled. The church has considered taking a special offering to replace it with a riding lawnmower, but that hasn't happened—you know Presbyterians have a reputation for being "tight."

Keys to the Kingdom – Aug. 16, 1989

Those of us who were sentenced to serve on the Pulpit Committee of the First Presbyterian Church breathed a sigh of relief last week. Our new preacher finally arrived. This ended a year of anxiety—not on our part, but for members of the congregation that had been worrying about what we were doing all that time.

Now that the new preacher is here, the story can be told. Our committee spent the past year losing and finding keys.

Jean Smith, who is best known for having made her husband, Verne, a success, was designated the keeper of the keys. I'm not sure why she was chosen, except that Smith is truly a modern day saint while the rest of us still have a long way to go.

Anyway, Jean Smith ended up with the keys to everything. She was the only committee member who could open the church doors and then unlock the historical room where we held meetings. At times, these gatherings became quite an adventure when Smith was unable to find the keys in the world's largest handbag. It is a purse that you wouldn't leave home without. It is indispensible—if you need to carry all of your household belongings along.

Don't misunderstand. I'm not complaining about Smith's purse. In addition to dozens of compartments for keys, it contains a mountain of goodies for our road trips—things like cookies, candy bars, cheese straws and even boiled peanuts for Carlton Greene.

But mostly Smith's purse is full of keys, originals and spares to everything. One of those keys led to the pulpit committee's most harrowing experience.

That happened one weekend when we sneaked into South Georgia hoping to steal a preacher from an unsuspecting church. Some congregations would be happy if another church took their preachers, but others don't like pulpit committees snooping around. The latter was the kind of church we found ourselves attending on that fateful

Sunday morning. We knew right away that we had to slip out of town as quickly as possible before we were recognized as a band of pirates.

We had driven only two blocks toward the city limits, when two church ladies pulled up beside our car and began waving their arms and shaking their fists. "Oh, no!" Smith exclaimed. "We have been spotted. Step on it!"

I happened to be the one driving the only car in town with a South Carolina license plate, so I put the pedal to the metal to make a getaway. Just as I wheeled Smith's Cadillac up to the last traffic light at the edge of town, a man in a pick-up truck pulled alongside and started pointing at our car. I knew we didn't have a flat tire (this was a tire dealer's car), but I pulled over anyway to see what was the matter. To our surprise, one of Smith's extra sets of car keys was dangling in the front door lock. Thinking everything was in her purse, Smith hadn't even missed the keys!

Needless to say, we didn't get that preacher. Actually, we ended up with a better minister, which proves (sort of) our Presbyterian-like theology "whatever will be, will be."

And Jean Smith still has the keys to the kingdom hidden away somewhere in the world's largest purse.

The New Preacher Showed Up - Sept. 11, 1996

It was a remarkably happier day than the Sunday six months earlier when a killer cold wave wiped out the peach crop. Our pulpit committee was on the road that day. By then we were such experts that we were splitting up and spying on two separate churches every Sunday.

Rob Hendrickson's team was on a 300-mile trip to Georgia. Only after the service began did they discover that the preacher they had come to hear was out of town. And Jean Smith was already an unhappy camper because there was no money in the budget for dessert with our Sunday dinners. So Smith had taken to carrying a purse full of candy bars. Not one treat made it back to Greer that day.

If someone had to hear the most renowned preacher in the state, I figured it might as well be me—so my group went in the opposite direction that Sunday.

Sure enough, this preacher delivered the best sermon I had ever heard. We were filled with such a glow that we didn't even notice the bitter cold wind as we walked back to the car and found it locked after the service. Fred Kiemle had the keys, and he was nowhere in sight. Finally I peered into a side window of the church. And there was Kiemle, filling out an application to transfer his membership.

"Fred's wasting his time," I told the others. I was confident we could lure this preacher to Greer with our incentive package. We were offering such perks as a membership in GARP, a personalized parking place in the church lot, two tickets to the Miss Le Flambeau pageant, and the rights to Ed McLeod's TV ministry.

While we were contemplating breaking into Kiemle's car, I felt a tap on my shoulder and heard the question "Who are you?" delivered by an angry voice. I turned and looked into the face Glenn Johnson, a member of my college graduating class. I hadn't seen him since 1961.

"I was watching you from the back of the choir loft," he said. "I thought it was you, except you didn't have gray hair back then."

"It's my job to spot pulpit committees," he continued. "We ran off two committees after the early service." He added, "So, what are you doing here?"

I might as well have been trying to talk my way out of a speeding ticket. But I gave it a shot anyway. Borrowing a page from a presidential campaign spin doctor, I put a different twist on our mission: "We're just passing through. And being very religious, we decided to stop for church," I stammered.

I looked around for a member of our group to corroborate my story, but the rest of my team had vanished. They were scrunched down in the floorboard of Kiemle's car.

It was either run or change the subject. So I told the classmate that one of my fraternity brothers had died recently. Actually that also was spin. The guy did have a terminal illness, and I thought I was going to die if we didn't get out of there. While my classmate stood dumbfounded at hearing the news, I jumped in the car, and we sped away.

"I guess we have blown another one," I said when we came up for air a few miles down the road. "Yeah," said Kiemle, his voice filled with resignation. "Besides, I have heard that this preacher plays golf twice a week."

"Anyway," Susan Tompkins chimed in, "the preacher's wife looked pretty frumpy in that flowery pants suit. She probably wouldn't have been accepted real well in our church."

Brad Clayton had the last word. Turning to me, he said, "All in all, it was a pretty good show today—especially considering that you only put a quarter in the collection plate."

Keys to the Kingdom II --March 12, 2003

I spent most of the weekend on a scavenger hunt, but not on purpose. I was assigned to prepare Communion for Sunday worship, an endeavor that, like going to war, is better suited for younger people.

The First Presbyterian Church's Rule Number One is "Nothing Ever Changes," but I quickly discovered exceptions during a day of shock and awe. Sam Clayton and I arrived at the church promptly at 9 a.m. Saturday to prepare the elements for the service, but we couldn't get inside. The church had installed a combination lock, and the pastor had given me the combination. But when I punched the numbers, nothing happened.

During the course of the next hour of fiddling with the lock, a Greer police officer pulled up, and I thought he was going to take us in as burglary suspects. It turned out he was looking for a couple of old men who had wandered away from the nursing home, and we matched their descriptions.

At that point, I phoned the pastor, Dr. Kyle, for help. "I'll be right down," he said.

Once Dr. Kyle got us inside the church, I recalled that we were supposed to find the key for the cabinet where the silverware is stored. We turned up many keys in various places, but none would unlock the cabinet. Eventually, we forced our way into the old kitchen where we discovered a bushy tailed gray squirrel embedded in a stove waiting to be picked up by Sanford and Son. Maybe the squirrel had figured out the combination. And maybe he had buried the key to the pantry. He wasn't telling.

As a last resort, I turned to the book that never made any best seller list, a 50-page tome of instructions entitled "How to Prepare Communion." The latest revision does not say you may be forced to break into the church, but it does state that you must get the pantry key ahead of time, before the office closes for the weekend.

So we had to call the pastor again. "Please come back, open the office and get us the key to the pantry."

When we finally got into the pantry, we were confronted with another surprise, plastic Communion cups. It took twice as long to fill the new cups with grape juice because they hold more liquid than the old glass cups. The church obviously didn't believe in doling out large beverage samples back in the 1930s when real wine was being served.

We decided to haul the Communion ware to the sanctuary aboard the elevator, but couldn't figure out how to operate the machine. So we set out pushing a cart on the half mile trek from the new kitchen to the front of the church, comforted by the knowledge that we would pass several water fountains and restrooms along the way.

Once everything was in place in the sanctuary, we covered the silver service pieces with white linen cloths, only to discover that the cloths didn't fit. They had been mixed up at the cleaners, and we had two top pieces.

A search of another closet turned up a bottom cloth, enabling us to finish the task just in time for Clayton to leave at 5 a.m. Sunday on a fishing trip to Florida. I reported for duty at 10:30 a.m. to review the game plan for serving Communion.

"You did prepare a separate Communion tray for the workers in the nursery and the deacons standing guard over the Dead Sea scrolls in the catacombs, didn't you?" asked Elizabeth Clayton.

"No," I replied. "I didn't get that far in the instruction book."

"Does everyone else know what to do?" asked Nancy Welch.

"No. You are supposed to tell us," John McWilliams replied.

"Well, I haven't read the book either. Y'all just draw numbers for positions and do the best you can," Welch ordered. "Let's roll!"

Amazingly, there was only one incident of collateral damage during the service. An overturned cup spilled its contents that disappeared into the new carpet, which fortunately is a Vatican shade of purple thanks to the foresight of the Decorating Committee.

Elizabeth Clayton graciously agreed to help clean up afterwards. After washing the silver trays, we discovered that the dishtowels had been lost in the move to the new kitchen. Paper napkins would have to suffice.

"Now we'll just put the silver back into the pantry if you'll give me the key," she said.

The key? Of course, I remember the key. It's at home on top of the chest in my bedroom. It will only take me 20 minutes to get it.

Providentially Hindered--Jan. 8, 1997

Dear Dr. Kyle:

Rev. Greg Sweet's timely Reflections column about church attendance in this week's newspaper jogged my memory.

For several weeks, I have had good intentions of getting in touch with you about my attendance on Sunday mornings. I know that you are anxious for all church members to be present every Sunday, but I also am aware that increasing attendance has caused a major problem at our church. Often times people who wait until 11 a.m. can't find a seat on Sunday mornings—at least not on our favorite pews. So we have to sit on the front row or in the extra chairs against the back wall.

Overcrowding has created what many think is an unsolvable dilemma. Some people want to expand the sanctuary. (That would cost money, and you know Presbyterians almost never spend any.) Others think you should preach two services on Sunday mornings.

I am very concerned about dumping additional work in your lap. Therefore, I have come up with an alternative solution to the problem of our sanctuary being too small.

You know, I have always said that everyone has a right to miss church now and then. I think you should consider giving members excused absences. This should help cut down on attendance.

I have obtained a 1997 calendar and used it to plan my entire year. I am requesting in advance that you excuse me from church for the following reasons, and the number of times, which is indicated at the right:

Bad weather (Snow, ice, rain, fog) 6

Specials on TV (Super Bowl, Daytona 500, etc.) 6

Time change (Springing forward, falling back) 2

Easter (Hiding eggs 1

Overslept (Forgot to set alarm clock) 2

Golf (11 a.m. only tee time available) 4

Anniversary (Second honeymoon)...........................1
School's out (Parents need a break before summer)................1
Deaths in the family......................................2
Yard work (Take advantage of sunny days)................3
July 4 (Shooting firecrackers)...........................1
Vacation (But we can always be reached
at home in case of an emergency)........................2
Family reunions (Mine and the wife's)...................2
Labor Day (National holiday)............................1
School re-opening (Recovering from kids
being at home all summer)................................1
Illness (One for each family member).....................4
Work (So I can play golf on Mondays)....................2
Clemson football games (As grief support group leader).....5
Unexpected company (You just can't walk out)...................2
Christmas (Last minute shopping)........................1
New Year's (Party lasted too long).......................1

As you can see, Dr. Kyle, that leaves only two Sundays during the coming year. So you can count on us to be in church on the fourth Sunday in February and the third Sunday in August, unless we are providentially hindered, of course.

Everyone May Live Happily Ever After--Mar. 5, 2008

A tempest in a teapot is brewing in Greer, also known as the Magic Kingdom.

It happened on the last Sunday in February, 2008, which coincided with the last eclipse of the moon until 2027. Not to mention that this is a leap year and strange things are happening.

As luck would have it, Feb. 24 also coincided with a membership drive—of all things—at the stodgy First Presbyterian Church. Among the drawing cards was a 10% discount on tithes, which can be quite substantial for the community's high rollers. Prior to the service, free donuts were served along with coffee to keep parishioners awake. Afterwards, a loaf of kosher bread would be given to everyone who made it through the service without the aid of a cell phone or I-pod. Topping it off were drawings for coveted prizes that included a free gallon of gas and the chance to take a spin in the motorized shopping cart amid the mountains of Chinese products at Wal-Mart.

Personally, I was there with an ulterior motive—hoping to get a laying on of hands for my demon- possessed golf clubs

At any rate, a huge crowd had packed the church to the rafters that morning in a scene reminiscent of feeding time at McDonalds.

As one might expect, there was a monster of a traffic jam outside. Cars were everywhere, despite the signs that warn: No Parking Any Time (but go blank on Sundays) and the curbs painted yellow (but turn white on Sundays). Vehicles encircled Greer's original City Park (the triangle in front of the church). Coupled with the Great Wall of China roadblock that occupies much of South Main St., there was total gridlock in downtown Greer.

The last time such an event occurred was during the first year of the reign of Doctor Cluck, AKA Police Chief Dean Crisp. That was on the final Sunday morning before Ed McLeod launched the TV ministry that enables folks to simply stay at home and watch the Presbyterian worship services on line at their leisure.

The church was built in the 1930s when most people walked to worship and there was one car to a family, unlike today's world with a family of cars to one person. Some 80 years later, times have changed to the point that one of Greer's Finest galloped upon the scene on a white steed, Cruiser No. 666 accented in blue stripes with a Krispy Kreme logo emblazoned on the hood.

After failing to reach the Chief Prince, Dan Reynolds, whose golf cart was out of radio range while rumbling through the woods in search of an errant shot, the officer simply emptied his ticket book, attaching citations to every vehicle surrounding the church. Then he marched up the steps and knocked loudly on the front door. Which was startling since it occurred during a protracted moment of silence during the service—the confession of sins.

The officer, a rookie, informed the Head Dwarf on Duty that the cars would be towed. That started a chain reaction of hand ringing among other Dwarfs who, by the way, are easily recognized. Most have gray hair, and all wear gold identification badges signifying a pecking order, such as: Ancient Elder, Greeter, Money Changer, Tithes Enforcer, Safe Place Patrolman, Ask Me About Predestination, etc.

The pastor, Snow White, descended from on high and assumed command of the situation. First she invoked the names of Nancy Welch, Sam Clayton, John McWilliams and other would-be saints. When that failed, Snow White raised her wand and with a single flick of her wrist turned the police cruiser into a pumpkin. Now it would take more than a tow truck to clear the monster jam.

In the next instant, City Administrator Sir Edward Driggers appeared and began pleading for mercy. Sir Edward feared that the city fathers would never raise taxes to purchase a replacement for the police cruiser, and he does not have the resources to convert a two-ton pumpkin into 15,000 pies. The City Council might just lop off Driggers' beard.

"Furthermore," Sir Edward declared, "when the Governor finds out, he will never again come to Greer to hold his press conferences."

Ultimately, Snow White relented and returned the cruiser to its former status of a cream puff used car.

Everyone is expected to live happily ever after since the Dwarfs threw the membership campaign into reverse by adding a 20% surcharge to tithes in order to establish a Super Fund to build a parking garage.

The Downside of Home Ownership

Showerhead from Hell--April 13, 2005

One day last summer, as I was walking out the door to play golf, my wife asked, "Don't you think we need a larger bathroom—one that is handicap accessible so we won't have to be put in the nursing home?" (We had built our house in the era of small bathrooms—back when people were happy that bathrooms had moved indoors from the back yard. In today's houses, the bathroom is the largest room, causing me to wonder what people do in there all day.)

Being in a great rush to make my tee time that fateful day, I replied, "Yeah, I guess so." Besides, the only goal I have left in my life is to stay out of the nursing home.

Several months of pain and anguish later, we are the proud owners of a larger bathroom. It has a big wide handicap accessible shower door so we can roll our wheel chairs through the entrance. The only minor technicality is that a wheelchair cannot pass through our bedroom door, which is the only means of getting to the bathroom.

Taking a shower was once my favorite pastime. That's where I got my ideas for this column. Alas, I am no longer inspired while bathing because our remodeled bathroom has a new showerhead from hell.

My wife bought this special showerhead at the suggestion of a close relative, like her brother. He has always gotten great satisfaction out of irritating me, going back to the days when he would lie under the couch and make strange noises while my (then future) wife and I were dating.

The showerhead is a huge, round heavy metal contraption the size of a small pumpkin. The head is attached to a long hose-like device that enables you move it all over the place. You could shower while sitting in the lavatory, or you could stick it out the window and wash the car if you so desired. That big head emits water at only one speed, however. That is considerably less brisk than the flow from an old fashioned garden watering can.

But the really unnerving feature of the showerhead is that it will not stay put in its bracket near the top of the wall. Once the water is turned on, the pressure causes the showerhead to start moving around. Eventually, it falls out of the bracket, hitting you in the back of the head.

If you happened to be a Georgia boy like me, you would never stand in a shower facing the nozzle, even though it may attack at any time. Georgia boys back up to such things as open fireplaces and showers. So I never know when the nozzle is going to conk me in the head—unless I feel the spray changing direction, and then I have a split second to escape a blow to the noggin. But sometimes, the showerhead pounces unexpectedly without warning, like a bobcat leaping out of a tree.

The threat of another knot on my head has forced me to concentrate on the water flow while taking a shower. That's not relaxing, since I must concentrate every other minute of the day just to survive. Like walking gingerly through the yard in case the neighbor's dogs have deposited a surprise; during meals—so I don't spill gravy on my shirt and get a ticket from the etiquette police; like placing typos throughout the newspaper to give our readers a challenging discovery-type game since we don't offer a crossword puzzle.

Our malfunctioning showerhead has me on verge of going bankrupt not only because the quality of these columns has deteriorated from poor to pitiful, but also because I am spending more money for deodorants since I am taking fewer showers.

We May Knock Out the Walls--Mar. 10, 1993

What I dislike most about the daily grind is television crews setting up cameras in my front yard every morning before I can get out of the house.

My analyst is encouraging me to talk about these issues as part of my therapy. I was recently diagnosed as suffering from extreme mental anguish. (In non-clinical terms, that means I have become a nut case).

The fault lies with ETV for producing a documentary about a carpenter. No, it isn't one of those do-it-yourself home remodeling programs. This is a series about how to extend one very small project into a lifelong career.

This particular carpenter shows up every morning at 7 o'clock, the hour that (at least until recently) was considered the middle of the night at my house.

No longer am I awakened by a nightmare. Just like the advertisement for Classic Coca-Cola, the "real thing" jolts me out of bed. This carpenter is banging away with a hammer. Or he is reducing a perfectly good piece of lumber to a pile of sawdust with his power saw. Or backing his 10-ton truck over my rose garden to collect a loose shingle that has fallen from the roof.

This activity continues until about lunchtime when either the carpenter gets tired, or the TV crew packs up—whichever comes first. It has been going on for so long now that I can claim the carpenter as a dependent on our income tax return.

The president of the bank drops by every Friday afternoon, looks at the house, and increases my line of credit by another thousand bucks.

A reporter from *Southern Living* magazine will be arriving tomorrow to do a story about our topless den for the July edition.

115

This massive undertaking had a small beginning—there was a leak in the den roof. But the leak really wasn't in the roof, a minor detail we belatedly discovered after the entire ceiling, boards and all, had been removed. The leak was in a wall.

By then it was too late to stop the project, so we installed a window in the den ceiling. That made me the only homeowner on the block who must wear sunglasses around the clock.

As you can guess, we didn't stop there either. Compared to the spiffy remodeled den, our kitchen floor looked shabby. After replacing the kitchen floor, we began working our way up the walls. We installed a new stove because the original was getting old—it possibly would break down, and we couldn't get replacement parts. And I mistakenly thought that concept only applied to people.

Meanwhile, the Burch household was honored for making the list of the Commission Public Works (our power company) mega consumers. The painter, applying assorted stains and enamels with the most pungent odors, fumigates the house on a daily basis. I arrive home after a lousy day at the office to find all of the windows wide open and the furnace running full blast with the temperature in the 30's outside. Our neighbors are beginning to serenade us with beach music.

We also installed a new washer and dryer in the kitchen. This move saves a lot of steps, but the new appliances occupy so much valuable space that it forced us to move the exercise bike downstairs. Now it is inconvenient to work off the energy that we are saving by not having the washer and dryer in the basement.

If you can figure this out, you are qualified to advise us whether to knock out the walls and install more windows.

Customer Non-Service--Sept. 27, 2006

Everything you need to know in life is learned in kindergarten. My problem is remembering those lessons. I was rudely reminded that I obviously had forgotten the kindergarten lesson "do not laugh at another's misfortunes." I had cackled at my neighbor's bad luck when a Bradford pear tree fell apart in his yard and took down the cable and phone lines to his house.

Revenge was just around the corner, however. When I was out of town for a football game, my wife called with the announcement: "you will never believe what just happened..."

She said that a large tractor-trailer truck had rumbled down our street late that Friday afternoon. A huge wind deflector on the cab, proclaiming in bold letters "reaching for heaven," snagged a low-hanging cable TV wire. The line proved to be pretty strong. So strong, in fact, that it did not break, but it snapped off the attached Commission of Public Works (CPW) utility pole. Before stopping, the truck continued several hundred feet, pulling down wires and ripping electric services out of homes while leaving a huge pile of debris in the roadway.

The CPW did a yeoman's job of replacing the pole and restoring our electrical power that night. Bell South made repairs by Monday afternoon. But getting the Cable TV service restored was another matter.

I was assured, after a half hour battle with the cable company's computerized phone system, that a repairman would be out on Monday. When nothing had happened by Tuesday, I went head-to-head with the computer again.

"This may take a long time unless you are trying to make a payment," the computer announced. I was instructed to press a number for the reason I was calling—new service, future service, TV difficulties, billing, etc.

That led to a second question-and-answer session with the automated customer response. I was instructed to answer yes or no. The first question was "are you experiencing difficulties?" I answered "yes."

"Are all of your TVs out?"

Again I said, "Yes."

"Then it is probably a simple problem that the cable company will soon have repaired."

"No," I injected.

"We do not understand your answer," the computer said.

"What part of NO do you not understand?" I asked

"You must want to talk to an operator," said the computer. "You will have to wait in line for the next available operator."

The operator that finally picked up 15 minutes later happened to be the Spanish-speaking expert. Unfortunately, English is his third language. "Are you having problems, senor?" he asked.

"Yes. A big truck ripped the cable line out of our house. It's lying in the street," I said.

"I see, your line is on the floor," the man offered.

It was the only time I have ever regretted forgetting most of the Spanish words I had ever learned in school. "No," I said, searching for the right words. "The line is not broken in my Casa Blanca."

"Oh, you live in the White House with President Bush," the man said.

"No," I said. "I'm sure the President has Direct TV."

"Then this will take a few minutes," the cable tech said. "While we are waiting, can I interest you in high speed internet service?"

"High speed and Charter don't belong in the same sentence," I declared.

After a five-minute pause, the man promised, "it will only be a leetle longer senor."

"That's good, because this conversation has consumed my entire lunch hour," I responded.

After a few more minutes of silence, the tech returned to the phone. "Do you like feetbol?" he asked.

"Yes. It's the only reason I have cable TV," I replied.

"Bueno! I can promise your service will be restored in time for the Clemson-Carolina game," he said.

"That's great, because I think the Tigers are going to whip the Tar Heels on Saturday," I responded.

"No, no amigo," he said. "I was referring to Clemson and the Gamecocks."

'But that game's two months away, in November," I protested.

"I know, I know senor," he said.

The Night Visitor--Jan. 13, 1993

A crew from "Unsolved Mysteries," the television show, is due any day at our house to film the story of The Night Visitor.

It started Jan. 7th of last year when I had just settled down for a long winter's nap only to awake with a start, my wife was punching me in the ribs. "Did you hear that!?!" she screeched. For someone who slept through the bombing of London, Mayor Don Wall's speeches and every noise-making activity in between, my answer was, "I didn't hear anything."

"Well, I heard something walking down the hall," she insisted. As usual she was right. The evidence, we discovered the next morning, was that the dog's breakfast had disappeared before the dog awoke.

It was the morning of Jan. 8, and I decided to spring into action. "But whatever you do, don't put out any poison!" I was instructed. So I set out a mousetrap to catch the critter.

Jan. 9 – I awoke to find the mousetrap had been sprung, the bait was gone and so was the critter. That called for Plan B. I went to the store and bought a giant, family-size rattrap.

Jan. 10 – The critter had not touched the giant trap. Instead, it had removed four small apples from the holiday 'apple tree' decoration on the dining room table and carried them to the kitchen. I went back to the store, bought three more knuckle-crunching rattraps, and baited them with apple slices.

Jan. 11 – The critter had not touched a single trap. It must have been running late that day, because at lunch time, Hazel opened a closet door and screamed when she saw a tail sticking out of her purse. The critter was munching on two cookies she had stashed away. Hazel fainted and was unable to describe what the critter looked like. I reacted by wedging balls of tinfoil around the opening where an air conditioning pipe was running into the attic.

Jan. 12 – The critter removed the tinfoil, but there was no sign of it anywhere. So my wife took over. She hired the world's finest exterminator who promptly arrived with a large trap that he set in the bottom of the closet.

Jan. 13, 14, 15 – The exterminator struck out, too. But the critter was still around, hauling off any food that wasn't behind lock and key.

Jan. 16 – I heard an old wives tale that critters are attracted to peanut butter. So I baited one of those new traps—the kind with sticky insides—with peanut butter and waited.

Jan. 17 – At 4 a.m. I was awakened by my wife punching me in the side. "Is this a re-run?" I asked. "No," she replied. "The thing is in the trap." It was true! I heard it thrashing around in the den. "Well, I'll throw it out tomorrow," I said, as I rolled over and went back to sleep.

Jan. 18 – I tiptoed into the den to remove the trap with the critter. But the critter was gone and the trap had been destroyed. That did it! One of us was going to have to go. I decided to declare all-out war. I marched back to the store for poison, put it out in places that only the critter and I could reach, and, for obvious reasons, did not inform my wife.

Jan. 19, 20, 21, 22, 23 – The critter has not been seen or heard from. All the traps were still empty. My wife was starting to ask questions. My response was, "we need to get to the bottom of this." I faxed an urgent message to 'Unsolved Mysteries.' They put my story on the schedule.

I admit 12 months is a long time to wait for an answer, but perhaps the TV crew will at last discover the identity of the critter. Since all of this began on Elvis' birthday ... well, you never know.

Newspaper Publishing Not for the Fainthearted

Management Is Not My Strong Suit--Sept. 22, 1999

Some people think I have it made in life. Like I only have to report to the office on Monday morning, write this column and spend the rest of the week on the golf course.

Unfortunately, the position of editor carries many other responsibilities such as emptying the trash and refilling the soft drink vending machine.

There is also the duty of overseeing the personnel. This amounts to listening when employees inform you what they are willing to do and when they plan to do it. I recently inquired, for example, if our ace education reporter Gala Mickle was ready for another Blue Ridge High football season. "No," she said. "I'm not covering any more football games. I've been going to games for three years, and I still don't understand what is happening out there." This from the person with the most education in the entire company—one who is on the verge of obtaining a master's degree.

I pointed out that education and football are a natural combination, like peaches and cream. Had she not heard of student athletes? "Besides, you can't play football if you aren't enrolled in school," I argued.

"No," she declared for the third time. "I'm not going." Even when I pointed out the benefits of strolling along the lush grassy sidelines in the cool, refreshing evening air, not to mention the added bonus of being mistaken for a cheerleader, she refused to budge.

For someone who once got the autograph of industrial magnate Roger Milliken, management is not my long suit. I gave up on the prospect of Mickle following my directives because, after many years at this job, I have learned that when you put employees in the corner for disobeying an order, they don't get any work done, period. I have considered implementing an incentive system, but the company can't afford to offer a reward.

I must also report that the perfect attendance award is already out of reach for Theresa 'Granny' Williams, and it is looking doubtful that she will retain the Employee of the Month trophy as well.

On the day I assigned Williams to check on the grades of the Greer High School football players, I looked up a half hour later and she had vanished. It seems Granny was enjoying a picnic. It may have been Labor Day, but that is not a company holiday. (The company allows only Christmas Day, and occasionally another half day off for a funeral—if it is your own).

Those who play hooky are soon caught, and Granny was no exception. We learned that Granny, accompanied by her grandson, climbed aboard a contraption ("with swings that whirl around," she explained later) at the picnic. Since the ride was filled with small kids, Granny's presence on the device gave real meaning to its name, the Tilt-A-Whirl.

With Granny on board, the contraption needed an extra jolt of electricity to get started, and that dimmed the lights in the Bi-Lo 'Rena. After it finally got going, the ride made only a few spins before Granny became deathly ill. She began waving frantically at the operator who merely waved back. He thought waving was Granny's means of expressing that she was having a wonderful time. When the

124

machine finally stopped, Granny staggered to the nearest garbage can where she deposited her midday feast of chili cheeseburgers and fries. Then she collapsed on a park bench.

Granny was still dizzy (more so than usual) the next day when she went to load the fax machine that (she said) was spinning like a top. As a result we failed to fax off a $1 million sales order for a customer and therefore he got fired the following day (I'm not making this up).

Our office manager, Tater Tot, the only one who gives commands that are actually obeyed, decided Granny could have the rest of the day off. Granny immediately headed for the chiropractor's office to get help for a sore arm. I failed to make the connection between a sore arm and dizzy spells, which is probably the reason I never got accepted to medical school and had to settle for a career in the newspaper business.

The only thing I can report with certainty is that everyone went home early last Wednesday when Hurricane Floyd was predicted to hit, even though the Governor did not order us to evacuate to the coast for a better look at the storm. I was left to board up the building by myself. Thank goodness Floyd proved to be a fraud.

The Cure for Insomnia--Aug. 31, 1988

I avoided them as long as I could, which was for more than 20 years. I'm referring to the monthly meetings of the Commissioners of Public Works that fall just short of PTA meetings at the top of my list of least exciting things to do.

Since the Commissioners occasionally make an earth shattering decision (like raising electric rates), someone has to be there to get the news. Unfortunately, most CPW transactions rank alongside Aunt Nellie's gall bladder operation when it comes to creating attention-grabbing headlines.

For that reason, CPW meetings never attract standing room only crowds. That means I can grab the empty seat next to the coffee pot, which is the best place to survive.

Everyone else fights for chairs near the end of the table where sits the tray piled high with homemade cookies. I pass the time by keeping a running tally of the number of cookies that each attendee consumes. It's like scoring a tennis match until it becomes more like counting sheep, making it even more difficult to stay awake.

A recent meeting opened with a 60-minute discussion of how the general manager should deliver the monthly financial report. That put me under the table like an over-served drunk at happy hour. Despite having guzzled a dozen cups of coffee, I slumped over and tumbled out of my chair.

After that interruption, the Commissioners devoted the next hour to debating whether new water customers should pay a high instal-lation charge and a low monthly fee, or vice versa. The last time I heard such a conversation was in high school when we tried to decide whether the chicken or the egg came first.

I fell sound asleep again, but this time my eyes were wide open, floating out on stems as the result of rapidly growing bladder pres-sure from having consumed the entire pot of coffee.

I roused slightly when the Commissioners were handed a bulletin that claimed many people's electric meters were running too slowly and must be checked out. The only thing I know about the meter at my house is that the dial spins faster than a ballet dancer in heat. If that isn't fast enough, then I can't afford to pay the next power bill.

Even the fear of bankruptcy couldn't prevent me from dozing off again when the Commissioners plunged into a discussion of the Peak Mean Shaving Plant. Although the name sounds like some sort of hostile barber shop, it has to do with delivering natural gas. If the Commissioners could only bottle the air in the meeting room, they could offset the shortage in the gas department.

Three hours into the meeting, I concluded that the Commissioners are sitting on top of a monumental discovery and don't realize it. They have invented a cure for insomnia! Now, if I can just convince them to sell video tapes of their meetings to people who can't sleep, the Commissioners can make enough money to cut our power bills in half.

Repetitive Motion Threat Apr. 14, 1999

Sometimes publishing a newspaper isn't fun. That's when you get tangled up with government red tape. I have been cowering in terror ever since I read that OSHA was considering eliminating jobs that cause employees to make repetitive motions.

Those fears were confirmed last week when a 50-page form arrived. It was an application for Workmen's Comp insurance coverage. The underwriter wants to know about every repetitive motion encountered in the newspapering work place.

After checking out the questions, I determined that repetitive motion is not responsible for poor health, absenteeism and other employee troubles.

I also decided to share here only the repetitive motions that affected former employees, on the grounds that my own health would be in danger if I wrote about our current employees.

We have had several employees who suffered Carpel Tunnel Syndrome, but for different reasons. One injured his wrist punching the time clock. Another developed Carpel Tunnel Finger from picking his nose. Yet another acquired Carpel Tunnel Elbow from raising and lowering a coffee cup to his mouth.

But those were nothing compared with an employee who came down with Carpel Tunnel Knees. The malady was caused by lowering his rump to the commode seat in the men's restroom. The first thing this employee did every morning was to head straight to the men's restroom, sit down and smoke a cigarette. He returned again and again to the same spot to smoke during the workday. This occurred so often that other employees were frequently waiting in line for the bathroom and 18-wheelers were delivering cases of toilet paper on skids. We never proved smoking was hazardous to this employee's health, but his repetitive motion was a double-edged sword: in addition to knee problems, he came down with toxic shock of the tush from sitting in one place for so long.

Another former employee had an even more unusual repetitive motion—passing gas. He was constantly enveloped in a cloud of toxic fumes. The fellow had to go into counseling for depression because no one would come near him.

A female employee once filed an insurance claim after developing cauliflower ear as the result of making hundreds of personal calls each day.

Another female came down with TMJ (an injury of the jaw) because her mouth worked faster than her brain. She blurted out things she hadn't yet thought of.

Several employees have been treated for writer's cramp. The affliction was caused by using old fashioned computers—pencils.

Because of the danger of keyboards causing Carpel Tunnel, some of our employees have had to limit their typing to one paragraph a day. If the disease continues to spread, we will have to make words three times as tall to fill up the pages of the newspaper.

Perhaps the most unusual case was the employee who filed for medical leave after licking 600 postage stamps to mail the monthly subscription renewal notices. She claimed that licking the backsides of famous State Birds of America was a psychologically damaging experience.

Even snacking has been declared dangerous. One employee was provided with a set of false teeth after wearing his chompers away while consuming crackers from the company vending machine.

All of this set me to wondering if anything that takes place in the DMV office could be classified as repetitive motion.

One Wild Ride--Dec. 16, 1987

The world's greatest mother didn't particularly appreciate what I had to say about her artificial Christmas tree in a recent column. But I topped that with a stunt that will erase any lingering doubts in her mind that she has raised a total idiot.

Anyone who puts in 70 to 80 hours a week as a newspaper journalist has to be a little daft, but the lengths we will go in order to get a story occasionally defy all logic. The day I found myself surrounded by feathered friends was when I realized my career is for the birds.

The owner of a steel erecting firm must have acquired the same insight, for he phoned to say that a great news photo opportunity was in the works at Allen Bennett Memorial Hospital where his crew was building the framework for a new four-story addition.

Since sticking a tree on a steel beam in the sky, known as the 'topping out ceremony', is something special, I was there in five minutes. It wasn't long until I had been persuaded to climb into the 'man basket' attached to a crane so I could be hoisted into the air to take a photograph LOOKING DOWN on the tree.

I have climbed the Washington Monument, gazed from the top of the Empire State Building, flown in airplanes and even ridden in the Goodyear Blimp. Yet it wasn't until I had been hoisted 90 feet in the air in the 'man basket' that I realized I am terrified of heights.

Twirling around like a Yo-Yo on a string, I was hanging onto the 'man basket' for dear life. There was no way I was going to let go with both hands in order to use the camera to take a photo. Besides, either my legs were shaking so badly that the basket would not stop vibrating or I couldn't get the building to stand still long enough for me to snap the shutter.

The cable and bolts holding the basket up looked as if they were shrinking, and the thin piece of plywood covering the bottom of the basket appeared that it might give way at any second. If the wire were to break and send me plunging to the ground, the only consolation was that the hospital emergency room was just a few feet away. And, in the event of the worst outcome, I could see the mortuary some three short blocks in the distance.

All sorts of things were running through my mind: I should have taken the advice of a multitude of life insurance salesmen who harassed me over the years and purchased even more policies; I should have sent someone else from the office out on this assignment, except they probably have the good sense to stay home. Finally, I decided to organize a 'just say no' support group to keep people from being tempted into agreeing to a crane ride.

All the while, I was waving to the crane operator to bring me down. He thought I was signaling to go higher, so the basket kept going up..up..up...until I was looking down on the light towers of the new Greer High football stadium across the highway. When I received a runway clearance from the Greenville-Spartanburg Airport, the crane operator threw the switch and lowered me to earth where I staggered off to my car on legs made of jelly.

We Need Truth in Absenteeism--Feb. 15, 1995

If anything good came from the most miserable wintry blast of the season, it was the campaign theme that should be adopted for the 1996 election. Term limits, welfare reform and truth in sentencing are out. I will cast my vote for whoever campaigns on a platform of "truth in absenteeism."

Whenever there is a hint of snow in the forecast, even if only in the wildest dreams of the weatherman, some of our employees immediately start making plans to take the next day off. After that, it doesn't matter whether we get snow or not. Some of them aren't going to come to work, no matter what. They may be able to make snowmen or go skiing for hours, but they would not dare brave the elements to come near the office.

With $1/1000^{th}$ of an inch of sleet barely visible on the ground on Friday morning, one employee phoned in at 9 a.m. to inquire if the office was open. He was informed that the place was open, and most of his co-workers had already arrived. "Oh," he said, and then added hastily, "By the way. I'm sick. I hope to get to feeling better so I can go to the doctor this afternoon."

By the time he got to the doctor's office, this hypochondriac had embellished his symptoms to include acute hearing loss. "I can't even hear myself coughing," he complained.

The doctor quickly dashed off a prescription, and the patient asked, "will this medicine improve my hearing?"

"No," the doctor replied. "But it will make you cough much louder."

His excuse is one of our all-time greatest for missing work. We have quite a collection of those because whenever it fails to snow, which is most of the time, Walter requires all absentees to submit an excuse.

Until last week, the best excuse had been, "I couldn't get in my car because the door was frozen shut."

A close second was "my refrigerator broke down." The solution to that problem would have been to shove the refrigerator outside, into the cold air, and open the door.

Then there was the time when a sewer line broke in an employee's yard and deposited a year's worth of fertilizer. He was out for several days on the cleanup. Our employees have missed work because of "ice on the windshield," and all of the ordinary excuses: dead batteries, flat tires, curling iron/stove left on, wife/husband/child/dog sick, etc.

Most excuses are very creative. The most well-worn is "I had to go to the grocery store." It's true. Everyone goes shopping when a winter weather advisory breaks. Snow was predicted so many times during the past week that by Monday morning one employee was trying to give away four gallons of milk and seven loaves of bread.

I've had it up to here with excuses. The next time it gets so cold that the post office snail refuses to come out of its shell, I want to hear someone tell the truth For a change, I'd like to hear: "I'm going to take tomorrow off and just stay in bed where it's warm."

Until truth in absenteeism becomes law, we have instituted a new policy at the office:

1. Sickness: Doctor's statement no longer will be accepted. If you are able to go to the doctor, you are able to come to work.

2. Leave of absence: (for surgery) will not be allowed. You were hired as is, and having anything removed would make you less of a person than was bargained for.

3. Death (your own): will be accepted, provided that you give a two-week notice. It is your duty as a responsible employee to train your replacement.

The Sky Is Falling--Oct. 29, 2003

No one at *The Greer Citizen* office had to buy a Halloween mask this year. We all look as frightening as goblins without going to any extra effort, just sitting around in hard hats with our lower lips stuck out far enough to give a hitchhiker a ride.

We have been in the middle of a construction zone long enough to complete a full term pregnancy. The city is building a new parking lot around us and moving overhead wires under ground. Unfortunately Duke Power, Bell South, etc. didn't get the message to remove their phone poles because downtown Greer has become a "no fly zone" for carrier pigeons. The poles are still standing, along with the wires, since the construction began in February. Ashmore Brothers paving has built curbs high enough to serve as hurdles in a track meet, but laid no asphalt so mud and gravel wash into the street with each cloudburst.

Until last week, I hadn't been complaining about having to park inside the paper dumpster—which is better than the plight of our customers who must either take a chance on parking in the middle of the street or wearing a backpack for the hike to the front door.

Then came a terrible clatter from above, as if someone were crashing through the roof. Walter rushed out to see what was the matter, and returned with his lower lip extended. "Richard (Howell) has started replacing the roof," he explained, adding, "He must have another payment due on his daughter's big wedding. There go our Christmas bonuses," at which everyone's lower lip jumped out.

Actually, we had arranged for Howell to repair the roof in early May, right after the parking lot was supposed to have been finished. But during the construction upheaval, Howell could not get his trucks close to the building. Since then, I have feared the roof would come down around us before he could get it fixed.

As the work continues today, the aroma of Howell's char-broiled asphalt is barely preferable to the scent of a skunk. And the pounding from above has left everyone suffering with Excedrin headache No. 283.

Since it hadn't rained for the seven previous years, we didn't know the roof leaked until January when the year of the monsoon set in. After each big rain, water would be dripping from many places across the ceiling, under which we have positioned the largest barrels money can buy. There are daily complaints about the buckets, especially those that block the paths to the men's room and the Coke machine. At least everyone doesn't have to sit at his desk under an open umbrella like Lori Sondov.

To make matters worse, the grading of new contours for the parking lot somehow funneled the rainwater runoff from Poinsett and Main toward our back door, which is far less substantial than the Apalache Dam. We have frequently arrived at work after an overnight storm to find water running through the building from back to front.

This has called for some dire measures. When the Blue Ridge Water Co. refused to buy our extra water, we were forced to bring in a water safety instructor to teach a seminar for our employees. We also became downtown Greer's only building with life preservers hanging on the wall.

The Chicken Little "sky is falling" syndrome hit us on a sunny day last week when Howell started the roof project. Since then, dust has been flying everywhere, and employees are worrying about asbestos in the falling ceiling tiles—completely ignoring my opinion that waterlogged asbestos isn't going anywhere.

Of course, I am totally immune at my desk, where I am surrounded by a six-foot-thick wall of paper, the best insulation available.

The last time we upgraded the building was in 1965 when we unplugged the window air conditioning unit, which no longer worked, and put a ladder underneath it in hopes that someone would steal the eyesore. The old unit is still with us.

On the brighter side, Howell is going the extra mile by making "gutter hats" for our roof drains. And we take consolation in the fact that our building, which ordinarily is a conflagration waiting for a match, hasn't been condemned by the fire marshal. Wet paper will not burn.

As for the parking lot that continues to proceed at a glacier-like pace, paving contractor Mark Ashmore promises it will be "finished by Christmas." He did not say what year.

Out of the Twilight Zone--Nov. 15, 2006

Men dressed in coveralls, wearing hard hats and speaking with strange accents hauled away an ancient piece of Greer history last week. They spent two days dismantling and removing our old News King printing press. Until a year ago, the King Press had printed *The Greer Citizen* every week since it was installed in 1971.

Making the transition from printing with "hot type" (a centuries-old technology of working in metal) was a quantum leap. We had to expand the building 35 years ago to accommodate the new press. At last, *The Greer Citizen* was on the cutting edge! We could finally print decent black and white photos.

Over the years, I figure the King Press cranked out more than 18 million newspapers with untold billions of words—and, yes, a fair number of them were misspelled to keep our readers on their toes.

Over time, however, our cutting edge press was no longer a match even for cutting hot butter. We were slowly enveloped by the Twilight Zone as the King Press evolved into a real monster. We began dancing to its tune every week.

The press habitually ground to a halt at the most inopportune time—publication day on Wednesday afternoon—on nearly a weekly basis as one part after another failed under the stress of wear and tear.

Promptly at 2:30 p.m. every Wednesday afternoon, all of our employees—except "Granny" Williams who watched the front door—gathered at the press hoping it would start. More often than not, we stood for hours just waiting.

There seemed to be a rhyme and reason to this madness as the press became a Murphy's Law unto itself. If anything on the press could break down, it did break down. Our pressroom guys would scramble frantically to make the repairs while customers stood in the front office, waiting for a paper. Frequently, replacement parts had to be custom made at local machine shops. On occasion we had to take the paper to another town to be printed because Fed Ex could not fly in a scarce part from Omaha, Neb. until the next day.

The earlier the staff got the pages ready to print, the later the press would start running. You could set your watch by this axiom.

Another certainty was that on the very Wednesdays when our staff had gotten a big scoop or an award-winning feature, the press would inevitably break down. Instead of getting the news out at 2:30-3 o'clock, it was 7, 8, 9 p.m. or later before the press budged. The monster repeatedly and thoroughly whipped us.

The company had a ritual of ordering pizza for employees if we hadn't finished printing and delivering the papers by 7 p.m. The staff consumed so many pizzas in recent years that we received a customer appreciation award from Papa John's.

We laminated a permanent sign, that was habitually delivered to the Post Office every Wednesday at 5 p.m., reminding postal workers not to lock the back gate so we could put the papers in the mail, no matter what time the press started.

Even as the press was wearing out in the 1990s, we foolishly attempted to make it produce color work, something that it was never intended to do. This only compounded our problems, often giving us papers with colors that never quite matched up. The effect was a 3-D like appearance. Unfortunately, we could not provide a pair of 3-D glasses for readers with each copy.

I wasn't sorry to see the cantankerous King Press leave town.

Walter also took it in stride. He did become emotional, however, after spotting a dime on the floor when a forklift removed one large section of the press. Said he remembered losing it on September 18, 1983.

Even as it was departing, the King Press was the centerpiece of one last delay. Two truckers stood in the street and argued over the right to haul off the pieces. The press wound up being transferred from one "low boy" to another 18-wheeler, a delicate process that took several hours.

As I write this, the King Press is on a 3,000-mile journey to the port of San Diego, Calif. We are told that it will be shipped overseas.

I secretly hope that the News King will wind up in the hands of the Al-Qaeda so it can foul up their propaganda program. It could delay terrorist news for years.

What Is an Editor Emeritus Anyway?--July 3, 2008

Thousands? of readers are pummeling me with questions: "What are you doing now that you are retired?" and "How does it feel to be retired?" and "What is an Editor Emeritus anyway?" Please, please—one question at a time. Here are the answers.

If I was retired, I would not still be writing this (potentially) Pulitzer Prize winning column every week and the other stuff in the newspaper that readers just cannot do without. I am, however, now working just part time.

That decision was not difficult. I made the choice after being informed: "we are cutting your pay, but you can stay on full time or just work part time."

It's nice to be at my old desk at the office a couple of days a week, but at my age it's nice to be anywhere. I plan to continue working part time until I check in at the Wood Mortuary or they run me off. Or maybe until other stuff just starts to interfere too much with work. For instance, I never punch the clock on frantic Wednesdays because working that day would interfere with my golf therapy sessions at SSI (Saving Seniors In denial).

I don't have a hard and fast schedule most days. Sometimes my wife wakes up old grump; other days she lets me sleep.

I never thought that I would ever get this old, but it beats the alternative. I don't worry about things like I once did, such as my health. It will simply go away.

I look so ancient that whenever I eat out, the waiters ask for the money up front. And flowers are beginning to scare me. But I really don't feel incredibly old, just chronologically challenged.

I sometimes sit in Bullock's Barbershop waiting room for hours, and that's just to get an estimate.

Other days, I do yard work. I have heaped pine needles on every inch of unpaved surface, even some areas that were once occupied by grass. I have dug thousands of holes in the ground and filled them with plants that led to the unintended consequence of having to water them every day. I've pulled so much water out Lake Cunningham that the ducks are padding in the mud, and some of my drowning plants are begging for life preservers.

And, wouldn't you know it, just as I sailed into the "golden years" our house started to fall apart. I have already had to repaint the entire sun porch and refinish the dining room ceiling. Next is converting an upstairs room into an office so I can work when I'm not at work. I've gotten the cart before the horse there, however, by piling stacks of paper everywhere so that the room already looks like my office at the newspaper.

I don't really feel retired, and I'm not sure very much has changed other than I have to put forth more effort to accomplish anything. But I do have the good fortune of being able to rely on my vast experience, which is a wonderful thing—it enables me to recognize a mistake when I make it again.

I was always taught to respect my elders. Since becoming Editor Emeritus, I no longer have to respect anyone since there is no one left to look up to except John McCain.

Editor Emeritus does have some advantages. I'm the only person in the office who is allowed to use his break time to take a nap.

The youngsters on the staff always ask me the historical research questions, like "Did George Washington really sleep in your parent's guest bedroom when he visited Greer?"

As a courtesy, I also am asked my opinion about many issues. But no one sticks around to hear my answers.

In addition to carrying a pay cut, the title of Editor Emeritus permits me to sweep out my office and empty my own trash can. But I'm not complaining. The value of working is that when I am here, I can't be out spending money. And there's nothing to buy here in the office.

But, if you really want to know what an Editor Emeritus is—it is an Old F...!

The Good Old Days

Remember the Good Old Days?--July 29, 1992

My high school class is planning its 35th reunion this fall. The shrinking number of us will sit around and reminisce about the Good Old Days, whatever those were.

Actually, I remember when Pepsi Colas were a nickel (a 12-ounce bottle at that), hamburgers were 15 cents, and gasoline was 29 cents a gallon. It didn't cost an arm and a leg to get in the movie theatres either. The downside of the Good Old Days was working for minimum wage, which was 50 cents an hour.

If we took a vote, I don't think many of us would want to return to the Good Old Days. Besides, in the past 35 years there have been more inventions to make life easier than in all of previous history.

When it comes to the Good Old Days, our memories play tricks on us. One's memory is a selective filter, weeding out the bad while allowing us to recall only the good times. For instance, do you remember the Good Old Days *when*:

Your paper grocery bag burst, spilling the contents all over your yard as you struggled to get in from the store. Not as likely these days with the advent of plastic grocery bags.

You looked in the freezer and there was no ice for the Kool Aid. Your little brother had forgotten to fill the trays with water. Would you trade that for your automatic ice maker?

Remember when you ran out of money and had to rush to the bank before it closed at noon? Now you can stay in touch with your money (assuming you have some on deposit) 24 hours a day at the automatic teller machine.

Speaking of plastic finance, do you remember being stranded at the cash register with more items in your buggy than you could pay for? Master Charge has cured that problem. It has made us a nation of debtors at the same time.

Do you remember waiting until a commercial break so you could rush to the bathroom during your favorite TV program? With the invention of the VCR, you can record the program and zap the commercials.

Another invention, the remote control, makes it possible to watch several programs at once, bypassing all the commercials in the process. Unfortunately, this feat cannot be performed by people with one-track minds, like me.

Remember spending hours on your knees in the yard with a pair of clippers trying to trim the grass around trees and along the edge of the walk? Since the invention of the Weed Eater in 1971, homeowners have been winning this battle with nature.

Ever forget a dentist's appointment or your anniversary? Thanks to refrigerator magnets (unheard of when I was growing up), the head of the war department now keeps all the important events posted in the kitchen so there will be no excuses.

Did you ever slave over a hot stove all day cooking a big meal? Hot stoves are a thing of the past, thanks to the microwave oven, which is the greatest invention since the can opener. The microwave also doubles as a dandy popcorn popper.

Do you remember the big controversy when fluoride was added to toothpaste? That was nothing compared to the importance of dental floss today. Don't dare leave home without your floss unless you want to hear a sermon from the dental hygienist during your next checkup.

Do you remember the world's foulest odor? It was that bag of dirty diapers you saved all week to be picked up by the diaper service. Disposable diapers doomed the diaper service to the same fate as the Railway Express.

Governor Carroll Campbell credits the fax machine with bringing BMW to South Carolina. Personally speaking, I have no use for the fax. It brings us numerous letters I would not open otherwise and memos not worthy of a Post-It Note (also a recent invention). What's more, fax paper costs $5 a roll. If there's one Good Old Day I yearn for, it is the time when the Post Office delayed and occasionally even lost my junk mail.

Why is That?

More Smug Than Ever--Jan. 15, 2011

I suspect that the ban on smoking in the City of Greenville is the reason that the movie *Leatherheads* was filmed in Greer. If the George Clooney production is true to its setting in the 1920s, a haze of smoke will color this movie blue because most people smoked in that era—especially movie stars. They smoked on screen and endorsed cigarette brands in advertisements on the pages of such magazines as *Life* and *The Saturday Evening Post.*

Some Greer folks continue to puff away in the tradition of America's 300-year love affair with tobacco that began when the Pilgrims joined the natives in smoking peace pipes. Exporting American tobacco back to the motherlands was like sending over a Trojan horse. The new thrill of smoking unleashed serious health consequences for generations to come.

This is no joking matter. No smoker has ever beaten the undertaker, although in some cases it has taken 80-90 years for cigarettes to get the best of them. As a super smug reformed smoker, I'm still taking up space—proof that quitting works.

My first memory of the noxious weed is from the eighth grade. One warm May evening, a group of guys bought a couple of packs of cigarettes. It was easy back then—no law against kids smoking. Simply pump some quarters into a vending machine. We pitched a tent in Denby Davenport's back yard, climbed into our sleeping bags for a spend-the-night party, and lit up cigarettes. Pretty soon the air was so thick you could cut it with a knife.

About that time, Denby's mom peeled back the tent flap "to check on us," and the smoke boiled out. The news of our misbehavior got back home before we did.

I didn't light up again for three years until all of my high school friends were smoking. Principal B.L. Frick responded to great clouds of smoke billowing from restrooms by designating a "smoking area" outside the cafeteria. There, students and teachers alike puffed together standing side by side. Our motto was "no relightable butts left behind."

Football coaches frowned on smoking, but chewing tobacco was different. Coach Eddis Freeman enjoyed Brown Mule, a cellophane-wrapped cake of tobacco that could pass for a brownie. I will never forget my first "chaw' of Brown Mule. I cut a "plug" off the block, stuck it in my cheek, and minutes later fell flat on my back. The world was spinning, and I wanted get off. I have never been dizzier in my entire life.

The temptation was too much when I arrived at college to find handfuls of cigarettes being given away to freshmen attending "smokers" thrown by fraternities. After that, I found a reason to smoke on every occasion—birthdays, non-birthdays, eating, dieting, going to bed and starting a new day.

Years later, after a small fortune had gone up in smoke, I joined the ranks of reformed smokers who are overbearingly inconsiderate of the rights of smokers to puff themselves into oblivion.

And so, when I recently accompanied my son to check out a car he wanted to purchase, I was immediately turned off by the odor of stale nicotine when we opened the door. We made a hasty exit, although I admit if someone had removed the scent of smoke from my first set of wheels, it would have fallen apart. Nicotine and tar were the only things holding that 1954 Plymouth together.

The federal government is paying farmers not to grow tobacco, and local governments are defending me from cigarettes, even though I wouldn't go into the same room with one. My only question is: Why are cigarettes illegal when it's okay to consume enough alcohol in bars and restaurants to get pie faced and smash your car into a tree?

Put your Congressman to Work--March 9, 2005

When there are so many vehicles parked in your driveway that your home could be mistaken for a used car lot, one thing is for certain—the family is spending a lot of dough on gasoline.

So it came as no surprise one night recently when, during a newscast, the announcer declared that the stock market had suffered its largest one-day decline in over a year. The reason, we were told, was because the price of oil had risen to $51 a barrel.

"We should all go to the filling station right now and get gas," declared my son, Joey.

"Nah," I said. "Let's wait until in the morning. The price of gas won't go up over night." Wrong! On my way to the office I discovered that the price of unleaded BP gas had gone up by 13 cents a gallon. That's for the same gas in the underground tank that was $1.69 a gallon yesterday. Joey was right.

At least new car dealers announce they are padlocking their doors while changing prices (but it could be to prevent customers from escaping.) Convenience stations don't lock up to change prices. They do it by computer, even as you are filling your tank with the precious liquid.

Gasoline prices are like a broken window shade. They roll up in a hurry and don't ever seem to get back down.

Politicians are continually talking about cutting taxes, saving Social Security and fixing schools that aren't broken. But I have never heard a single office seeker campaign on a platform of lowering gasoline prices.

America is spending billions on all sorts of research—except finding a fuel that will eliminate the nation's dependency on Middle East oil. Why not nuclear-powered cars? The only drawback would be having to drive in a lead suit.

And why doesn't the U.S. have a direct oil pipeline to Iraq? The Iraqis could pump the stuff over here in exchange for the billions of dollars that we spent to put Saddam's head in a trophy case.

Not even the talking heads on CNN have answers to those questions. So the best I can do is imitate the 11 o'clock TV news which offers tips on all sorts of things, like 10 reasons why you shouldn't open the front door after midnight or ways to stay dry if you live on a river boat. I have come up with a list of suggestions for easing the pain of high gasoline prices.

Another son, Preston, measures his gasoline consumption by how many dollars worth go into the tank. Preston puts aside the same amount of cash for driving every week, and when prices go up, he simply drives slower to avoid running out of gas. He holds the world record for a Ford Explorer—30 miles a gallon. That's tip number one. Drive slowly. Not only will you get better mileage, you will thoroughly confuse police radar operators.

Tip Number Two is to go on a diet of cabbage and beans. You will be surprised at the kick in the pants from natural gas. At times your car will coast uphill.

Don't drive on flat tires. Not only is it bad for the rubber, square tires require more energy to roll than round ones. If Tip Number Two doesn't improve your mileage, at least it will help you keep the tires property inflated.

You can improve gas mileage by taking a page out of the NASCAR handbook. Learn how to 'draft' as the Nextel Cup drivers do at the Daytona Speedway. You can get so close behind a tractor-trailer truck that all wind resistance is eliminated and thereby improve fuel mileage. The money saved at the pump can be used to pay the fine when you are ticketed for 'following too closely.'

Tip Number Five is drive a lighter weight car. If you can't afford to trade for a subcompact, then throw out all of the junk you are hauling around including the roof rack, spare tire, etc. Experts say that a vehicle's mileage improves two percent for each 100 pounds removed. And while you are at it, join Weight Watchers to reduce the size of the driver.

Idling, that is sitting in one place with the engine running, is a terrible waste of gasoline. If everyone would cut the motor off at some of Greer's "traffic lights from Hell," such as Wade Hampton at Buncombe Road, Main at Poinsett, Wade Hampton at Poinsett, etc., millions of dollars could be saved annually.

The best way to save at the pumps is to buy a pair of walking shoes and hit the pavement. Taking a bicycle is another good alternative. America could put OPEC out of business if everyone parked their cars and pedaled to work. It would also put fitness centers out of business.

If all else fails, put your Congressman to work earning those big bucks that elude the rest of us. Write letters demanding that he do something about lowering gasoline prices.

Compulsive Hoarding--April 14, 2010

I have been diagnosed with a new disease. While watching television recently, we stumbled upon a PBS documentary about compulsive hoarders, those people who collect things—massive amounts of stuff that eventually forces them out of house and home.

The hoarders appeared to be perfectly normal before the investigative journalists took cameras into their homes. In every house there was only a two-foot-wide path for the occupants to walk from room-to-room amid floor-to-ceiling clutter.

Each compulsive hoarder was asked why he collected things. One explained, "the reason I never throw anything out is because I think that I might need it sometime."

"Why Leland, that sounds just like you!" my wife exclaimed. "Don't you realize that you're a compulsive hoarder, too?"

My wife was right, as usual. I do hoard things, although I don't have much to show for it because she's constantly throwing out my junque. I'm still grieving over the loss of my gas grill that she packed off to Miracle Hill in 2002. We haven't grilled a steak since then.

Last week, my wife cleaned out the laundry closet and chunked a box filled with tubes of caulk and caulk remover. "But you never know when we might need to caulk something and then have remove it," I protested—to no avail.

Over time, I've become somewhat adept at hiding stuff that should hit the dumpster. I keep things like my high school sweater with a big block letter G that I was awarded as a member of the golf team. That sucker is 52 years old and full of moth holes, but it is out of sight in the back of my closet. I'm the only one who knows its there, although my wife recently warned me, "your closet is next on the list for spring cleaning."

In another closet, I have a huge bag of 500 well-used golf balls. All golfers are on the lookout for balls, but I have the advantage of a 20-foot-long retriever to fish them out of lakes and briar patches. Finding balls is the best part of playing golf. Besides, I never know when the urge to practice might strike, and I will need balls. At least once a year, I get the fever and hit a few dozen balls into Thomas Grady's yard next door. Since Grady insists on bringing them back, my horde never shrinks.

I come by hoarding naturally. Like my arthritis, I inherited it from my mother. Among the things she saved were every letter that any family member ever wrote to her, empty glass fruit jars, old magazines and huge balls of string. It took months to clean out her attic after she passed away, so I feel that a similar inheritance task should be handed down to my own kids.

It's a miracle that our ceilings haven't collapsed under the weight of the stuff that I have stashed away in the attic. "Our house would burn for days if the attic ever caught fire," my wife says. I have hundreds of old magazines, books, my collection of model trains and eight sets of worthless old golf clubs stored in the attic.

I have also amassed several hundred black plastic flowerpots of various sizes—just in case I decide to start raising plants one day. These pots now occupy a sizeable area of the basement, and my wife doesn't go there because gardening isn't her thing. Otherwise, I would have no pots.

There is a basement cabinet filled with glass vases for roses. I have more rose bushes than anyone needs, but not nearly enough to fill so many vases. But then....who knows when a bumper crop of blooms might come along.

Unfortunately, Medicare doesn't cover the malady of hoarding. There's no magic pill that would send me into a spring-cleaning mode and fill several trash dumpsters with stuff that I will never need.

I should follow the example of a customer who ordered 50th wedding anniversary invitations. "Please put NO GIFTS on the invitations. We don't want any gifts. We don't have room for anything else," she said.

I don't feel that way—yet. But just in case, I added a book on "coping with hoarding withdrawals symptoms" to my collection of 500 paperbacks.

Old Hackers

Beach Bloomers Blunder--April 18, 2007

A gloomy overcast could not dampen my excitement as I hastily threw my clothes into a suitcase and lugged my golf clubs to the waiting car that was already slam full of hearing aids, walking canes and extra pairs of eyeglasses. I was leaving for the annual geezer golf excursion to the coast! Nothing could possibly go wrong—could it?

While unpacking at our destination five hours later, I realized that in my haste I had forgotten to bring my undershorts. Not a good thing, as Martha Stewart might say.

It would be downright embarrassing to have to admit to such a blunder, especially after I had kidded Hal Jones about forgetting his T-shirts the year before. From that experience, I knew there was no store with underwear anywhere near where we were staying. As a last resort, Jones had to by a pair of undershirts, emblazoned with the image of a huge pig, at a nearby supermarket.

Hoping for the best, however, I said nothing about my plight—thinking that when we were out looking for a restaurant, I might spot a men's clothing store. No such luck. We passed dozens of real estate sales offices, numerous hammock shops, sunglasses huts, and restaurants of every size and shape, but no clothing stores.

My lone pair of Fruit of the Looms that I was wearing made it through the first morning of golf the next day. At lunch, I noted the other guys were hopping around like contestants in a cake-walk. They were trying to grab a chair as far away from me as possible when we sat down to eat.

My one and only pair of underpants had stood by itself in the corner our first night, and, barring a miracle, it would have to move outside to the deck the second night. Desperately looking for a solution, I checked the yellow pages and located the nearest TJ Maxx store some 31 miles away. "I have a gift certificate for T.J. Maxx, and it's going to expire April 15," I announced.

"No way," said Jones who was driving. "It would cost $10 worth of gas to go there and back."

Finally I had no choice but to confess that I had forgotten my unmentionables. It was my most embarrassing moment since I dropped the collection plate during a church service.

Taking pity on my plight, Jones gave me a pair of his old Calvin Klein boxer shorts. Since my posterior had never come in close contact with such upscale intimate apparel, it dawned on me how Cinderella must have felt—both dazzled and conspicuous.

Then Rob Hughes suggested, "Why don't you just wash your dirty underwear in the sink. That's what women do with their delicate lingerie every night."

So, decked out in the hand-me-down Calvin Kleins, which Jones refused to take back after I had worn them, I set about removing the skid marks from my own briefs.

Naturally, there was no washing powder in the condo, so I had to use the complimentary bar of milk and honey facial soap at the lavatory. Some time later, I put my increasingly off-white, sopping wet Jockey shorts into the clothes dryer and set it on high, timed for two hours, while we went out to look for supper.

The minute we returned to the condo, I dashed to the dryer to find that the elastic in my underpants had turned to toast as the result the heat treatment. My once tight-fitting briefs now flapped around like the Calvin Kleins.

"When your underwear keeps falling down, it's a real handicap playing golf," I grumped during another dismal performance on the links the next day. Denby Davenport had no sympathy. He refused to give me any strokes. He did get a handicapped sticker for my golf cart that stated: "In case of emergency, do not resuscitate so the pace of play can continue uninterrupted."

Arriving home Saturday night, I was unceremoniously dumped out of the car amid a torrential downpour of rain. Even as my underwear was again soaking wet, I asked "if I am out of rehab by then, do you guys want me to make reservations for next year?"

"Our calendars are already booked for next March, April and May," my three ex-pals responded in unison.

Old Grump, Times Four--Mar. 19, 2009

The verdict is in from our DOA (Department of Aging) fact-finding excursion to determine how long geezers can survive on their own in the Neon Sandbox.

We (Old Grump times four) made it for barely three days thanks to some extremely patient folks, especially one waitress at the Ocean View Restaurant. We arrived there at 4:45 p.m., just in time to get the early bird dinner pricing, and then managed drag out the meal for so long that eventually we were eating elbow-to-elbow with the high rollers who were seated at 8 p.m.

We had barely sat down when our waitress, who appeared to be hardly old enough for the high school senior prom, walked into a buzz saw—us.

"What's this so-called 'no wine' item on the wine list?" Hal Jones demanded immediately.

"I think it means you can't put new wine into your old skin, seeing as how you might explode," I interrupted, noting that the waitress did not have to ask for an ID before handing Jones the wine list.

The waitress patiently explained something about California champagne that I didn't understand, but Jones chirped, "I knew it! I knew it all along!"

"I'm thinking about ordering sautéed crab. What ingredients are in the sauté?" Denby Davenport asked.

"I don't know," said the waitress. "No one has ever asked about the sauté."

"Well, how long have you been working here?" Davenport inquired.

"Nearly two years. But I'll find out about the sauce," she said, turning and making a dash for the kitchen.

While we awaited the answer, Rob Hughes peeled off his purple cardigan sweater, revealing a bright yellow sweater underneath. That confused the waitress who wandered about for some time before spotting us. "It's sautéed in butter," she announced, confessing, "I was looking for the purple sweater table."

"In that case, I'll have something else," Davenport declared. "Butter is not good for my diet."

I ordered a second glass of iced tea to cope with the hot air, but the waitress brought out a glass of red wine and handed it to Hal. "That's not for me. Denby's drinking red wine," Jones said.

"And I don't want any more wine," Davenport informed the waitress. "By the way, what's your name?"

"Misty," she replied.

A few minutes later, Misty brought out two plates of fried shrimp piled high with French fries. "Take that back," said Hughes who had peeled off another layer and was now wearing a coral pink sweater. "I ordered a shrimp cocktail."

"And I ordered a baked potato," I said. "We're old. We can't eat French fries any more."

"I'm sorry. Please keep the French fries, and I'll get you a baked potato," Misty insisted.

As soon as her back was turned, everyone grabbed a fork and began spearing the fries.

When the baked potato arrived, Davenport asked for a second glass of red wine like the one he had recently rejected.

"Can I get you all dessert?" Misty inquired some time later.

"Maybe," Davenport responded. "What kind of ice cream do you have?"

"Vanilla," Misty said.

"No, no. I mean what brand of ice cream," Davenport said.

"I don't know, but I'll find out," she said.

"It's Pierre," the waitress reported a few minutes later.

"I never heard of that brand, but I guess I'll have a small dish, just to taste it, even though it's not good for my diet, you know," Davenport groused.

Misty soon returned with huge bowl filled with a half gallon of ice cream.

"I didn't order this much ice cream!" Davenport screeched. "I'm on a special diet."

"I know," the waitress said. "This is for all of you to share. It's free."

"Oh! In that case, we'll take it," I said.

"Our waitress is the best part of this dinner. I think I'll give her a $10 tip," Davenport declared between spoonfuls of ice cream.

Jones collapsed with a sneezing spasm when Misty returned with the check. "I always do that. I'm allergic to picking up the tab," Jones halfheartedly apologized.

"Sorry, but could you bring us separate checks?" Hughes asked.

"Denby, did you really give her a $10 tip?" I asked as we were walking to the car.

"No," he said. "I had second thoughts, especially after Rob was the only one who got a hug."

"Maybe she felt less threatened by Rob," I speculated. "He's constantly shrinking." By then, Hughes had peeled off another layer and was down to a baby blue sweater.

"Actually, I brought 15 sweaters, but I'm saving a couple for the golf course," Hughes explained.

"Does a salad come with this?" Davenport asked, poring over the lunch menu in the golf course restaurant three days later.

"I don't know. This is my first day," the waitress said.

"By chance, is your name Misty," I inquired

"No!" she huffed, and vanished.

A half hour later, another waitress emerged. "I'll take your order now," she said.

"What happened to our first waitress?" Davenport asked.

"She quit," was the reply.

"Our golf has gone from bad to worse. We should try shuffleboard next year....we could be a traveling team for The Bayberry and take our game to the beach," Hughes suggested. He quickly added, "I'm going to call for reservations right now, before I forget Misty's table number."

Going and Going – April 19, 2006

I have learned another lesson the hard way: after years of macho independence, the older a person gets, more like a toddler he becomes. This reality check occurred last week when our group of very old timers headed to the beach thinking we were taking a mini golfing vacation. As it turned out, however, we spent three days heeding the calls of nature—not the call to be one with the great outdoors in the glorious springtime, but frequent and insistent bladder calls. Our old wine skins can't hold much liquid of any sort.

We failed to recognize the tip off when we had traveled only 20 miles and someone raised his hand to request a "pit stop."

After that, the most frequently asked question was "How many more miles?" Not to the Neon Sandbox, but to the next rest area. We also pulled off at most of the major exits along I-26 in between, pretending to be looking for cheap gas. "While we're here, we might as well check out the restroom," I suggested more often than not.

At one stop, I became concerned after a long wait and headed inside to round up two members of our party. "Did you see two old men in the restroom?" I inquired of a boy who was doubled over, waiting outside at the door of a two-holer. "Yes sir," the kid replied. "One of them can't get started, and the other one can't stop."

After that, we posed as DHEC restroom inspectors in order to spend as much time as we needed while pretending to check out the accommodations.

The only bright side of our situation is that no one had to set an alarm clock to arise at 7 a.m. Someone was awake using the restroom every half hour throughout the night.

We discovered that drinking six glasses of iced tea for breakfast, even though it may be 90 degrees outside, is not the best way to start a new day. A few minutes later on the golf course, we were like Energizer bunnies—we were going and going.

164

"Hal!" I yelled on the fourth hole, "what are you doing over there in the bushes? Your drive landed in the fairway for the first time today."

The next afternoon, the groundskeeper at the posh resort golf course questioned us. "Did you gentlemen see anything unusual out here yesterday? Some of our big azaleas turned brown, just over-night."

And so, it came as no surprise that after hundreds of ups and downs Denby's zipper snapped off during our last pit stop before heading back to Greer. "I can't get out of the car like this before we get home. I'll probably explode," he grumped.

The long ride had barely begun when we dozed off for afternoon naps, only to be rudely jolted awake a few minutes later by the sound of a siren. It wasn't a parade but a fund raising event at a forlorn low country crossroads known as Andrews.

I looked in the side mirror and saw a silver belt buckle approaching from a dingy brown, unmarked police car. Pretty soon the rest of the policeman followed his big belly up to the front door. "Mr. Jones," he asked, "why didn't you stop at the four-way sign back there?"

"I did, officer," Jones said. "I stopped behind the car in front of me, and when he pulled out, I did too."

"No. That's not how you are supposed to stop. I'm going to have to write you a ticket," announced the poster boy for Krispy Kreme donuts.

A half hour later, Rob spoke up and said, "I do wish the cop would hurry up. It's 18 miles to the next rest stop."

Finally the officer, who could star in the next Dukes of Hazard remake, waddled back to deliver the traffic ticket. "If you come back here to court next Monday, I can get your fine reduced," the officer suggested.

"In the first place coming back would cost more me more in gasoline than I would save on the reduction," Jones pointed out. "And we

165

have to stop so many times that we only make about 30 miles an hour. So I would lose one entire day of my retirement as well."

"It could have been worse," I suggested helpfully. "If the cop had noticed Denby's broken zipper, he would have hauled all of us off to jail."

Hot Wheels

You Never Forget Your First Car

"You never forget your first car."

I heard that gem of wisdom frequently when growing up, and years later I can confirm that it is true. I was reminded of my first car upon hearing of the demise of another textile giant when Pillowtex shut down. The textile industry put me on the road. I spent an entire summer working at Greer Mill to earn enough money to buy my first car.

My quest for a set of wheels began one Saturday afternoon when it took me four hours to thumb a ride home from Wofford College, only 18 miles away in Spartanburg. That was in another time when many motorists weren't afraid to pick up hitchhikers, so my struggle to get home indicates that I appeared to be as weird then as I am now. Prior to that day, I had regularly borrowed the car of a fraternity brother, Bill Belk, but we had a falling out when I snagged the right rear fender of his '49 Plymouth on a telephone pole. I made a mental note that day never to let anyone borrow my car if I ever got one.

By a stroke of luck I landed a job working the third shift for J.P. Stevens Co. for $1.29 an hour. It was a princely wage compared with my previous summer's salary of 50 cents an hour at Taylor's Peach Shed.

After three months in the textile mill, I had saved $650 and set out to find a used Ford or Chevy. When those brands proved to be too expensive, I settled for a 1954 Plymouth coupe because the price happened to be $650. Actually, I jumped at the chance to buy this five-year-old, high mileage car. Not only was it all I could afford, it was also "two tone" blue, my favorite color. Otherwise the Plymouth was a plain vanilla six-cylinder, straight drive car—the vehicle of preference of old maid school teachers.

I became a big man on campus when that Plymouth drove through a series of snowfalls like an SUV. I taxied my friends who got stuck in their cars with automatic transmissions.

Even my professors could spot me. One day, I had a heck of a time eluding Dr. L.P. Jones, faculty advisor for the college newspaper. He began pursuing me in his big black Nash that resembled a pregnant whale because I was late turning in an advertising sales contract. I managed to shake him off, picked up the contract at a downtown store, and beat him back to his office in the History Department. "I tried to catch up with you a few minutes ago," Dr. Jones said. "Your Plymouth must be some more automobile."

"Oh, it is," I replied.

The best gift I received that Christmas arrived from my future bride. It was a new set of seat covers for the Plymouth.

The car contributed as much to my education as any class I ever took. It taught me that the more things you own, the more problems you have looking after them. I also learned more about automobile mechanics than I ever wanted to know.

I had never heard of a vapor lock until the Plymouth quit running one day in downtown Spartanburg. Seeing my predicament, a guardian angel ambled out of a nearby barbershop and inquired if I needed help. "Yes," I said. "My car won't start." The man went back inside and soon returned with a pail of water that he showered on the motor. That freed the vapor lock and the car started instantly.

I learned how to change the oil—every 1,000 miles for that model. I learned tire changing, too. The treads barely made it 5,000 miles before wearing out, so I bought many a recapped tire for $10 apiece. After running to Winthrop College every weekend, the Plymouth developed serious engine problems. Much of the money I earned working at Greer Mill the following summer went to have the motor rebuilt.

The day after the car came out of the shop with the motor purring, we hit the road to visit relatives in Atlanta. When we were heading home a day later, the car began making a strange knocking sound. Glancing in the mirror, I observed a plume of blue smoke. It wasn't long before the Plymouth quit in Lavonia, GA. It was a Sunday afternoon, and the only place open was a filling station. The proprietor, truly a good Samaritan, persuaded one of the town's two mechanics to come in and work on the Plymouth. The mechanic quickly determined that the car had thrown a rod. Upon dropping the oil pan, he discovered nuts, bolts and bearings that connected a piston rod to the crankshaft. The parts had not been tightened during the final step of rebuilding the motor. Three hours and $200 later, we were on the road again.

Despite its woes, I have always regretted trading my first car for a newer model.

Get That License--Oct. 18, 1989

If you think the stock market crash is a problem, it is merely a minor inconvenience compared with getting your driver's license renewed. This is a chore that can require weeks of advance planning, especially to gather all of the necessary paper work.

And once you arrive at the DMV office, there are numerous obstacles to overcome. For starters, it is not easy to figure out which line you need to camp in. Each line has its own name like: tags, titles, transfers, license renewals, road hazards, weight station, road maps, one-way, blind, handicapped and eight-items-or-less. The line labeled license renewals is the one with all the laughs.

If the line is moving fast, you still have time to eat a box lunch and take a nap before you get to the window to match wits with the harried clerk.

It is only then that you discover the DMV will no longer issue you a driver's license unless you can prove your identity. The law says you can't get a license unless you have your Social Security card. The other side of that problem is that you can't get a Social Security card without a driver's license. You can't vote without either document, but that's another story.

The DMV may be a nice place to visit, but I would not want to work there, especially when someone like me comes though the line. I waited three hours recently to get my license renewed and went home boiling mad because I forgot to bring my Social Security card.

Then too, the clerk took a look at my old driver's license and saw a smiling George Clooney with dark hair. Looking up at an old geezer with gray hair standing at the window, the clerk declared, "you aren't Leland Burch." The obvious reason that you simply cannot exchange your old license for a new one is that no one can recognize you from your old photo.

When the week-long license renewal process continues, you note that the Highway Department may be operating the newest cruisers on the market but are still using the same vintage cameras that snapped George Washington signing the Declaration of Independence. To get your new driver's license photo, you must stand on a set of footprints in the general vicinity of the camera. Then, while your head is in motion obeying a sign that orders: "look over here," the camera snaps your photo. This is the reason there are a lot of one-eyed people pictured on South Carolina driver's licenses.

When the machine spit out my new license, the clerk inquired if I wanted to wait for an ambulance or just go straight to the mortuary. I've seen better looking Halloween masks than my driver's license photo. No respectable post office would put my picture on the wall.

The man standing in line behind me said he had not seen any victims of a tornado that looked as bad as I did in that photo. I was a disaster waiting to happen, but no one has sent me any relief funds.

I may yet cash in because a TV station is offering to buy the worst drivers license photos to air on a new horror series, 'Night Gallery.'

Red Neck Test Driver —Dec. 15, 1999

When the invitation came in the mail, I figured the BMW Manufacturing computers had become early casualties of a Y2K disaster. Why else would the world's most elite automobile maker invite a red neck editor to test drive its newest creation, the X-5 sports activity vehicle?

Never mind. I jumped at the chance. Test driving new cars and writing reviews for pay is the ultimate dream of any reporter.

Like the night before Christmas, I didn't sleep a wink before we were to take the new X-5 to the hill country of Georgia for a rugged, off road test. Just moving from our motley assortment of company cars into a plush BMW was like going from a flea market to Tiffany's for a private showing of rare gems.

Soon after sunrise, I carefully wiped my feet and settled into the captain's seat, surrounded by fine grain leather. Actually, surrounded is not quite accurate. My rump overlapped the seat, serving as a grim reminder that I must start on a diet—after Christmas of course.

Every review of a BMW that I have ever read included a sarcastic comment about cup holders. I will dispose of this issue at the outset: If your friends chew tobacco and drink beer at the same time, then the X-5 does not have enough cup holders to take three of them on a Sunday afternoon spin.

As for the rest of my review: I gave the X-5 one thumb up for its all-time four-wheel drive system. It is ideally suited for most off road activities including hauling moonshine from liquor stills on logging trails in the back woods.

The X-5 is an acoustic wonderland complete with Dolby CD and multiple speakers. I had no choice but to give it one thumb down, however, because the radio selector automatically screened out all country music stations.

Unlike its first cousin, the Z-3, the new SAV failed to pick up any women. And for that I gave it two thumbs down. BMW engineers should have had the foresight to give the X-5 a coating of heavy window tint. The car turned a lot of heads as we drove past. Females, however, quickly looked away after observing this white-haired geezer who was clearly visible in the command seat that sits tall above the road.

My test model came equipped with a powerful V-8 engine. We rocketed from 0-60 mph in 7.1 seconds across a Georgia pasture while dodging cow pies and flattening fire ant mounds. This fine piece of machinery gets a thumb up for giving Orkin a run for the money as a fire ant exterminator.

I gave the X-5 two thumbs up for its real-time self-leveling system, rack and pinion steering as precise as a Swiss watch, and extra wide wheels. The combination makes the X-5 a peerless hunter. Possums, squirrels and rabbits are no match for an X-5. Scurrying animals that dare to cross the road in front of an X-5 are sure to end up on the dinner table.

The challenge of bringing home a day's road kill makes a case for BMW to outfit the X-5 with a truck bed. Unfortunately, this is not a pickup truck, although BMW is definitely on the right track. I am holding out hope that the next BMW introduction will have style sides, a gun rack and knobby tires for taming muddy barnyard floors.

Nothing "like a rock" that Detroit advertises, the X-5 is truly a pearl and one of great price at that. Parked in your driveway, it makes a statement: you have surpassed the Joneses next door by qualifying for a really big loan from the bank.

Unlike my "Exploder," the X-5 was passing everything in sight as we cruised toward home on I-85. The BMW was kicking butt and taking names—until we blew the doors off a Ford Crown Victoria that looked like an unmarked patrol car. I glanced down at the speedometer and was horrified to see we were sailing along at 95 mph. I immediately put the four-wheel disc braking system to an emergency stopping test, which smoked the tires coming down to the speed limit.

The performance convinced me that the new BMW will relegate the Mercedes SUV to the ranks of a taxi cab—a role that brand has played for decades in Europe. On a more personal note, they had to pry my fingers off of the steering wheel to get me out of the X-5 when it pulled up at the Zentrum in Greer.

Better Than a Yugo – June 6, 1990

When I drove up to inspect the new automobile models recently, the dealer threatened to call a tow truck. He said my clunker sitting on the lot might scare his good customers away.

And then, I nearly keeled over when the salesman explained how my current set of wheels had depreciated a whopping $10,000 in just three years. My car's value couldn't have dropped much faster if I had driven it off a cliff.

I can remember the day when houses cost less than that car. Now I have been informed it is a practically worthless heap of metal that is only good for a huge paperweight or a doorstop.

"Your car was really a great one in its time," the salesman said consolingly as we negotiated over whether my chariot was worth $100 or $200 as a trade in.

"But that was only a few years ago," I argued.

"The factory realized they had a made a big mistake when they built this car," the salesman countered. "They quickly discovered there wasn't much demand for cars with 75 horsepower that get five miles to the gallon."

I had to admit that my car does have some drawbacks. It behaves like an 18-wheeler because you have to build up considerable speed to climb over the next hill.

It does break down on occasion. But I really did not mind when the air conditioning quit because I simply rolled down the windows and kept going. The radio doesn't work either, but I never listened to the radio anyway.

The fact that the gas gauge is broken is only a minor irritation. I buy gas every day whether I need it or not.

The salesman informed me that the factory is making bigger and better cars "to smash the Japanese and Koreans." It sounded like a very patriotic approach to manufacturing.

The manufacturer's latest brochure claims quality goes into every car. When I asked about 'always low prices,' however, I was informed that I was in the wrong store.

The salesman recommended that I purchase the new Roadhog V-8. This 880 horsepower gas- guzzler deluxe is equipped with four wheel anti-lock disc brakes, all the better for stopping at every filling station. It features an eight-way power seat that separates the cash from your billfold (a less painful way to make the monthly payments).

The new model is outfitted with 500 pounds of chrome, custom stripes and two-tone paint. I'm afraid the car will go so fast that no one will have time to admire the wonderful color scheme.

Purple is the only color of the model the dealer has in stock right now. The salesman offered to use the computer system to locate a different color car at another dealership. "Of course if we find a car like you want, we will have to go get it, but they will charge us more for it because we are selling one of their cars. So you will have to pay more," he explained.

The man added, "You could order one like you want from the factory, but it might not get here for six months." That is a tempting thought, because I can get the options I want like tires with white letters and a trailer hitch in case I decide to buy a boat. There is a catch, however. For this week only, the purple car is selling for $1,000 under invoice plus a $2,000 rebate from the factory because they can't unload this particular color. It seems like a once-in-a-lifetime opportunity, except I don't know whose lifetime we are talking about.

After gulping down six aspirin to clear my head, I remembered all the cars I have already outlasted in my lifetime. Then I decided to keep my old crate. It may not be much, but it's better than a Yugo.

An Adventure in Motoring--May 29, 1991

It was one of those times when you don't know whether to laugh or cry. We set out to Atlanta to collect a box of old family photographs on Sunday. The entire collection of Burch ancestors, of no interest to anyone except a few relatives, might bring 25 cents if sold for paper recycling. But it cost us a cool $175 and five hours to get that box home.

It was another adventure in family motoring, of which I have had more than my share.

There we were, less than 90 minutes from home, trucking along in our tough, four-wheel drive, off road "Exploder." We were prepared for rain, mud, snow, rocks, gullies, mountains and anything else that Mother Nature could throw at us—except the highway. I mean I-85. That's what did us in.

Anyone who has ever driven to Atlanta knows that the DOT is always working on I-85 somewhere, and this day was no exception. We came upon the latest improvement project that happened to consist of spreading another layer of fresh asphalt.

Nearing the South Carolina state line heading for Greer, we hit the newest layer of paving. The impact of one-inch of asphalt had not phased the 100,000 or so vehicles immediately ahead of us. Yet it produced an instant cacophony of screeching under our hood, sending us scurrying off the highway at a nearby exit.

Unfortunately, our only option was a convenience store in the Georgia countryside where no one on duty knew anything about vehicle problems. In fact, no one there could even operate a can opener.

So, it was up to me to raise the hood. And, in spite of never having studied auto mechanics, I could see that a bolt had sheered off and dumped the alternator, air conditioning compressor, belts and attached bells and whistles into the radiator fan. Not a pretty sight.

After making several phone calls, we finally got a tow truck. The operator, Dinky Dewdrop (not his real name) said he would be right out to help us—in an hour or so. It seems he was in the midst of cooking a big pot of chili and could not leave it unattended.

After the chili was done, Dinky arrived in a cloud of dust and gave us two options. One was to spend the night and wait on repairs to be made, if and when parts could be found. The other was to take a ride to Greer on the back of his skid truck, at the New York City taxicab rate of $1.75 per mile. Even that outlandish price was more appealing than spending the night in the backwoods of Georgia.

There wasn't enough room in the cab of Dinky's skid truck for four Burches. After drawing straws, Walter and Susan won the right to ride in the beached SUV aboard the back of the skid truck. There was just one small catch: they had to lie down during the entire trip in order to avoid detection. Dinky informed us that it is illegal for anyone to ride in a vehicle that is being towed or carried.

This made for a scenic return trip as Dinky kept pulling off I-85 and driving through the countryside to avoid the state weight stations. Otherwise, the two Burches in the "Exploder" might have been ticketed as lawbreakers.

We did not fare much better up front in the cab. Dinky was not interested in hearing about my roses. Instead, he gave me a lengthy description of his six kids, ages 2-10 who spend their days playing in a big mud hole in his front yard.

Dinky, who was only 4'6" and could barely see over the steering wheel, was addicted to cigarettes. I was addicted to the weeds before the invention of nicotine gum, but I wasn't allowed to smoke in the house, let alone the car. When Dinky lit up in the truck cab, however, he was tolerated—at least for a short while. Then my wife finally resorted to putting a handkerchief over her face and enduring the final 50 miles looking like a member of the Iranian royal family.

"You got a sick vehicle?" asked the night watchman when we unloaded the "Exploder" at a local auto trauma center in Greer. "Not just sick," I replied, "it is in cardiac arrest."

178

And so was my billfold. When I settled up with Dinky, I realized I had spent our entire vacation savings during that Sunday afternoon in Georgia.

Curmudgeon in a Ragtop--Nov. 13, 2002

It was enough excitement to jump start a dozen pacemakers. I am referring to the opportunity that members of the "local" media were given to take the awesome new BMW Z-4 roadster on a test drive.

I was one of the lucky ones to get their hands on the newest model coming off the assembly line at BMW Manufacturing in Greer. My only obligation was to write a review of the hot new rag top, which is no problem, as you will see. A crusty old newspaper editor like me has plenty of experience venturing onto the battlefield after the war and shooting the wounded. I was sure I could find a lot of things about the new model that need to be improved upon.

Getting into the Z-4 is like strapping on a book bag. Once you wiggle your oversize belly under the steering wheel, you have become part of the machine.

With its stout six-cylinder engine, the Z-4 gave me a whiplash as it rocketed out of the parking lot. Telephone poles were flashing past like broom straws less than five seconds later.

Cruising along the highway, I had forgotten that a convertible ride could be so exhilarating. My hair was flying everywhere, acting like a furnace filter combing pollen out of the air, as I sailed along winding mountain roads. When the day was over, I looked like I had been sitting on the front row of a presidential candidates debate.

I had driven the Greer plant's original car, the Z-3 roadster a couple of times, and I can attest there is no comparison. The Z-4 is completely new from the ground up.

Not only did I feel "cool" sitting behind the wheel, but as someone who enjoys shifting gears, I was also in hog heaven motoring down the road. The Z-4 has a six-speed gearbox that is as smooth as butter. This car is larger, handles better and is much faster than the Z-3. The only thing the two roadsters share in common is the hood ornament.

The Z-4 has the strongest frame of any car I have ever driven. You can take posted 10-mph mountain curves at speeds of up to 40-mph and the Z-4 never bends or sways. I was thankful there was no back seat with a passenger screaming for me to slow down.

You are sitting only a couple of inches above the pavement in a Z-4, and that must be by design—to fly underneath police radar. While it is disconcerting to look up at motorcycles passing by, it is educational to be able to inspect the under carriages of buses and 18-wheelers creeping along ahead of you.

The wind chill of 25 degrees was no problem. The Z-4 has heaters in the seats to warm your buns. I didn't need the heater, though, having nothing left to warm as the result of years of getting my rear end chewed away by irate readers.

By my calculations, the Z-4 shaved a half hour off the trip to Caesar's Head and Brevard, offering the potential of converting those North Carolina mountain outposts into bedroom communities of Greer.

This curmudgeon did decide that BMW engineers must have overlooked senior citizens when designing the Z-4. For example, getting out of the roadster is a problem for those of us who can no longer climb. When the door opens, you are sitting there at ground zero thinking, "I have fallen and I can't get up." That's why nursing homes have installed chest-high commodes. The Z-4 should be equipped with ejector seats, like jet fighter planes, that pop you out.

This car could also use an alarm to wake up elderly motorists like me who fall asleep while waiting for the traffic lights to change on Wade Hampton Blvd.

As a safety feature, the Z-4 should have a silhouette of a teenager with a ponytail painted on the driver's side window. That will prevent other motorists from running off the road while craning their necks to see if an old coot like me is really behind the wheel of the Ultimate Driving Machine.

Bargain Hunting

Mall Shoppers Similar to Marines--Dec. 16, 1992

Do the television pictures coming back from Somalia seem familiar? It's because the U.S. Marines invasion is similar to a Christmas shopping trip to the mall.

When the Marines hit the African beaches, the bright glare of television lights and flash bulbs was there to meet them. When shoppers hit the mall, they are welcomed by a blinding display of neon signs.

There are many other similarities. The Marines are on a mission to rescue the starving Somalis. The mall shoppers' mission is to rescue merchants who don't have time to wait for the President to save the economy.

Getting to the mall can be just as risky as an infantry landing on a foreign shore. Soldiers must sidestep land mines and dodge showers of machine gun bullets. Mall shoppers must take to the freeways where two million cars are banging fenders and fighting for every square inch of asphalt. And that's just in the lanes where the traffic is moving.

I always get stuck in the wrong lane behind a blue-haired lady who hasn't driven in years. Typically, she has just inherited the family's Patton tank-like 1972 Buick from her late husband and has summoned up the courage to venture forth. It is barely possible to ascertain that her vehicle is moving forward when she reaches top speed.

Even when you finally get to the mall, there are no vacant parking places near the doors. If you are lucky, and if you get to the mall before dark, you may actually see the building off in the distance.

If you thought getting there was half the fun, you may need the help of a psychiatrist to deal with the stress of making a purchase.

You find the shirts that were advertised for sale but not a single one in the size you need. In fact, the only ones on the shelf have size 17 collars with 22-inch sleeves.

Would a clerk know if the store has any more shirts in the stock room? Well, it's tough to find a clerk, let alone one who knows anything. So you get in the line waiting at the cash register and work your way up to the front, hoping to get an answer. By the time you finally are informed that no other shirts are available, the early bird extra 20 percent discount has expired, and that's why you went to the mall in the first place.

So you settle for the strange size shirt in hopes that the lucky man in your life can exchange it after Christmas. You get back in the cash register line, work your way to the front and then the computer rejects your credit card. It seems you have nervously rubbed a hole in the magnetic strip while waiting. Therefore, you must make your way to the office on the second floor to get a check approved.

By now, you are ready for a guest appearance on Oprah. But it isn't over. You still have to get your purchase gift-wrapped—it's Christmas you know.

And that is the crowning experience. Just when you finally arrive near the front of the gift-wrap line, the lady ahead of you dumps a dozen pairs of socks out of her shopping bag. She wants each pair individually boxed and wrapped in different colored paper. They must be done one at a time so she can affix the appropriate card.

Some 20 minutes later, when the next available teenybopper arrives to wrap your package, wouldn't you know it, she is called away to take a phone call from the boyfriend and disappears into the canteen.

Bigger Than a Bread Box--Nov. 17, 2010

What could be worse than the first Friday night since mid-August without a Greer High football game? Easy. A trip to the mall. My wife suggested that adventure, and I could not protest since she had just endured another 12-week-long football season at home alone.

The mall reminded me of a football stadium because you are lucky to find a parking spot within sight of the place. With that many shoppers out, one might think the recession had ended except that no one was carrying a package. My observations were cut short when my wife announced, "I want to check out the Crockery Barn."

I reluctantly went along, reflecting I have never understood what attracts women to these places. They flock to pottery stores like hummingbirds to a flower garden. Females vacationing at the Neon Sandbox are still having withdrawal pains years after Waccamaw Pottery was bulldozed to make way for a roller coaster.

Contrary to the name, there was everything except pottery in the Crockery Barn, and my wife quickly spotted a huge desk. "I really need a desk," she said, "with all the projects I have going. My things are scattered are all over the house, and I don't have any place to work."

What could I say? It's true. She needed a desk. Besides, I have a desk, although it is like a Mini Cooper beside an 18-wheeler when compared with the desk in the store.

The Crockery Barn desk is modeled on the cockpit of a 747 except that it wouldn't fit into a jumbo jet, which, in turn, probably couldn't fly with such a massive amount of wood on board. Another six ounces, and the Chinese boatload of such desks would never have made it through the ever-shallowing Charleston harbor.

Even though Black Friday was still two weeks away, I asked, "Would you like this desk for Christmas?" in hopes that I had just completed all of my holiday shopping.

"Drive around to the back, and I will get someone to load it up for you," offered the giddy clerk who floated to the cash register having just exceeded her November sales quota with two weeks left in the month.

"That's good," I thought, "because this thing must weight a ton." I was right. Eventually an overhead door flew up and out rolled a huge cart piled high with boxes. I was expecting a couple of lumberjacks to follow. Instead, a small woman who had been waiting on customers a few minutes earlier was pushing the cart. She quickly bent down, cleaned and jerked a 100-pound box and dropped it on the tailgate like tossing a five-pound bag of flour into a grocery cart. I attempted to pick up an identical box, but too many birthdays have taken their toll. I couldn't budge it. "Let me give you a hand," said the Wonder Woman who promptly launched the five-foot-square cardboard cube into the car.

Even in the truck mode with the back seats folded flat, we couldn't cram all of the pieces of the desk on board the Exploder. We had to make two trips to the mall to bring it home.

"If we were buying this desk by the pound, it was a steal," I declared while congratulating my wife on such a smart purchase. Then I remembered what mother always said, "When something is too good to be true, it is too good to be true." That instant, my wife's phone rang and the overjoyed sales lady nearly burst into song, "Please come back inside. I forgot to ring up the acrylic surface protectors for the desk top." I reached for a nitroglycerine pill when the cost of the glass-like panels amounted to nearly the price of the desk.

I needed the help of three sons and two grandsons to wrestle the boxes into the house. Eli figured out how to put the desk together, or else we would still have mountainous pieces of it scattered about. Finally, our curb was piled high with enough empty cardboard to build a New Delhi subdivision.

The desk fills most of our sunroom. It's wings stretch into different Zip Codes, and the top can accommodate a 36-inch flat screen TV, computer, printer, fax, typewriter, adding machine, telephone, cabinets with drawers for paper supplies, matching lamps, dish garden, and a pair of potted palms. Underneath are four drawers worth of hanging-file cabinets, an electrical panel and other gadgets befitting a command center.

And I do feel good about finishing shopping early because I have 13 months to pay off the balance.

Learn Your Vegetables—Before It's Too Late--June 9, 1993

This is the tenth anniversary of downtown Greer's famous Square One Farmer's Market. Since very few people are continuing to hold out hope that a real farmer will ever show up in the heart of Greer, city leaders are considering turning the place into a museum. This seems to make the statement that Greer is either (1) very far ahead of the times or (2) very far behind.

A museum might not be a bad idea since we have started beating our plowshares into bumpers for BMWs. It may not be many more years before the last remaining peach orchards have been annexed and a business license placard plastered on each tree.

Home economics classes are being rooted out by Weight Watchers and jazzercise in schools. A growing number of housewives' culinary knowledge is limited to following simple instructions like "microwave for 1:30," "do not thaw in boiling water," "refrigerate after opening," etc. In another 10 years, no one will know how to shop for food, let alone how to cook.

So I urge you to do something educational for the kids this summer. Take them out to the country to visit one of the rapidly vanishing roadside vegetable stands—to see and touch real food before it disappears into a can or a plastic freezer bag.

The only special equipment you will need is a black light. Any vegetables that give off an eerie purple glow probably have received an overdose of pesticides. Remember, too, that you must have a hands-on experience to get a complete education about vegetables.

So test-drop an English pea. If it shatters the sidewalk, it probably isn't ripe.

The best way to buy corn is to look for a worm in the tip of the ear, not that you would get meat as an added bonus. If a worm won't have anything to do with the corn, it probably isn't very good.

If a tomato looks like something out of a Burger King ketchup packet, it is over-ripe. On the other hand, if you break a thumbnail squeezing one, it probably is not ripe.

Using your toe, carefully brush aside the piles of sawdust on the floor. Any vegetables you find there may be going on sale after 5 p.m. Unless you've forgotten an important date and need a last minute floral offering to make peace, stay away from broccoli in full bloom.

Buying onions can be a smelly task, particularly if you are trying to figure out if you're getting real Vidalia Onions. If you've ever seen a map of Georgia, note that Vidalia does not stretch all the way from Macon to Tallahassee. Yet Georgia onion farms cover an area larger than most states. So, claiming an onion came from Vidalia is an even greater exaggeration than claiming that the BMW plant is in Spartanburg.

If you're into athletics, take home some squash. Overgrown zucchini and under grown acorn varieties will keep the kids occupied for hours in games of roll-at-the-bat.

If you wander into a pick-your-own orchard, never try to take a peach away from a yellow jacket.

When picking strawberries, remember: There's no way your pie is going to resemble those served at Shoney's.

Be sure to thump the cantaloupes (an age-old tradition). When you find one that sounds like the church handbell choir, buy it.

Do not attempt to lift a watermelon unless the farmer has workman's comp insurance. Otherwise, the doctor bill for curing your injured back will be coming out of your own pocket.

Speaking of medicine, unless you're into raising penicillin, skip celery that is wearing a hairy gray beard.

New Expert On Women's Clothing--March 31, 2004

You never know when some new adventure will turn your life upside down. Just last week, for instance, I was enjoying a peaceful dinner when my wife suggested that "we" go to Atlanta so she could shop for new spring clothes.

"But I don't know anything about women's clothes," I protested. "Besides, I don't like to go shopping, either."

"Well, if you can take an entire weekend off to play golf, you certainly can take one day off to take me shopping," she countered. It is impossible to prevail against such logic, although I did point out, "I have a compulsive urge to play golf because I am finally within reach of my lifelong goal of shooting my age—on nine holes that is."

Needless to say, I was heading down I-85 to Atlanta, along with three million other motorists, at the crack of dawn on Friday. The nightmare had become a reality.

My wife began darting in and out of women's shops the minute we arrived at Lenox Square. The only store that even slightly interested me was Victoria's Secret, but she forbade me to go inside because an advanced life support unit was not on duty at the mall.

So I sat on the bench in the middle of the mall alongside several other hen-pecked old men and watched people pass by. I observed that many shoppers were talking on cell phones. They can qualify for inclusion in the latest Federal Bureau of Labor Statistics report of new manufacturing workers since they are making something—phone calls.

Despite being engrossed with keeping a running tally on the number of women displaying tattoos on various parts of their anatomies, eventually I realized we had been there for five hours, and my wife hadn't bought a single stitch. That's when it hit me that if she didn't find something to wear, we would have to do this all over again next weekend. Terrified, I dashed into the next store behind her and began yanking clothes off the racks.

My wife quickly dismissed every item I suggested. Each time I thought I had found the perfect suit, the skirt was too short, or the sleeves were non-existent, or the color was wrong. "Fitting Cinderella wasn't this difficult," I grumped.

"You don't know anything about women's clothes, do you?" my wife responded.

"No, but I do recall saying that very thing only a few days ago," I replied.

Not giving up, however, I began taking an even closer look at the women's wear and observed that every garment in every store had been made in China. The newest spring fashions are black, orange and brown as if the designers had created them during a three-martini lunch at Halloween. Since all of my wife's winter clothes are black, I suggested a fancy orange dress.

"I don't look good in orange," she said, flatly dismissing my selection.

"But you could surprise everyone at church as an Easter pump-kin," I contended.

I was learning more about women's clothes than I ever wanted to know. I observed that pink colors had been splashed with orange that converted them to peach shades, and most of the spring greens are the color of pond scum. No wonder the economy is still in a recession.

Come nightfall, I suggested in desperation, "Why don't you try my method of buying a suit? It only takes five minutes."

I explained that upon entering a store, I head for the racks with last year's suits, which are 50 percent off, and sort through them until I find one my size. I try on the coat and slacks to make sure they are large enough. The secret is selecting a tie to wear with a new suit. I can find the ugliest tie in the store in one minute flat. Then, when I wear that tie, the new suit gets all sorts of compliments.

As fate would have it, though, we arrived home empty handed at the stroke of midnight. Well, almost empty-handed. Just before Bloomingdales closed, my wife snapped up the world's strangest looking pair of black sandals. They will go with the clothes in her closet that she has decided to recycle from the winter season because black is leading the spring fashion parade.

Shoppers Anonymous--Nov. 30, 1994

I don't think I have Alzheimer's yet, but I'm beginning to wonder. This time every year, I make a resolution to never again go Christmas shopping during the Thanksgiving weekend. But 12 months later, I've forgotten about the last ordeal. That's why I am easily persuaded by my wife, who is chomping at the bit, to again venture out on Black Friday, the opening day of the Christmas rush, along with 20 million other bargain hunters.

As quickly as my frazzled brain forgets, my feet remember. Those dogs, which have no trouble tramping all over a golf course, start giving me trouble after 30 minutes of pounding the hard tile floors in the stores. While tempted to rent a bench in the lobby of Kmart, I resolve that the first person to reinstate the Sears catalogue will have me as a lifelong friend.

Our mission was to find that special men's dress shirt that was advertised for 25 percent off the fourth and final 50-percent price reduction. (I'm not great at math, but adding up all those reductions probably indicates the store should pay you to come and take the shirt off their hands.)

I soon discovered that anyone who wants this holiday special sale shirt for a normal-size human being is out of luck. There are only two shirts left, even during the early-bird hour. One size would fit a midget with 23-inch-long arms and the other is made for an NFL defensive lineman with a neck bigger than most people's thighs.

"Sorry, we're sold out of those shirts in your size," the helpful clerk said. Hardly skipping a beat, she points to rows upon rows of the correct size but overpriced shirts that are not on sale. "Those shirts look fine," my wife announces. "As long as we're here, we'll take one of those."

And so it goes. It is far easier to spot a UFO than to find a Thanksgiving sale item for someone on your shopping list. Price soon becomes unimportant as long as your credit limit doesn't exceed the value of the store.

I always get choked up during the holiday season as I watch a year's worth of Christmas Club savings going down the drain in a matter of minutes. But there is little time for sorrow. My wife has given me two assignments to carry out on this shopping mission. One is to douse our credit card in the water fountain when it overheats and is in danger of melting. My other job is to lug armloads of purchases to the gift wrap department and wait while they are boxed and wrapped in colorful paper and ribbon.

By the time I've dumped my third load of parcels on the counter, the happy holiday smiles have vanished from the faces of the gift wrappers. Even though they out number my wife three-to-one, the wrappers cannot keep up with her shopping prowess.

Three hours into the shopping foray, I can find the gift-wrap department blindfolded. The clerks can spot me coming a mile away. As I rounded a distant corner with yet another load, I noticed one of the girls ducking down behind the counter. Since the store was open an hour longer than usual, I decided to wait her out. Ten minutes later, the clerk poked her head up, and exclaimed, "Oh no. It IS you! I thought I saw you coming."

"I have a deal for you," I replied. "If you'll just wrap these last 15 packages, I promise not to bother you again until next year."

"Doesn't it feel good to have all of our Christmas shopping done?" my wife asked as we drove the store's forklift loaded with boxes out to our car in the parking lot.

"The only thing I can compare it with is the feeling I get stepping out of the dentist's chair," I replied.

While undergoing counseling for holiday stress, my psychoanalyst suggested that I start a chapter of Shoppers Anonymous. Anyone interested in joining should call me at 911.

Geezer Super Heroes--Jan. 10, 2007

"Remember how it was back in the Fifties? We were probably the only generation that knew what it was like to believe that you could actually change things for the better."

That was one of my old college classmates, Jim, reminiscing about our world before it was thrown off axis by the first Vietnam debacle. (Jim married my wife's college roommate, Sara. After all these years, we were reunited when they bought a vacation home on top of a North Carolina mountain, and we made a down payment on a double wide in a nearby valley.)

"So now we have a second chance to save the world," said I, one who sees the glass half full, during one of our recent weekend get-togethers. We had hit upon a grand idea to change the course of history in a way that would make Ralph Nader proud: we took a vow not to buy anything new—never, not ever again, ever.

Our mission is simple. We will recycle other people's stuff. That is what would occur naturally if the boatloads of Chinese textiles and plastic gadgets sank in the ocean.

Need I list all the reasons why this is a brilliant idea? It will cure the nation's trade deficit. It takes a lot more time to find and buy something used, so money can't burn a hole in your pocket. Your children will appreciate you more for not spending their inheritance. Retail abstinence will also save valuable space in our nation's landfills.

If our new movement gains a foothold and takes off, Goodwill will make Wal-Mart look like the Corner Mart. That would make us Geezer (and Geezerette) Super Heroes.

We put our new shopping theory into practice on a recent Saturday, setting out to visit as many flea markets and "nearly new" shops as possible, and to bring back unexpected treasures that were others' trash.

The first rule is never carry a shopping list. You won't find a thing on any list. Rule number two is when you see something you can't live without, buy it on the spot because it won't be there next week.

"You must be local yokels. You want everything for half price," grumbled a grizzled old fellow operating a booth at a flea market. "Wrong! I said. We're from Greer, so we're poor but proud. We already own so much junk that we don't really need anything more unless it's a bargain."

Eventually we found a T-shirt for $1.25. It must have cost $25 new, because it was the official T-shirt of the 1996 Olympics in Atlanta. We bought it to hang on the wall as a reminder that we didn't get to attend the Olympics.

The most expensive item we purchased was a cookie that cost $1.50. It was so fresh it could not have been baked in China.

I ran across a Confederate States of America Army belt buckle that had me drooling. Then I recalled that my great-grandfather also had one and lost it when he was shot in the head near Richmond in 1864. After that, he didn't remember much at all, a trait that he passed along to all future generations instead of money and Civil War memorabilia.

We had to show our IDs at the door of the Bedpans R Us. (No one under 65 is allowed).

Inside the 'Used But Not Abused' antique mall, I ran across something I've always wanted: an ancient globe with all the countries of the world named just like I had learned them in school. I couldn't resist. Besides, if we are patient, those names will be recycled, making the $1 globe ultra modern again.

As part of our mission, we made helpful suggestions everywhere. I advised one shop owner who was stuck with several thousand ancient, rusting golf clubs to have them bronzed and insured. "Then, maybe some thief will steal them, thinking they're copper," I explained.

At the end of the day, I had the deep satisfaction of having killed eight hours for a noble cause when I don't have than many hours left to kill.

Now that I have shared our little secret, I am inviting you to join the white-collar hippie movement and take the pledge to buy used. Any pangs of retail withdrawal will be more than offset by the comfort of knowing that you are helping to save the world.

Lurching Toward Christmas--Dec. 11, 2008

The Burch family does a lot of things, but planning ahead is not one of them. Not at our house where even green bananas are unwelcome. We typically lurch like a drunken sailor from one season to the next, and so it wasn't until last weekend that we finally stumbled around to thinking about Christmas.

As usual, Nancy Welch was far ahead of us, having put up a tree and decorated her home before Thanksgiving.

As usual, our timing was bad because the customary after-Thanksgiving sales had already taken place. For example, the decorative tree ornaments we needed had disappeared from the shelves by the time I hit Hobby Lobby clutching a 40% off coupon in my hot little paws.

Despite that setback, we jumped at the chance when Welch suggested that we venture to Filbert, a place the size of Tooter Town near the metropolis of York. Stacy's world famous greenhouse was having a sale on poinsettias. Welch wanted several of the traditional holiday flowers to top off her decorations. We needed a few poinsettias just to start our decorating.

"We could end up with a lot of poinsettias," my wife observed. "Why don't you rig up something in the back of the Exploder so we can bring a lot of them home."

As luck would have it, of course, I was unable to find a single scrap of lumber, plywood or cardboard the size to fit the rear of our SUV. So I rigged up something that resembled a house of cards. It promptly collapsed in a heap when my "Exploder" hit the first bump in the road.

When I expressed concern that my fallen contraption would be the only way to bring home a greenhouse full of poinsettias, Welch said "no problem. We'll get Louiege to load the car. No matter how much we buy, he can get all the stuff in there."

As Bob and I emptied Stacy's coffee pot while washing down a plate of free cookies, the women filled carts with an assortment of poinsettias and other must-have items for the holidays. They bought candles, a tray of pansies to replace those that a varmint dug out of our planters, and a wreath to replace the fresh one that had turned desert tan in a single day after being left sunning on the porch under a piece of plastic. We also could not resist a colorful banner proclaiming "Noel" to be hung from the useless rod on the lamppost in our front yard.

Welch even spotted the world's largest chrysanthemums on sale and snapped up a matching pair covered in glorious yellow blooms.

"We can get all this in the car," I declared confidently after sizing up the load that put my VISA card on track for a federal government Bailout. That was before Louiege emerged, took in the situation with a single glance, threw up his hands and scurried back inside the building.

That left it up to me to pack the SUV. I was afraid to put the mums on the luggage rack for fear we would not get under the bridges on I-85, but I wasn't overly concerned, having re-rigged the two-story contraption in the back of the SUV. Then I belatedly discovered that the poinsettias were too tall to fit, so I had to dump the cardboard and planks in a heap in the parking lot and try a new tactic.

With Welch's help, everything was soon crammed into the SUV. The minor technicality was that stuff was hanging out the back and the lift gate would not shut. So we pulled everything out and repacked. Three times. With each pass, the poinsettias became more compact, taking on the appearance of slim red peppers instead of flowers. Shattered and crushed mum blooms rained down on my growing pile of debris like yellow snowflakes as these plants began to resemble a pair of daisies. If the temperature had been any warmer than 38 degrees, the parking lot could have passed for Sanford & Son in sunny Hawaii.

"We couldn't even put a pine needle back there now," said Welch when, on the fourth try, we finally slammed the lift gate shut.

As luck would have it, the "Noel" lamp post banner is far too wide to fit the rod, so it had to be scrunched up and now reads: "NL," which passersby assume stands for "Non-noteworthy landmark."

Living Healthy

The Health Test--April 12, 1989

I'm afraid I have just flunked a health test. I have no idea why the Greenville Hospital System (GHS) published this test in the newspaper, although I have my suspicions. On the surface, the hospital appears to be promoting healthy habits. In reality, perhaps GHS wants to identify those of us who have one foot in the grave and the other on a banana peel to justify expanding its bedpan patrol team. That really has me worried.

Some of us truly enjoy bad health. Like the weather, poor health is our universal topic of conversation. As you may have guessed, bad health is also a front-burner issue that can help fill this space in the newspaper.

Someone once remarked that death is a bad side effect of poor health. That thought prompted me to take the GHS health test to confirm that I am still alive.

My first discovery was that you really have to be a brain to take a modern health test. When I was studying health back in middle school, the only principle I had to know was "an apple a day keeps the doctor away." Today you must also know everything about the apple, especially the type of pesticides that have been sprayed on the orchards to prevent insects from carrying off the fruit.

There are other tough questions on the health test like: "has any-body in your neighborhood ever suffered a heart attack?"

Continuing to plow through the exam, I came across a paragraph of instructions that ordered me to pause and find my pulse. Which proved to be impossible. My pulse has been lost in the fat for at least a decade.

Next I was directed to check my resting heart rate. My heart always rests, except when I am getting my annual prostate exam and during the mud wrestling competition that replaced the Chili Cook-Off in Greer.

A new math formula that was provided with the test indicated I have an ideal body weight. Unfortunately, that weight is not distributed in the right places. Like, I can't look down and see my shoes.

The next section of the test inquired about my typical daily diet. I immediately lost 10 points on the first question because when I am called on to cook, I rush out for hamburgers and French fries. When I had to admit that I do not drink skim milk, and I absolutely refuse to eat certain foods including broccoli, all creatures with feathers and fins, and not to mention Brussels sprouts, I was docked another 40 points.

At that point, my test score had plummeted to such an extent that the next instruction advised me to dial 911 for medical attention. It was then I decided it would not be a bad idea to check into the hospital. That surely must be the only place in the world you don't have to worry about coming down with some new medical affliction.

Another way to look at the health issue is to consider the possibility that we humans weren't designed to reach the ripe old age of 125. The lifestyle decision therefore becomes: would I rather joyfully feast frequently on steak and stuffed potatoes but only live to be 65, expiring on the cusp of the magic age for Medicare—or would I prefer to endure a daily diet of oatmeal and skim milk so that I could exist in a state of misery until the age of 95?

Clinton Has Lost the Red Neck Vote--Aug 16, 1995

Aug. 16, 1995, was a day that will live in infamy. That's the day President Bill Clinton lost the Red Neck (myself included) vote by attacking cigarettes.

I don't smoke myself, not now anyway. So, from my unbiased point of view, I don't think it was fair to suggest prohibiting cigarette manufacturers from sponsoring NASCAR races.

This was like the Greenville County Council attack on nude dancing in nightclubs. Obviously I could not attend such an exhibition because it might short-circuit my pacemaker, but I cannot imagine a better way to go when the time comes. Just knowing that nude clubs are open for business adds one more item to my "bucket list."

Like nude nightclubs, cigarettes have never been fully appreciated. The statistics may be disputed, but I believe smoking has kept more old people out of nursing homes than any other remedy known to the medical profession.

There is nothing on earth that can get the adrenalin flowing like running out of cigarettes in the middle of the night. Cigarettes are responsible for 24-hour convenience stores that we enjoy only in America.

Clinton's argument that cigarettes are too influential in racing does not hold water. To my knowledge no car powered by nicotine ever won a race. I don't know how many NASCAR drivers smoke, but they probably figure to get killed in a crash before lung cancer takes them away.

Another important fact has been overlooked. By breathing second-hand cigarette smoke at racetracks, spectators have less chance of being poisoned by the noxious, leaden fumes emitted by the race cars.

If denied cigarettes, there is the risk that race fans might start chewing and spitting. Streams of tobacco juice running across the pavement could cause drivers to lose control, creating monstrous crashes at racetracks. So I say smoking is safer than many things—like standing in the middle of the track during a race.

There may be other major industries, like clothing and insecticides, just waiting in line to get on the NASCAR bandwagon, but a name like *"Fruit of the Loom Cup"* does not have as much snap as *Winston Cup*. And *Black Flag Cup* would be disastrous.

Even worse, if the government substitutes soccer for NASCAR racing, I predict that millions of sports fans will commit suicide out of sheer boredom.

That's only half the problem. There is also the farmer to consider. If the government banishes cigarettes, what will farmers do with all the tobacco that they grow? The federal government would have to find somewhere else to spend the money that they pay farmers not to grow tobacco on the other half of their lands.

How will the government get the money to prop up the price of tobacco? Will we have to pay higher taxes to provide agriculture schools to retrain tobacco farmers to grow exotic crops like green beans, corn and watermelons?

I just can't cope with all these unanswered questions at once. It has given me an uncontrollable urge to reach for a cigarette. Come to think of it, I've never met a cigarette I didn't like.

Getting Fit--June 25, 2009

It's tough to ignore announcements at the fitness center because the bulletin board hovers just above the most popular spot in the place—the water fountain. That's where I learned that the week of June 15-21 is national Men's Physical Fitness Week. The announcement urged males to get fit—at least we should work hard enough to shrink our stomachs so we can see our shoes again.

One simply can't ignore such an invitation because it could send you on a guilt trip like one that arises from refusing to buy cookies from a Girl Scout. Besides, the younger generation is really into physical fitness. And what if you had to answer this query from your kids: "What are you doing for Physical Fitness Week?"

Even so, I managed to put off doing anything on Monday, Day One.

The next day, I got around to considering starting to get fit, beginning with the recollection of dipping my big toe in the swimming pool on the first hot day of summer. The shock of just plunging into the water or a fitness routine all at once would be too great. I simply couldn't risk starting out with a great deal of exercise.

That thought stayed with me another day. By Day Four, I had devised a plan that began with calling Dr. Doom to remind him that the instant weight loss scheme, a colonoscopy, was now a full year overdue. Then I put wheels on my dining room chair so I could push back from the table. That backfired, however, when the wheels mired in the deep pile carpet.

Before I knew it, Day Six had arrived. My back was to the wall. I had to spend the entire day exercising to make up for lost time. But my wife wanted to ride up to the mountains to cool off, so my only accomplishment was chalking up a few calories spent walking to the car.

That left Day Seven when I had to forego a trip to Spartanburg to take in the Gay Pride Parade in order to burn an entire week's worth of

205

calories. The only problem was that the rain-delayed U.S. Open Golf Tournament, golf's annual greatest spectacle (other than the Masters Tournament) was being televised from 9 a.m. to 9 p.m., and I simply couldn't miss any of it. I put on my best golf shirt and hunkered down in front of the wide screen TV in the den. Any exercise I was going to get would have to be done in my easy chair.

I started by working my brain on the Sunday crossword. I ended up burning only three calories while leaving most of the crossword blank because, well the Sunday puzzle is hard.

I exercised my arms by squeezing a red rubber ball in each hand for five minutes, and gave my thumbs a workout by punching the pound button on my cell phone for more options.

I figured my eyes were burning many calories watching the ups and downs of Wade Hampton High School grad Lucas Glover. Not to mention my ears, straining to catch every word uttered by the team of peerless golf commentators led by Johnny Miller.

"Have you noticed how high the grass is getting in the yard?" asked my wife during one of her trips through the den.

"Yeah," I replied. "But, I break into a sweat just thinking about yard work in this heat."

That did give me an idea, though. During commercial breaks thereafter, I went outside and moved the hose around. Heavens no, I wasn't watering the lawn. I was just staying in practice for whenever the next drought hits.

"Do you think this is change that anyone could believe in?" my wife asked when I returned to my chair.

"Give me a break. This is the 20th year of my mid-life crisis, after all," I replied.

When I requested that she serve lunch on a tray so I wouldn't have to get up, my wife suggested, "Not even a federal stimulus could get you out of that chair."

So I strapped a pedometer to my ankle to record trips to the kitchen for snacks. I ended up walking 1.5 miles over the remaining nine hours of the telecast.

"I've really been hoping you would set out that new ground cover, you know the plants in the flat that I bought before Easter," my wife mentioned at mid-afternoon.

"I guess I got a little carried away when I was spraying with Round-up the other day," I said, confessing that the ground cover had gone the way of the unwanted crab grass and wild onions.

I continued exercising in my chair, burning 100 calories bending my elbow while consuming a half dozen Diet Cokes. Another 50 calories went into tossing peanuts in the air and catching them in my mouth.

And so, I avoided a case of writer's cramp the next day while entering my week of exercise in my personal logbook at SSI (Seniors Superfat & Indolent).

Shaping Up--Jan. 9, 2008

I once laughed at people who made New Year's Resolutions to lose weight and get fit.

That was before I had an attitude adjustment after losing sight of my shoes. Over indulging during the recent Thanksgiving holidays left me unable to buckle my belt, and I waddled back to the gym for the first time in months.

Thankfully, I still had my bar-coded ID implanted in my sneakers to gain admission. I don't know why security is so tight there. Are they afraid that someone will try to sneak past the front desk and start lifting the weights?

I noted that my photo was framed on the bulletin board, like an Amber Alert on a milk carton, underscored with the question: "Have you seen this geezer? He has been missing since March."

"You could have at least thought up a good excuse and called in sick," was the greeting offered by my 'wellness' coach.

The really bad part was trying to regain the ground I had lost over eight months. After four weeks, I had managed to shed two pounds. Then Christmas came along, and I had worked up a huge appetite at the gym. So I ate high on the hog. Heck, I ate pretty much the entire hog—for several days hand running. By New Year's Day, I had taken several steps backward by gaining ten pounds, naturally all in the same place.

Adding to my health woes, I found myself constantly out of breath trying to dodge the only people who give me a second glance—recruiters for The Bayberry assisted living home.

Although the odds are much greater that I will get struck by lightning than I will shed 20 pounds, I renewed my annual New Year's resolution and headed back to the gym. After getting thorough security, I had to weigh in. The trick is to start off with six rolls of quarters in your pockets. You can show a dramatic weight loss by leaving the coins at home the next time you face the scales.

As I looked around the gym on Jan. 2, there was standing room only, indicating that working out was about to become a spectator sport again.

I observed several fitness buffs wearing tight fitting outfits. I was too, but it was not by design. I had more than grown into my nearly new (even after all these years) sweat pants.

Some folks were moving around with Blue Tooths in their ears, I-Pods in their pockets, and MP3 players stuffed in their pants—any distraction to take their minds off the fact that working out is more about work than anything. It's like digging ditches or breaking up rocks.

There was a waiting line at the treadmills, a device that interests me because it has a built-in TV screen that keeps track of the few calories you are burning. For those really dedicated, unlike myself, the screen shows a running tally of your progress for the day. After a half hour of jogging, a small cup of yogurt appears with the message, "Well done. You have earned this." You can work up to a larger reward, like a Whopper with cheese, in six hours. Earning super sized fries requires a day and a half on the treadmill.

There's no stronger emotional bond than standing shoulder-to-shoulder while fighting the battle of the bulge. Even so, there have been no takers each time I attempted to persuade someone to help me lift my iron for a few reps so I could get home sooner.

I do receive inspiration from my co-workouters. Just the other day, Scott Tompkins was grunting and groaning like a sumo wrestler attempting to lift hundreds of pounds. "Why don't you back off a little, Scott?" I asked.

"I can't," he replied, explaining, "I don't want to end up like you."

That, plus a funeral planning circular from the mortuary with the price list of big and tall caskets, was all the motivation I needed. I am taking out another time share in the sweat shop with the good intention of exceeding my previous personal best of three months in the custom designed 'Geezers on the Go' workout program.

I must admit that it does feel great after you finish working out—just knowing that you won't have to come back for a day or two. I invite you to join me. For more information, check out my web site: www.lard.com

Let Me Show You My Scar

Down in the Back

Broken Back--Feb. 10, 2012

One day I was perfectly healthy. The next I was struck down by excruciating back pain that sent me on a torturous path in search of relief. The red hot, poker-like pain was much worse than a political campaign back stabbing. It was like being nailed with an Olympic javelin. I was in agony when standing for more than a few minutes or walking a short distance. I could only get temporary relief by moldering for hours in a straight-back chair. I was quickly degenerating into a vegetable that could pass for Turnip of the Month on the USDA food chart.

I am sharing my unwanted poor health adventures as a public service because the odds are overwhelming that your back will also go out.

I never knew that back problems are as complicated as a computer breakdown until I became the object of two months of concentrated medical attention. I got a hint from the doctor's wall poster of the human spine depicting a maze of wires, transistors and circuit boards. The clincher: "At least 80 percent of golfers have back trouble," the spine guru declared during my first office visit.

"But I have back problems 80 percent of the time," I countered. "Furthermore, my health insurance company is refusing to pay, claiming it is a pre-existing condition, like before I was born."

As I was describing the pain, which often drives me to gnawing on nails, the doctor grabbed a rubber hammer and whacked me several times. "How do you feel now?" he asked.

"Much worse after being kneecapped," I moaned. "When I came in, my back was hurting. Now my front is hurting, too."

Incessant pain makes you do strange things, like dive head first into a sewer pipe. That's how I got an MRI. Once inside medicine's version of a Disney World ride, you are trapped. You cannot move a muscle while anti-bodies make noises like hammers clanging on a soup kettle. The booming sounds impart a sense of doom. Even worse, you can't scratch your nose when it starts to itch. Just as you conclude that health care has gone too far, the machine spits you out like a wad of used bubble gum.

Later, my head throbbing and my eyes glazed like a shell-shocked combat veteran, I asked the doctor, "did the MRI show what happened to me?" I was hoping to hear that I am suffering from some exotic multi-syllable aliment, like lumbarscolosisstenosis, that would make me a candidate for a new miracle drug or a Mayo Clinic trial study.

But the doctor's depressing diagnosis was, "your problem is that you have lived too long." He explained, "the human back is only designed for 30-35 good years. After that, it degenerates. You're living proof."

Since the Kevorkian Institute of Geriatrics has closed, I was referred to a pain management specialist. He prescribed a medication that had two major drawbacks: the pills did not relieve my pain, and, unlike Oxytocin, there isn't a street market for your leftovers.

My useless medicine bottle came plastered with warning labels: "Do not take this medication if you think you may be pregnant."

Which was an insult because I only appear to be pregnant. Another sticker warned: "This medication may cause dizziness." Heck, I was already dizzy without this drug.

Yet another label warned: "Do not operate heavy equipment when using this medication." Really? Really! Are these pills routinely prescribed for bulldozer operators? Do I look like a candidate to jump on a John Deere and plow through Piazza Bergamo in downtown Greenville?

"You may never be pain free," was the spine guru's gloomy assessment after the pain pills failed. "But I'm ordering injections that may help. Meanwhile don't lift anything heavy, like a dinner fork."

"Oh, I only take small bites," I replied. "But the repetitive bending motion has caused carpel tunnel elbow. That, coupled with my back pain, surely qualifies for morphine."

I Can Top That--(Bad Back story continues)--Feb. 17, 2012

Being ordered to the hospital for an injection grabs your attention—either the doctor is serious about curing my back pain, or my condition is serious. Those fears were heightened during my pre-op visit when the nurse suggested "by the way, bring a copy of your living will when you come for the procedure tomorrow."

Arriving at the crack of dawn, I was ordered to strip and put on healthcare's instrument of torture, a hospital gown, along with a pair of baby blue knee-length socks and a pink net cap. I glanced in a mirror and was shocked to see a ghost—my great-grandmother dressed for bed. That sent me scurrying back to my pre-surgery cubicle, mooning everyone along the way because I could not tie the strings in back of the hospital gown.

Every few steps, a nurse would approach and demand that I repeat my name and birthday. Finally, I asked, "are you baking a cake? If so, you will need a pickup truck to carry that many candles."

The pain specialist was wearing dark green shades to deflect the glare of my shining backside under the mega watt ceiling lights in the operating room. He greeted me by declaring, "this will only hurt a little bit." I'd heard that false promise before when trapped in the chair of the painless dentist. I couldn't hold my tongue and shot back, "If that's so, why have I been strapped down to the operating table?" I was informed, "OSHA regulations require certain precautions."

A dose of painkiller failed to mask the hammering on my spine and noises like a jackhammer drilling concrete. "I can't get the needle in," the pain doctor grunted. "Your arthritis is so bad that it's like I'm having to dig through a gravel pit."

"The lower back is not the ideal spot for a scratch 'n sniff Band Aid," I groused to my wife after being discharged. "Especially since the doctor warned me not to touch it for 48 hours."

Since then, I have been amazed at the number of people who suffer back ailments and willingly share their stories, even the nitty-gritty details. I don't have to ask—it's like I seem to be truly interested. In recent weeks, I have heard dozens of back pain tales, but not one could top my injection experience. That is, until I met a woman in SSI's water aerobics class.

"You should have a calaminectomy," the woman suggested when I complained of unrelenting back pain. She explained, "It's really a simple procedure. The surgeon makes a neat incision along your spine and lifts up a flap, like opening the hood of a car. Then he scoops out the old stuff with a spoon, like you'd clean out a cantaloupe."

"My word!" I gasped.

"Then the surgeon fills the cavity with a paste that he makes using a special Rachael Ray recipe," the woman continued in a somber voice. "He mixes flour, milk and cream cheese, tosses in a handful of minced garlic—that prevents all kinds of diseases, you know. Then he cures it for five minutes in an oven pre-heated to 450 degrees. The doctor packs the paste into the cavity, smoothes it out, sprinkles on a little paprika, and drops the flap back in place like slamming a trunk lid. Finally, he sews you up."

"You don't say," I managed to croak, fighting not to lose my breakfast.

"And here is the best part. Three hours after having a calaminectomy, I was up walking the halls," she claimed. "The only downside is having to constantly chew breath mints, or else no one will come near me."

Her tale left me in an unusual state—speechless. While wondering if I could substitute parsley for garlic should I have to be calaminectomized, I managed to stammer, "Have you ever considered sharing your story with Ripley's Believe It Or Not?"

215

There's No Place to Sit in Chair Yoga--March, 2012

I am extremely reluctant to try anything new. I won't go to a restaurant unless it has been open for two years, and a movie must be recommended by at least 10 friends before I will invest $7 in a ticket. Thus, it is easy to understand why I ignored physical fitness for nearly my entire life—up until the day I learned researchers have found that physically fit people have a 70% better chance of staying out of the nursing home. I immediately began working out at the fitness center. Even then, however, I never gave yoga a second thought. Until last week.

Robert Hannon, a member of my SSI Golf Fitness Class, suggested that I join him in the Chair Yoga Class. He believes yoga might help my ailing back, but I was hesitant. I had always considered yoga to be nothing more than sitting on crossed legs on a mat and contemplating your navel. And since I have my naval so far out front, I don't have to strain to contemplate it.

"I need a different kind of exercise class, like something for weight loss," I suggested to Robert.

"No, no you don't understand," he said. "In Yoga, you exercise muscles that you don't even know you have. Yoga also also very stimulating."

"Is it like being surrounded by *Sports Illustrated* swimsuit models?" I asked hopefully.

"Oh, no. It's not like that at all," Robert said. "But we do get to watch Alison Howard lead the class."

"There's no way we can watch Alison. The human eye is not fast enough to keep up with her," I argued, speaking from experience after having barely survived Alison's water aerobics class.

"Well, if we were 50 years younger, you and me both would be going after that girl," Robert huffed.

"And if we were both 25-years-old again, I'll bet we still couldn't catch her," I shot back.

Disregarding that jab, Robert contended that chair yoga had helped him recover from a recent automobile accident. Despite seeing no evidence of that, I reluctantly agreed to give the class a try.

I assumed that chair yoga amounted to nothing more than sitting on your feet in a chair while listening to a CD of an East Indian snake charmer producing mournful sounds on a flute. "At least this might help clear the cobwebs from my brain, although that could take months," I thought.

Yeah, right.

Everyone was issued a chair to start the class, but we were not allowed to sit down. I soon learned that the object is to hang onto your chair while attempting inconceivable body-altering twists. These contortions, that put you in a variety of pretzel-like shapes, are undertaken at a deliberate pace that can be quite painful. It's very much like slowly pulling a strip of adhesive tape from your hairy leg. It's as bad as having a nurse stick your arm five times attempting to find a vein for drawing blood.

"Swing your right foot over your left shoulder, and strrreeetch!" Alison barked. I got my leg up as high as my waist when I felt something snap. The next thing I knew, I was in the floor. The room was spinning as the group went on to rising on their tiptoes and pointing to the ceiling.

"Help! I've fallen, and I can't get up! Call 911!" I screeched.

"Hush! Pull yourself up on your chair!" Robert exclaimed. "That's what it's for, you knucklehead."

When the class came to a merciful conclusion, I hobbled frantically for the nearest door, bent nearly double in pain.

"I've never seen anyone leave chair yoga with tears of joy in their eyes," declared a woman as I squeezed past, hurrying toward the front desk to enroll in grief counseling.

"These are a different kind of tears," I sobbed. "I have just lost everything that I had gained in water aerobics."

Kidney Stones

Answered Prayers--June 23, 2010

Good deeds really don't go unpunished, do they? Count me among the idiots that touch a hot stove twice. Even with my wife's car still in the shop several days after one round of good deeds, I talked her into whipping up more dishes for folks who are ill and/or bereaved. She remarked that I was going on her prayer list for making that suggestion, which I thought is really awesome.

And then came a premonition that my run of bad luck had only just begun. My wife sent me to the supermarket to buy ingredients for a batch of banana crème pies that she was planning to make for shut-ins. The first person I saw in the parking lot was one of my old high school classmates, Larry Bright, who was wearing a frown. "What's wrong, Larry?" I asked, and he quickly replied, "I've had better days. I'm just sitting here waiting to pass a kidney stone."

I know all about kidney stones, having suffered through three of them many years ago. They must be contagious since the Center of the Universe, Greer, S.C, is also known as the Kidney Stone Capitol of the World. I rushed on and left Bright to cope with the misery in solitude.

Less than 24 hours later, I experienced terrible pains in my side and back. I knew immediately that I, too, had a kidney stone, and informed my wife. I was expecting a sympathetic ear, but she said, "I must confess that I have been praying you would have a health problem this summer that would make you truly appreciate the suffering that I went through last summer."

"But...but...but I really did appreciate all your pain, especially when the medical bills started pouring in," I protested.

My kidney stone attack subsided but returned in the middle of the night. I was up pacing the floors at 3:30 a.m. causing King Gabby, our 20-pound attack dog, to mistake me for an intruder and start barking.

"Your prayers definitely have been answered. I am really suffering," I informed my wife as she drove me to the emergency room at the crack of dawn.

I only had to wait five minutes—amazing—before being asked for my insurance information. But then, I was the only patient in the ER.

"On the scales!" ordered the second person I met. I stepped up and was told, "No, not you. We only need to weigh your wallet."

Then I was presented with the item that no one would ever steal, a hospital gown, which instantly multiplied my misery.

"How much pain are you in, on a scale of 1-to-10?" asked another nurse. "About a 12," I confessed.

"Would you like some morphine?" she asked.

"Why not," I replied. "This kidney stone has already whipped four extra strength Tylenol tablets."

One shot of morphine later my world was a wonderful place. Republicans must have been giving morphine samples to Democrats when they voted Alvin Greene into the U.S. Senate race.

After being stuffed in a CT scanner like a hot dog in a bun, I was informed that I was the proud owner of not one, but three kidney stones. I was totally unconcerned, however, floating on the morphine-induced cloud.

The folks at the ER then hustled me off to see a specialist. The doctor prescribed that I should "go home, relax and watch a movie. You may pass the first stone, and we will deal with the others later. If your pain becomes too much, you can always go back to the ER for more morphine."

That was music to my ears. Forget about marijuana, morphine ought to be legalized.

Mistakenly thinking that the Greer Idle opener would help relieve my suffering, we headed downtown. It wasn't long until we met up with an off-duty nurse who said, "It's real easy to get rid of a kidney stone. Just drink a few beers. That'll wash it out." But I don't like beer.

Leaving downtown in even greater pain, I rented an evil vampire movie thinking it would scare the you-know-what out of me. Still feeling great pain, I sat back to enjoy the movie, but nothing happened. Upon closer investigation I discovered that a bolt of lightning had struck our new flat screen TV during a predicted "widely scattered" thunderstorm earlier in the day. The flat screen set was stuck on Fix News. Watching Glenn Beck was more frightening than any vampire movie, not to mention depressing since we can't afford a new TV set. I could have bought two flat screens for the price of one alternator that went into my wife's car last week.

Several more hours of pain followed, but eventually I birthed the kidney stone and immediately gave it up for adoption. So far, there have been no takers.

I'm headed back to the specialist today with hopes that I will get a prescription ordering, "no more good deeds—ever."

The Common Cold

New Year's diet lasted only one day--Jan. 10, 2001

Isn't it disgusting when you greet someone with the expression "how ya doin'?", and they respond by launching into a discourse about their latest ailment, going into minute detail about their newest prescriptions and their doctor's bedside manner (or lack of). *Disclaimer*: You may not want to read the remainder of this column because it tells how I'm doin'. This is about my latest near-death experience.

I can say for certain that it started on New Year's Eve, when the wife and I spent six hours huddled in sub-zero cold in the corner of an over-priced ski lodge that had no fireplace. Two days later, we had come down with the worst colds imaginable.

It was the first time in my life I have ever felt as bad as I look, and I quickly forgot all of my other afflictions—acid reflux, dandruff, halitosis, toenail fungus, gas, etc. I was actually in worse shape than when my appendix blew up five years ago. My only consolation was the thought that I might kick the bucket just in the nick of time to take advantage of the after-Christmas casket clearance at the Wood Mortuary.

My nose was swelled up big and red, like a miniature Bill Clinton. It poured so much water that I expected the Commission of Public Works to dispatch someone to put a meter on it.

While I was complaining about modern science being able to cure everything from malaria to pneumonia but not the common cold, my wife did something about it. She rushed out to the drug store and scooped up $100 worth of off-the-shelf cold remedies: cough syrup, vitamin C, sinus tablets, Tylenol and Alka-Seltzer cold remedies, etc. Not to mention several herbal cures such as Echinacea-Goldenrod, a mix of dried grasses like tall fescue, alfalfa and crabgrass. You name it, and she had all the stuff to battle colds.

Sampling some of everything left my mouth with a taste like a birdcage floor. Then my nose stopped running and clogged up like a traffic jam on I-85. That, in turn, caused a tremendous headache. My head felt denser than a concrete block, which is how most folks have described it over the years.

With eyes bulging from the pressure buildup, I improvised an adult size vaporizer. I climbed in the shower and turned on the hot water, full blast. In a few minutes, great clouds of steam had engulfed one end of the house. "Leland!" my wife screeched as she ran down the hall. "Get out of there this instant. You're peeling the paint off the walls."

"Here, take these," she commanded, handing me a hand full of $5 zinc tablets through the dense fog. What I really needed was a plutonium pill to nuke my clogged sinuses. Several zinc tablets later, all I had to show was a heavy metal head. It set off the alarm system at the entrance of the Belk store when I went in to exchange a Christmas gift for a larger size.

Later that day, I finally remembered the age-old advice: "feed a cold, starve a fever." So I cleaned out the refrigerator for supper, finishing off two Christmas cakes, a dozen cookies, a turkey sandwich and a slab of dressing, in that order. As a result, I am my jolly fat self again. The downside is that my New Year's Diet was over just one day after it had started. I can also attest that we did recover from the colds in one week's time. Otherwise, it would have taken the usual seven days.

Stamping Out Foot Disease

Stamping Out Foot Disease--Sept. 25, 2008

While writing about the walking wounded, I became an unwilling soldier in the army marching to stamp out foot disease. I began limping one morning and realized this was not just another health issue that comes with the Golden Years, the sort of problem that could not be addressed with a new miracle drug like Flomax.

I assumed the reason my big toe was swollen was because a fire ant had gotten inside my shoe. Wrong! Dr. Anthony Mathis, who helps keep my legs attached to the ground, took one look at my toe and declared, "you have an ingrown toenail. I'll have to cut it out." And he did.

Fortunately the shot of Novocain was worse than the surgery. With one whack, Mathis extracted a strange looking object the likes of which can be observed floating in bottles of formaldehyde in the Smithsonian Museum.

"You do want to keep this—to show your friends, right?" Mathis asked.

"No," I replied. "You can have it. I don't want to scare anyone."

With that, he wrapped my ailing toe in the world's largest bandage.

When I was unable to squeeze my softball-size toe into my shoe, Mathis suggested "just try wearing sneakers for a while," adding, "this is going to slow you down, you know."

"If I get any slower, I will be going in reverse," I said, explaining that my golfing buddies are constantly hounding me to speed up when I am only trying to enjoy the moment—moments communing with nature while looking for stray balls in the woods, in creeks and lakes.

Sure enough, I got no sympathy on the golf course. No one gave me any strokes, although I was basically playing on one leg in a shoe that could not be laced, a feat that not even Tiger Woods would attempt.

I quickly learned that you can't do a lot of things with your big toe out of commission, things like picking up your soiled underwear from the floor without bending over; making a withdrawal from a drive-thru ATM; steering your car while combing your hair and talking on the cell phone at the same time.

I began to feel like a real loner when no one wanted me on his team for the annual fanny-kicking contest at the office. I even got no sympathy from Jim Fair. "Your big toe! That's nothing!" Fair screeched. "The batteries just exploded in my defibrillator, and next week I'm getting an entire knee replacement. I'm even beginning to act as if I were older than you."

When I checked in at SSI (Super Sized and Infirm), I was unable to walk on the treadmill. The computer that keeps tabs on everyone's heart rate sent me a hate message when I checked out: "You failed to complete your workout today. Go to the sauna and sweat it out. Do not pass go. Do not collect a smoothie as a reward."

When my toe turned the color of an overripe tomato, I considered peeling and slicing it. Then I remembered Dr. Mathis advising "your toe will look like it's infected, but it's not infected. Just soak it in Epsom salts." He also pointed out my predicament isn't life threatening since the big toe is a long way from your head.

I happened to know all about Epsom salts. I buy it in 50 pound bags to spread around my rose bushes to encourage them to sprout new canes. I would think my other body parts could use the stuff more than my feet, but I followed the doctor's orders. I went to the drug store and bought a one-pound box of Epsom salts that was only $2 less than the 50-pound bags of the stuff at the feed & seed store. I soaked the ailing foot, big toe and all, and it felt noticeably better than a fire ant sting—it didn't itch.

The next day, I limped into the Bistro restaurant wearing my AARP-approved white Reeboks. In a flash, an entire party of eight got up and headed for the door. "Why are they leaving?" I asked the hostess.

"Judging by your shoes, they thought this was a John McCain campaign rally," was her response.

I was still in the Reeboks on Sunday when I arrived at church. "You can't come in," declared a greeter at the front door. People in outfits like mine are directed to the Grand Strand-style contemporary service in the social hall where anything goes in the way of fashions. It was a long way to limp, but at least it was downhill.

The Killer Toe--Aug. 28, 1996

I'm living proof of the old saying "if I didn't have bad luck, I wouldn't have any luck at all."

Take my vacation for example. I spent it sprawled out on a recliner with my left foot soaking in a tub of hot Epsom salts solution.

I didn't plan it that way. I was overjoyed about the opportunity to play golf for three straight days. I had saved my money and sent off for a new 'Killer Bee' driver that is guaranteed to hit the ball 50 yards farther off the tee. Then I had mailed a deposit that amounted to more than I paid for my first car to rent an ocean view condo. I was ready to go.

Everything was fine when we arrived at the condo. I set the clock for a 9 a.m. tee time and hopped into bed. But disaster struck when I got up in the middle of the night—a problem that afflicts all males over the age of 50.

I don't recall if I was checking on the commode that was running endlessly, thinking for a moment that we were in a Gatlinburg motel listening to the flowing Pigeon River. I just remember suddenly realizing that it was extremely cold in the condo. My wife had turned the thermostat down to 60 degrees, maybe as a reminder that we have never taken a winter vacation. The chill sent me sprinting back to the bed for the warmth of the covers.

In my haste, I failed to take into account that the room was filled with oversized, overstuffed furniture that might have been designed for an NBA basketball team of seven-footers. I snagged my big toe on a chair that was protruding five feet from the wall. There was a sickening, crunching noise like when you step on a light bulb. Then I felt a searing flash of pain. I collapsed on the bed, thrashing around like an overturned beetle.

"Will you please be still! I'm trying to sleep," my wife grumped.

"But I just broke my toe!" I howled in pain.

"How do you know it's broken?" she demanded.

"It sounds broken, it looks broken and it feels broken," I explained.

"Maybe you should call Dr. (Bill) Alverson," she suggested.

"What?" I replied. "It's the middle of the night. Besides, this is his day off, and we are 250 miles away. I would have to ask him to visualize my foot with four toes pointing in one direction and the other going the opposite way," I continued. "Then he would probably tell me to take two aspirin and go back to bed."

Needless to say, I spent my three vacation days indoors. I wasn't even able to walk down to the beach to gawk at girls sunbathing in bikinis.

My one-year-old grandson kept looking at me like I was crazy because the only thing I could do was to crawl around on the floor alongside him, dragging my left foot behind.

One morning I did manage to hobble out to the swimming pool. A little kid paddled up and said "Look Mom, that old man is getting into the pool wearing a blue sock."

I straightened the brat out pronto. "That's no sock, kid. That's my foot."

I decided the head cover of my Killer Bee driver would fit my wounded foot. So I put it on and limped over to the pro shop to check out the golf equipment. As I stumbled through the door, the clerk hit a bell on the counter and yelled, "Get security over here now! A deranged old man has come in wearing a head cover on his foot!"

After that, I stayed in the condo in front of the TV, watching the same programs I would be viewing at home, except that I was paying $40 an hour for the privilege of being in the Ocean View. The food wasn't bad either, if you like chicken soup seasoned with Epsom salts.

Headed to Surgery

The Eyelid Opener-- May 14, 2014

"Who referred you?" demanded Dr. John Siddens, world famous plastic surgeon, during my first visit to his office.

"My wife, of course." I replied. "She is weary of living with a lizard."

It seems that Dunlap Disease had claimed another part of my body. My eyelids done lapped over my eyeballs to the point that my eyes were closed down to narrow slots. I looked like a lizard, and my skin was becoming kind of scaly, too. The only difference between me and a lizard is that I don't have a tail, not even a small semblance of one.

The only place I can look is down. This impairment actually has some benefits, like always being able to see when my shoes are untied or my fly is unzipped. The sun never gets in my eyes so don't have to wear sun glasses, and I am always the first one to spot a stray golf ball burrowed down in a bed of honeysuckle.

But narrow vision also has numerous drawbacks. I bump into low hanging tree branches and miss seeing girls in short shorts driving the beverage carts on golf courses.

"Actually, I had rather be getting a butt lift because mine has fallen into my shoes," I told Dr. Siddens as our conversation continued.

"When it comes to needing surgery, the rest of your face isn't far behind—all those wrinkles. Some people like to say those are experience, but I doubt that even an Otis elevator could lift that face," Siddens remarked. With that, he reached out, grabbed my ears, and pulled them upwards to the extent that I could get a role in the next Star Trek Movie. "However, for an extra $3 grand, I could remove those bags from underneath your eyes." Siddens continued.

"No way! If you unpack my bags, our friends would think we had stopped traveling," I countered. "Besides, one of the shortcomings of Obamacare is that it doesn't cover beauty treatment."

But Medicare does cover eyelid surgery, "otherwise I would not be here," I informed the nurse during the customary two hour grilling known as 'pre-op.' I had to fill out a stack of papers about my medical history including why Cialis is right for me if only I could get my hands on a bottle of the stuff.

The nurse wanted to know if I had been subjected to a cardiogram and MRI in recent weeks, like I should get those in to help the hospital's bottom line. After that, I had to explain whether I have a 'living will' or a 'dying will.' I'm not making this up. Finally, I had to sign a document guaranteeing that I would mortgage my house to pay the bill if Medicare did not pick up the tab.

One week later, after having had nothing to eat or drink for the previous 20 hours, I was required to report 90 minutes early for surgery, as if they would start without me. I was ordered to strip off my clothes, and, if that's wasn't scary enough, I had to get into an infernal hospital gown that can only be tied in the back by double-jointed people. "Look, I'm only having surgery on my face. Besides, if I had any butt at all, this gown would not cover it," I complained. The nurse responded by jabbing a huge needle into my arm and starting a bag of IV fluid that was no stronger than tap water but cost $95.

After lying on a gurney for 90 minutes, I was informed that Dr. Siddens was running behind because another patient had decided, at the last minute, to get his bags unpacked. By then, the IV bag was empty, but my bladder was about to explode. I asked to be catheterized, but instead was forced to struggle down the hall to the bathroom while towing the IV contraption.

The only thing I recall about the surgery was that it lasted barely ten minutes. When I opened my eyes, Dr. Siddens was hovering above me wearing a green beret cocked at a jaunty angle like a Seal Team leader who had just zapped a terrorist. "You look better than before so the surgery was successful," he declared.

"Did you remove all the wrinkles?" I asked.

"Goodness no! I can't work miracles!" he shot back. "And do me a favor, don't ask again."

After soaking my head in ice for the next three days, I no longer resembled a lizard. Instead, I looked like another member of the animal kingdom—a raccoon.

"How did you get those black eyes?" inquired Rev. Wayne Cole when I showed up for Sunday School. "It looks like you were peeping through a keyhole when someone pushed the door open and the knob hit you in the eye."

"Actually," I replied. "It's like I didn't learn the first time and blackened the other eye as well."

Appendicitis

The Atomic Appendix--Dec. 4, 1996

"You could be suffering from a bad gall bladder, considering that you are an old coot with varicose veins," the doctor observed while reviewing the results of my colonoscopy plus 65 other diagnostic tests. "But we have found a mushroom-shaped cloud where your appendix should be. This is something that usually only happens to teenagers."

"You don't say! What does this mean?" I asked. "I could have sworn the pain was the result of an upset stomach because of eating something revolting, like broccoli."

"It means your appendix has exploded. Or it could be something even worse," the doctor replied. "We've got to go in there and whack that sucker out. Don't make any long range plans, like renewing magazine subscriptions."

After a week's delay while haggling with my health insurance company over the tab, I was dragged, kicking and screaming, to the hospital. The first order of business was putting me on a strict diet of beef bullion and Metamucil. That made surgery seem like a wonderful escape.

Since I was investing much of my life savings in the experience, I tried to get a two-for-one deal. I begged the surgeon to throw in a fanny transplant, because unhappy readers had gnawed mine away over the years. But no deal. A donor could not be found.

On the morning of the big day, moments after the business office put my billfold on advance life support, the preacher came by and gave me the last rites.

After that, I don't remember anything except being forced to wear an aluminum hat. I felt like a member of the cast of the latest Star Trek remake ready to board a space ship, although I was being wheeled down to the operating room.

Fortunately, the surgeon videotaped my entire operation. Not only so I can treasure it forever, but he also hopes to sell it to the Surgery Channel and earn a royalty from Sun Sweet Prune Juice.

I had hoped to bring my appendix home in a jar so I could show it off on the mantle next to my collection of kidney stones. But there wasn't enough of it left after it had disintegrated.

After escaping from the recovery room, the Robbie Gravley pre-game radio show kept me in a state of near unconsciousness until I could get another shot for pain. When the Yellow Jackets football team finally kicked off for the last time that Friday night, I awoke with the realization that I was freezing. It seems the heating unit had gone out in my hospital room.

Grabbing the portable radio in one hand and clutching my Tommy Hilfiger designer bedpan in the other, I lurched down the hall in search of a warm room.

"Leland! Stop!" my wife shouted. She pointed out that infernal invention of the Devil, my hospital gown, "is flapping wide open in the back!"

"That's okay," I said. "I paid a lot of money for the privilege of mooning everyone in the operating room. This time I'm getting to moon others for free."

Red Tape Bad for Your Health

Another Form of Terrorism--Nov. 14, 2001

My research into the War on Terror has turned up evidence that we are being terrorized on another front. I attempted to Call the Homeland Defense Department to sound the alarm but could not find the number in the new *&%@#*&+%#@ business numbers-only phone book!

The least I can do is alert our readers about this new form of Chinese Water Torture. The simple act of trying to open a line of communication between your health insurance provider and your doctor's office has become such a hassle that it is enough to drive anyone to the funny farm.

My troubles began the other day when I received a notice from the insurance company that denied my medical claim because the physician did not submit the request through the PPO (whatever a PPO is) for review. Since I am already paying a king's ransom in insurance premiums, I was HOT, in fact downright PPOed myself.

My first call was to the insurance company where a computer answered and rattled off a five-minute message that merely served to raise my irritation level another ten notches. I rocketed from a two to a ten on the frustration chart as I listened to the menu and pushed button after button. I had the mistaken notion that any minute I would actually get to talk to a real, live person who could give me the definition of a PPO.

After wasting my entire lunch hour, the computer finally informed me that a human being would pick up the line. In the meantime, however, I was instructed to have the following information at my fingertips: insurance policy number, driver's license number, Social Security number, date of birth, license plate number, Visa Card number, copies of income tax returns for the last five years, library card number, blood type, daytime and after hours phone numbers, mother's maiden name, nearest of kin and SAT score. I had to take the rest of the day off to compile all that information.

The next morning I placed another call to the insurance company and proceeded to punch all of the buttons to get back to the same place with the phone computer, like playing a Nintendo game. Finally, I was given a warning message: "this phone call may be monitored for quality assurance purposes."

"Huh?" I said, thinking, "they must be kidding. No one in their right mind would ever listen to one of these calls unless they were undergoing treatment for insomnia."

Eventually, a real person came on the line and informed me that my claim was rejected because the doctor had put down an incorrect code number on the submittal form.

That meant I had to notify the doctor of the error. The doctor's office answered with a less sophisticated computer that put me on hold immediately until, "the next available operator will take your call." Yeah, right.

Five minutes later, the canned music was interrupted for another announcement: "Please continue to hold because all of our operators are busy." Translation: the little old lady at the front desk is on her lunch break.

I was grinding my teeth so hard that my mouth was filling with enamel dust when the computer cycled over to deliver a health care commercial. It was presented by a voice like one of the bikini-clad women that advertise the 900 phone numbers of dating web sites in TV commercials. She was urging me to come in for a PAP Smear. She claimed that would prevent every known disease from anthrax to PPO or whatever ails me. "You are never too old for a Pap Smear," she purred, making me feel like a teenager again.

I was tempted to drop everything and rush over there. But not daring to hang up after having waited on hold for hours, the best I could do was to stretch the phone cord out the front door to Rita's Beauty Salon next door. I stuck my head in and inquired, "Do y'all compare notes about Pap Smears while sitting under those dryers?"

"I think I've been wasting time getting prostate exams, which are no fun," I hastened to add, but not quickly enough to prevent Rita from slamming the door in my face.

I have concluded that the result of a PAP smear and prostate exam is the same: your billfold weighs a lot less.

And I have been thoroughly defeated by the disingenuous phone system that the health insurance industry has implemented to discourage all contact with customers. "I surrender. Here's my checkbook. You can have my money, but please do not ever give me another toll free number to call."

"Your Call Is Important to Us"--Feb. 20, 2008

A long time reader of our newspaper cornered me the other day to complain, "why do you always write about things that don't turn out right? Doesn't anything good ever happen in your life?"

Sure, just once I would like to have a happy ending, but the only way that may happen is if I were to invent the whole thing. So I'm sticking to writing about real life, where the rubber meets the road, like last week when I was caught between Godzilla and King Kong in the battle of health insurance titans. Medicare and our company's health insurance provider were warring over my most recent medical expense.

My arthritis doctor's billing department, the health care equivalent of a SWAT team, left me a message to call within 24 hours—or else.

Returning the call was a dose of pain and suffering. I had to take a day off from work to resolve this issue by dealing with telephone answering machines, some programmed with more riddles than the college entrance SAT. The doctor's office machine cut right to this chase: As soon as I convinced the device that "me no habla Espanol," the machine barked: "please listen carefully to the following menu because it has changed."

"Just my luck," I thought, "after I had finally memorized the old menu."

So I kicked up my hearing aid a notch and was informed, "if this is an emergency, hang up and dial 911. We don't operate an ambulance service. Also, we cannot give tips over the phone for removing your gall bladder for fear of being devoured by hungry lawyers."

The answering machine then rattled off a number of new options, including: "If you cannot get the child-proof cap off your bottle of Viagra, dial 911." "For the best deal on a cemetery lot, dial extension 42." "If you are a bill collector, dial extension 666." "To ask if Cialis

238

is right for you, dial extension 23." "For the list of pit stops on I-85 provided by the makers of Flomax, dial extension 72." "If you are on hold for longer than 40 minutes, dial extension 44 to have your blood pressure checked." "If it has been four hours, call an ambulance."

Ten minutes later, I finally made contact with a real person. I was informed that Medicare had reduced the charge for my office visit by 60 percent, and then would not pay the remaining 40 percent because the government's claim that the Med Cost Preferred is my primary insurer. Med Cost, in turn, also reduced the doctor's fee by 60 percent, and then refused to pay on the grounds that Medicare is my primary insurer.

"That's 120% off," I noted. "Therefore it looks like the doctor owes me 20% for stopping by."

"That's not funny!" scolded the bookkeeper, one of the world's top female wrestlers in an earlier life. "I will give you 24 hours to get this matter straightened out."

The perfect storm of frustration continued to brew when I called my insurance company, Med Cost Preferred (the Preferred part has no connection with paying your medical bills). I spent another ten minutes continuing to punch numbers, by now so many that my arthritic fingers were in worse shape than ever.

While placed on hold again and listening to music that would make most callers hang up, the answering device interrupted occasionally to declare, "your call is important to us."

"Yeah, right," I said. "If my call is that important, you would hire enough people to answer the phones."

Eventually, a live Med Cost person came on the line and informed me that they will not insure anyone with the word "emeritus" in their job title.

My next call was to Medicare where I punched many more buttons and eventually was put on hold to listen to music so lousy that no one has ever considered downloading it to their I-pod. As I waited for an hour, the answering machine interrupted frequently to repeat: "You will be answered by the next available operator. The wait will be 30-to-60 minutes if the operator has not had a call of nature or a Big Mac Attack."

Finally, a Medicare employee came on the line and declared, "we are the primary insurer of old f...s like you, but you will have to call and inform the other parties that it will be 145 days before we can make the change in your coverage."

Back to dialing the same places again, I was gritting my teeth so hard that I might as well be putting them to something useful, like grinding stumps. My brain was fried, as if my head had been in a microwave oven.

I spent the rest of the day hanging out in Bullock's Barber Shop where the debate was raging over voting for the presidential candidate who declares, "everyone is entitled to health care." And I injected, "they are also entitled to the misery of settling the tab."

What's Wrong with Our Schools

School Requires a Big Load--Aug. 7, 2002

There isn't much to be said for reaching senior citizenhood. But one good thing is I don't have to scurry around trying to get small children ready to go back to school next Monday morning.

That opinion was reinforced by Larry James, a man on a mission to see that everyone gets a good education, whether they want one or not. James stopped by the other day to ask my advice (everyone else must have been out-of-town) for the best way to provide school supplies for less fortunate kids. I agreed to share my ideas, but only because James was shoving a stack of papers at me. These were the lists of supplies that teachers require kids to have on opening day.

After checking it twice, I realized that each child will need the help of Two Men and a Truck to get to school with the pile of stuff on those lists. And without a set of hand trucks, at the very least kids should wear a brace to avoid a serious back injury while lugging their supplies into the building.

The mountain of provisions required for a kindergarten student will outweigh the kid himself. One elementary school requires each five-year-old to have a dozen glue sticks. That's enough cement among them to build a new classroom from the stock of wooden ABC blocks.

Kindergarten kids must have crayons, but no more than 16, at this school. I wonder what the penalty is for possession of a box of 24 colors.

Kids must also have four pocket folders, but in solid colors only. This rule will be enforced by the Fashion Police.

A box of a dozen pencils is required. Four pencils must be pre-sharpened, which means the classroom pencil sharpener is behind lock and key.

Students must have two or more spiral notebooks which, put together, must total at least 180 pages—this for kids who cannot add two plus two.

The kindergarten supplies list also includes clipboards, safety scissors, notebooks, assorted markers, Zip Lock baggies of various sizes, Band Aids, baby wipes, tissues, not to mention "waterless antibacterial hand sanitizer" which surely will come in handy for tackling brain surgery in the science lab.

Topping the list is a box for storing all of the above items. The size of such containers obviously will be similar to those Sea Paks rumbling down Hwy. I-26 on 18 wheels, bound for an ocean-going freighter in the Charleston harbor.

Another local elementary school's kindergarten list is color conscious. Their post-toddler must possess two packages of solid color construction paper, but only in purple and yellow. Their one dozen pencils must be solid yellow (not decorated). They are required to have two reams of white copy paper (that's 1,000 sheets), which indicates the school is affluent—the copier is in operating condition.

Six-year-olds need four times the amount of stuff for the first grade: three dozen pencils (all sharpened, but no Eagle brand pencils for some reason—perhaps because such birds are considered an endangered species); 4 bottles of Elmer's glue, 4 boxes of crayons, 6 composition books totaling 420 pages, a roll of film, etc. But no rolling book bags with wheels, please—the school does not have enough space to store them because the supplies take up so much room.

Second graders need composition books WITHOUT spirals; gender identity index cards—large for girls, but small for boys; paper plates, colored (not plain) file folders, envelopes and a pack of name tags so the kid will remember who he is.

Third graders are instructed to write their names on four packages of notebook paper (for identification purposes) and to add a package of pens to all of the above.

When a kid makes the fourth grade, his pens must be red; he must have a set of indexes for his notebook; the notebook paper must be college ruled, not wide—for getting an early jump on the SAT. But fourth graders get a break on crayons—they are required to have a box of only 8 colors. No kidding.

This school requires fifth graders to add the following to all of the above: a disposable camera, colored copy paper instead of white, a ruler and protractor for designing better storage boxes to handle school supplies.

When it comes to buying all this stuff, I'm sure Governor Jim Hodges' tax free weekend was appreciated, but not as much as the fact that interest rates are at an all time low for those who had to take out a second mortgage to get through the checkout lines.

What's Wrong with Our Schools--Sept. 20, 1995

I've just returned from the pharmacy with a new supply of sleeping pills. I've been lying awake at night worrying about why our students' SAT scores are declining.

It doesn't take a genius to figure out that test scores would be higher if only they would ask better questions. I have come to the conclusion that we should stop insisting on testing students. I believe any court of law would decree that tests are cruel and unusual punishment which cause a great deal of stress.

And we don't need to inflict more stress on students. They are already burdened with such problems as needing a AAA Tour Guide to find the new high school campus. Furthermore, an entire math class was diagnosed as suffering from burnout after trying to count the members in the Greer High School Hall of Fame.

Even in the best of times, the kids can't decide whether to wear Tommy Hilfiger or Calvin Klein, not to mention what color sequined evening gown to purchase for the Miss LeFlambeau Beauty Pageant. Furthermore, not one student has learned the meaning of GARP.

I say we should look for other ways to improve education. We should start by throwing computers out of the classrooms. If God had wanted us to have computers, He would have given us rectangular screens for eyes and put Intel inside our heads.

Did you realize that test scores have gone down in proportion to the number of computers installed in schools? In the good old days of chalk and blackboards, test scores were much higher. If you look inside a computer, you will understand why—it's a jumble of wires and transistors that cannot pick up any channels, even on the cable.

Most computers will not operate without a modem. At old Central Elementary School, the modem was located next to the lavatory.

You can't write a love letter on the computer and slip it to your girlfriend because it might be intercepted on the Internet. You can't

245

tear a page out of the computer, wad it up into a spitball and throw it at the teacher when her back is turned.

You really have to wonder about the uproar over having more education anyway. Once you master the TV remote control, what's left to conquer? Since our Greer phone book has been discontinued, there is no longer any need to know how to do research.

In one semester, you can memorize all the English you need to know to get a good job: "Welcome to McDonald's. May I take your order please?" For continuing education, you can devote the second semester to learning conversational Wal-Mart greeter language.

I'm glad Greer High School has resisted the computer stampede and is still using the same science labs we had in the golden era of education in 1950. The science department was good enough to help us understand such important inventions as the wheel, but not so advanced that we got off into the deep end into rocket science. And for good reason. Look how the world has declined since the invention of nuclear missiles.

The first thing each new family from New Jersey does when they move to Greer is to criticize our SAT scores. My response is "why do you want to live here with all of us stupid folks?"

Grading Our Schools--Nov. 12, 2003

If they haven't already done so, Greer kids will soon be bringing home report cards with a grade for their schools. The even bigger news is that education gurus find the report cards to be so complicated that most parents will not be able to comprehend them.

Like most other state endeavors, the report cards come with no funding attached. The kids are carrying them home because the schools can't afford to buy stamps to put them in the mail. If the state really wanted to do something about education, it could refund taxes to parents whose kids flunk out of school.

Since that will never happen, my advice is to pinch yourself when your kid's school report card arrives, because it is like living in a TV reality show that could be called "Revenge of the Nerds '03."

If your school made an "excellent" grade, it may mean only that a lot of smart kids took the test, and the dumb kids called in sick that day. Or the kids on the back row forgot their number two pencils. Or the students practiced taking the test for months until they got it right. On the other hand, if a bunch of Spanish-speaking kids took the test, which is given in English, your school may not be at the head of the class.

If none of the above applies to your school, then you've got to figure that teachers laboring in under-achieving schools didn't accomplish a great deal more with a great deal less money as was expected by the state legislature.

That being said, I note that the report cards don't factor in such important school activities as athletics. Greer High's girls and Blue Ridge High's boys won state cross country championships last Saturday. That should be worth something in the ratings.

Winning the region football championship should earn a ton of points for Greer High and confirm the community's high expectations for success on the gridiron. But it doesn't count, even though there has never been a high school stadium filled with people cheering for a group of kids taking the SAT. And a Beta Club member has never earned a million dollar bonus for turning pro and signing an employment contract.

In its current form, the school report card measures only what the bookworms and computer geeks have accomplished.

Nowhere, for instance, is there a rating for school lunches. If your school cafeteria is serving cuisine fit for an upscale restaurant, it should improve the school's overall rating by several notches.

The size of the kids would be a good yardstick for measuring school cafeterias. That would be simple enough: put all the kids on the scales and divide their total weight by the number of students. If the students are overweight by an average 100 pounds, then the school could be rated "excellent"; if kids are 50 pounds overweight, "above average"; and so on. If the kids are 50 pounds below average, the cafeteria should get a grade of anorexic.

Schools should also be rated on the quality of their playgrounds, athletic facilities, etc. An indoor swimming pool or skateboard park should be worth a much higher grade than a set of simple swings. Any school with an indoor roller coaster, such as Space Mountain, should go straight to the top of the A Honor Roll.

There's nothing in the report cards about good manners, either. When students exhibit such boorish behavior as engaging in a food fight or setting off the fire alarm, the school rating should be lowered.

Finally, I would eliminate the word "Absolute" used in the ratings. When I was in school, Absolute was the brand of an adult beverage hidden under lock and key in the teacher's lounge.

The Parents Entrance Exam--August 20, 1991

In an effort to improve the quality of education, the state recently passed a law requiring all parents to pass a back-to-school test before junior will be admitted to classes this fall. I happened to get my hands on an advance copy of the exam, which I am printing here to help you bone up on the answers before school opens tomorrow.

Instructions: Mark the answer that you think best suits the situation. (P.S.: The correct answers are printed at the end of this column.) Each correct answer is worth 10 points. You must score 80 or above before your kid will be allowed into public school.

Consider carefully: WHAT WOULD YOU DO IF:

1. The PTA president resigns unexpectedly and you are drafted to be the replacement?

(a) Change your name and move to a new neighborhood.

(b) Have junior transferred to another school.

(c) Grow a beard in hopes no one will ever recognize you again.

2. Your insurance agent phones to inquire if your teenager is enrolled in driver training so that your premiums will merely double instead of triple?

(a) Sell the car.

(b) Send your kid overseas in the foreign exchange student program.

(c) Change your name and move to a new neighborhood.

3. You are notified that your daughter's cheerleader costumes will cost $1,200?

(a) Take out a second mortgage on the house.

(b) Hold up the 7-11 convenience store.

(c) Move away while the kid is at school and hope she finds a good home.

4. You receive a special invitation to eat lunch in the school cafeteria?

(a) Stock the medicine cabinet with Pepto Bismol.

(b) Throw your own luncheon at home so you will have a 'previous commitment.'

(c) Don't risk your gall bladder. Go to the hospital and have it removed first.

5. The price of Airhead Jordan sneakers increases to $298 for "back to school?"

(a) Float a loan.

(b) Apply for food stamps.

(c) Give your kid up for adoption.

6. Your daughter elopes with the star quarterback?

(a) Hope your new son-in-law signs a big bucks contract to play in the NFL.

(b) Remove your daughter from your Last Will and Testament.

(c) Grow a beard and leave town under cover of darkness.

7. You stay up all night working on your kid's science project that earns only a grade of C?

(a) Give the kid a tip about how to make a stink bomb.

(b) Put out a contract on the teacher.

(c) Change your name, grow a beard and hope nobody finds out you do such lousy homework.

8. Your kid's new teacher, who is fresh out of college, was just voted first runner-up in the Miss South Carolina Pageant?

(a) Volunteer to wash the blackboards after school.

(b) Have new batteries installed in your pacemaker.

(c) Grow a beard in hopes it will make you look younger.

9. Your kid's new teacher turns out to be the same old bag that gave you an "F" in Senior English back in 1969?

(a) Put out a contract on the witch.

(b) Take up donations to buy her a one-way ticket to South America.

(c) Grow a beard and hope she won't recognize you.

10. You are asked to serve as a Cub Scout Den Mother?

(a) Get a commitment to Marshall Pickens (mental health hospital) for six months rest.

(b) Enroll your kid in a Brownie troop instead.

(c) Grow a beard.

11. Your kid stays up until 1 a.m. playing the tuba while practicing for playing in the band?

(a) Recycle the tuba into something practical, like aluminum cans.

(b) Buy some earplugs.

(c) Set the house on fire, but only after making sure your homeowners insurance hasn't lapsed.

12. Your wife volunteers you to operate the neighborhood car pool each morning?

(a) Relocate to a new neighborhood.

(b) Get another wife.

(c) Trade your station wagon for a motorcycle.

Answers: 1-c 2-c 3-c 4-c 5-c 6-c 7-c 8-c 9-c 10-c 11-c 12-c.

Homework for Parents--Feb. 18, 1987

We are observing Homework for Parents Week. Actually that would be a more meaningful title for the annual hullabaloo that area schools refer to as "science fairs."

I have spent several days producing another science fair project, something that was unknown when I was a student. Just as well, because I probably could not have tackled even a simple science project until I was over 35.

This year, the school sent home a list of suggested projects that would have baffled Albert Einstein. One called for demonstrating the 'Doppler Effect.' Having watched the 'Cosmos' series on ETV, I recalled that the famed astronomer Carl Sagan demonstrated the Doppler Effect with a freight train speeding at 90 mph. A check with the Norfolk-Southern Railroad revealed there were no spare locomotives available for science fairs. Then too, the principal probably would not approve laying a set of railroad tracks through the building.

After some hair pulling and gnashing of teeth, we decided to tackle a photography project. I had an ulterior motive for teaching my youngest son, John David, how to take pictures: he works cheap, only $1 a week.

We decided to use various shutter speeds of the camera to photograph the motion of blades in an electric fan. This required taking apart our household fan and mounting the motor and blades on a large board. We placed the project on an artist's easel that John David swiped from his mom's closet.

Just as we plugged in the fan, a huge gust of wind arose and toppled the contraption. "Dad, we could get killed doing this science project!" John David exclaimed watching the motor fly apart while the blades bounced along the driveway before rolling out of sight.

John David, who had succeeded in learning how to use the camera, spent the rest of the afternoon photographing my attempts to put the fan back together.

I gave myself a grade of 'F' for frustration on the project and warned John David not to include any of my comments in his report.

On the Horn

Answering Machine Speaking--Oct. 15, 1997

Like a Chocoholic in the Hershey candy factory, it feels so good to gripe about things that I could not resist bringing up one of my greatest pet peeves: answering machines.

What happened to the good old days when everyone had a three-digit telephone number like 138? You really didn't even need to know a number. Just pick up the phone and ask the operator for a particular individual, and she would connect you. It was that simple. If you did not get connected, either the line was busy or no one was at home to answer the phone.

Today, we have answering machines to complicate our lives. No matter whom you call, it is all but inevitable that you will talk to a machine.

Talking to machines makes me feel stupid. In the first place I never know at what point in the recorded message I will be given the opportunity to say anything. Some folks' answering machines, after reciting the Gettysburg Address, continue to yuck it up with an endless series of beeps and noises before you can chime in.

Some people screen calls with machines that announce the name of the caller. When the phone rings, they sit by the machine and laugh while I mumble something incoherent about returning my call.

The answering machine that irritates me worse than poison ivy is the one that businesses use to require you to punch an endless series of numbers to reach a particular person or department. When it finally instructs you to "press pound for more options," I feel like hammering the phone right into the floor.

Forgive me if I don't like to talk about phones and phone books. We have four separate telephone services connecting us at home, the office and on our persons. For some reason, I do not feel extremely blessed by this expanded ability to communicate. Our combined monthly phone bills amount to more than the house payment.

If you asked me for the phone numbers of my closest relatives and friends, I couldn't begin to tell you what they are. I'm not real anxious for you to call and talk to my answering machine either. That means I will have to return the call and talk to your machine.

Callers who manage to get past my answering machine make me feel like a target. The last time I picked up before the office machine took the message, the caller wanted me to switch long distance phone services. I refused.

"Why?" the sales lady demanded to know.

"Well, my present company does not send a 50-pound phone book to our house, only to the office," I replied.

The next caller asked me to give them the phone number for the library. My arthritic fingers walked through thousands of pages, failing to find the number listed under the headings of books or reading or even the proper name, The Jean M. Smith Library of Greer. It has been years since the new library opened, but the phone company has not changed the 1920's name, the Greer Davenport Memorial Library.

Most of the calls I receive deliver bad news like, "This is Principal Marion Waters speaking, and you need to come to the school this afternoon for a conference about your son." And "this is the bank, and your account is overdrawn again."

The only time I really want someone to call, it never happens. Like all of the times I did not hear from Publishers Clearing House about winning the $1 million prize.

And during the Lions Candy Day fund raising project when I was the unlucky slob drafted to serve as a team captain. I had mailed letters a week in advance to all members of my team with just one request: Please call if you cannot take your turn. Only one Lion did not show up and did not call—club president Ronnie Bruce. When Bruce phoned to apologize several days later, I didn't even pick up. I retaliated by allowing him to talk to my answering machine. Bruce mumbled a weak excuse about being called out of town for an emergency meeting of the Gamecocks Grief Support Group.

It's Here Again – The Phone Book--Oct. 8, 1997

"You sure are lucky," a woman said to me the other day.

"Why?" I asked.

"Because you can gripe about something every week in your newspaper column," she explained.

I never intended to be a constant complainer, although I will admit that it is fun to gripe about everything under the sun. After hearing her comment, however, I made a resolution to stop complaining. But that lasted less than 24 hours.

As fate would have it, one thing that irritates me greatly occurred the very next day: the new 50-pound phone book was delivered. It is about as welcome in our office as a mound of fire ants. One of our employees is filing for workmen's compensation after injuring his back from picking up the phone book.

The huge publication, listing the phone numbers of 400,000 people whom I will never call, is obviously another setback for the local chapter of the Sierra Club and other conservation groups fighting to save America's forests. Never have so many trees been sacrificed for such a questionable cause.

Then too, the Girl Scouts will suffer. Years ago, the Girl Scouts delivered phone books to raise funds. But this day and time, none of them have earned the required merit badge for learning how to drive a forklift needed to heft a phone book.

My first impulse after receiving the phone book was to call Job Service to send over several sets of fingers to help me do the walking through this new mountain of paper. Then I remembered what my good friend Bill Millwood said: "I just keep tearing out the pages until I get to Greer in my phone book." A great idea. Except I'm going to wait until the next recycling drive so I won't have to pay the sanitation service to haul away the torn out pages.

But for the added weight, it is difficult to distinguish the new phone book from last year's. Both covers are done in taxicab yellow. The color is a reminder that you probably can call a taxi to visit someone by the time you can dig his phone number out of the book.

This latest monument to the logging industry features photos of the Greenville Symphony Orchestra performing at the Peace Center. (Which is ironic considering there has been little Peace in the symphony in recent years.)

That brings us to another problem: what to do with the old phone book. It is unlawful to dump the used books in the landfill with other garbage, for they will never deteriorate. Instead, old phone books are supposed to be recycled. But the Athletic Clubs Association of America has obtained a court order preventing people from moving their old phone books out to the curb. It seems that such an activity may erode the clubs' aerobic body building business.

Then someone suggested using old phone books instead of sandbags in case of a flood. But it hasn't rained in months.

The really scary thing that comes to mind is that none of the numbers for cell phones and pagers are in the book. It would take a 100-pound monster to hold the listings of all the phones that we have plugged ourselves into.

Costly Excursions

Remind Me Not to Go Skiing Again--Jan. 3, 2002

Dear Savings and Loan:

Enclosed, please find my application for a second mortgage on my house. I hadn't planned it this way, but I need to borrow the money to pay off my credit card that is double maxed out because of Christmas, followed by a skiing trip last weekend.

As my mother always said, "there's no fool like an old fool," and once again I have proved her correct. Who else would go to Syrup Mountain when two million other people were already there for the holidays?

I should have gotten the message when we had to park in Overflow Lot No. 15, some 2,000 feet below the two-mile high clubhouse. What a climb to get up there! After 500 feet, I had to stop for oxygen. At 1,000 feet, I went on a heart monitor. At the 1,500 foot for mark, I experienced a nosebleed. I was too feeble to complain when we reached the top and fell in a line of 300 people waiting to buy lift tickets.

While we were standing in line, we were handed brochures, suitable for framing, listing 20 different rates. It would take a CPA to estimate how much of the children's inheritance we would be spending at the ticket booth, especially when I got to the fine print that stated: "the highest rate, $50 an hour for adults and $40 for kids, will be in effect during the holidays, from November 1 through March 1."

To my relief, the gracious hosts refused to rent me a set of skis. They weren't afraid I would get hurt. They explained that I could not see the tips of the skis over my belly and would not know which direction to point them when coming down the slopes. Also, insurance would not cover the loss if the skis snapped under my weight after I strapped them on.

Instead, we decided to rent snow boards for a son and grandson. We were asked for an $800 deposit on the snowboards in the event that we did not return the boards, but the only thing we could offer was another grandchild as a hostage. When we returned the snowboards at the end of the day, they admitted to worrying that we might not return to claim the kid.

While the two lucky members of our group struggled out to the chair lift to tackle the slopes, the wife and I looked for a comfortable spot by the fireplace. There were no vacancies, so we followed a cloud of smoke that led us to the bar where we discovered dozens of prowling singles in tight ski pants and sweaters with sun glasses on top of their carefully coiffed hair for glamour effect. They had no intention of hitting the slopes. Instead, they were puffing cigarettes, drinking beer and hitting on each other.

A few minutes later, a whistle blew, and the lift shut down as the operators ran everyone inside on the pretense of 'grooming' the mountain. The real reason was to prime the food vendor's pumps. Naturally we followed the crowd and snapped up a pile of tiny pizzas—the size of Susan B. Anthony silver dollars—for five bucks apiece. When the whistle blew again, everyone rushed outside to grab another $50 ride, even a lady who never removed her full-length mink coat while warming her buns in the 20 below zero wind chill.

Soon the snowmaking machines came to life—giant water pipes spraying mist high into the night air. The spray quickly turned to a grainy while powder, and wind gusts blew the dust down the mountainside onto the parking lots. In a couple of hours, everything was covered with an inch of man-made snow.

By then, the bus that had been hauling people down the mountain had called it quits, and I was afraid we had been snowed in. With great care, however, we slid down to the parking lot, fortunately not breaking anything.

"None of our 60-year-old friends would dare do anything like this, my wife observed." We escaped by using the four-wheel drive gear for the first time ever in my three-year-old "Exploder."

PS: Maybe it was because the air was thin and I wasn't thinking too well, but please remind me not to go skiing again.

Travel Series Cancelled--July 11, 2007

I was excited leaving town, but not for long, as I was scoping out Hotlanta for the new travel section being planned for the newspaper.

It is the first time in years that I had visited the home of the Braves, and I almost didn't recognize the place, especially the section of the city known as Buckhead. I remember when Buckhead would have been hard pressed to overshadow the town of Duncan. Now it has more skyscrapers than in all of South Carolina. Most of them are 30-40 story condos, going like hotcakes for $1 million and up per unit. Move in today and tomorrow enjoy the view of your neighbors just a few feet away on the 40th floor condo in the building next door.

I am getting bad vibes about the travel series as I turn the corner and observe a flock of penguins at the entrance of the Grandiose Hilton. Actually, they are not penguins, but hotel employees in black jackets and caps, white shirts and black bow ties. This is a friendly bunch, all with hands extended-not the right hands fellowship, mind you, but hands expecting a tip.

I learn that you can never have enough dollar bills for running this gauntlet, even if you are carrying a backpack full of cash.

I barely come to a stop before the bell captain is opening my door and prying my fingers from the steering wheel. "Psst…..be sure and tip the captain more than the others," my wife whispered.

Many unkind thoughts are racing through my mind, like "why should I give this guy a big tip? He's probably taking in at least $500 an hour. I'd rather tip the minimum wage people." And, "How does he think I ever managed to get in the car by myself?"

Another attendant ceremoniously unloads our single suitcase—with one hand no less, leaving the other free to collect a tip. The sound of a cash register ringing in my ears drowns out the music being piped through the lobby.

I realize it is going to cost mega bucks to get to the registration desk which is inconveniently located at the opposite end of the main floor from the entrance. I can't look like a red neck and drag our lonely suitcase through the half-mile long lobby, but my dollar bills are going fast. I've got to have one of those luggage carts.

So I sneak up behind a cart near the doorway while a bellhop is looking the other way. The instant I grab the cart, however, he latches onto the other end like a duck on a June bug. A tug of war ensues. Finally I give in, fork over a tip and he loads our suitcase onto the cart.

Having observed the action, a parking valet grabs my keys and the rest of the money I was saving for a car payment. He is taking my wheels next door to the overnight garage where an 8-by-12 foot slab of concrete rents for $24 a night. I've stayed at places where the rooms were less expensive.

The wife, bellhop, and our bag make it past the vehicle check-in lady (after another tip) to the registration desk and beyond. Nearing the elevator, I ask innocently, "How much do most guests tip around here?"

"Oh, about $1 for each floor," the bellhop responds.

I dash back to the registration desk and, after some intensive negotiation (translated: begging), succeed in changing rooms, from the 38th floor to the second floor. Unfortunately, the basement is booked solid.

Broke, but safely inside the room, my heart sinks when my wife announces, "you must have left my special pillow in the car."

That means sending the parking valet to retrieve the car from the garage, a mission that requires deficit financing like the war on Iraq. Unlike the government, however, I cannot print more dollars. I have to borrow them from the ATM conveniently located in the lobby.

Announcing, "mission accomplished" as I return with the hallowed pillow, I decide to celebrate with a bottle of spring water on a tray by the bedside table. Then I note a small sign: "water: $5 per bottle." It wasn't, however, nearly the sticker shock that I get from hotel's $85 Sunday brunch that cannot touch breakfast at Southern Thymes.

Walking around the block that evening, we pass the exclusive Blue Pointe Restaurant. Seated at a window table is a familiar face devouring a gourmet filet mignon, market priced at $69. It is the bell captain, kicking back after a long day of opening doors of Mercedes, BMWs and Cadillacs.

We leave early the next morning, having spent an entire week's vacation worth of cash in less than 24 hours. Like feeding slot machines, but with no hope of ever winning, it costs just as much to get out of the Heartless Hilton.

Getting in the car when the bell captain finally opens the door, I hesitate momentarily before inquiring, "how can I get on here as a bellhop?"

"You must be a disadvantaged minority," he answers.

"It seems that being broke and from Greer meets those criteria," I reply.

I have learned that the grass may be greener in Atlanta, but only because the place is paved with greenbacks. That is why we're abandoning the travel series.

Fasten Your Seat Belts--Dec. 5, 2001

I arrived back in town at 3 o'clock that Friday afternoon. Which means I missed the first hour of the Robbie Gravley pre-game radio show when he informed everyone of my adventure.

Yep. It's true. I interrupted my annual vacation at Disney World to fly home for the Greer vs. Union football game. I plead guilty to having had less than a mustard seed's worth of faith in the Yellow Jackets' chances of going that far in the playoffs when I made vacation plans several months earlier. Then, after the team advanced to the upstate finals again, I was torn between my love of football and fear of flying. What tipped the scales was Principal Marion Waters' threat to erase my name from the press box if I ever missed a game. Actually, that plus Walter agreed to pay for the plane ticket because he has never learned which end of the company's camera to hold.

Of course I'm writing the trip off as a business expense since I was engaged in researching both airport security and the safety of flying. I don't know many people who aren't terrified of getting on a plane after the recent hijackings and jetliner crashes. I congratulated myself on planning ahead by having made the final payment on a cemetery plot.

I got through the metal detector easily enough at Orlando International after the guard determined that it was not my head, but a gum wrapper in my pocket that set off the alarm.

But then a girl in a Pinkerton uniform pulled me aside for a "random search."

"Do I look like a terrorist?" I asked, waving my arm toward the waiting area filled with numerous swarthy travelers, some of whom looked as if they had just ridden up on camels.

"Well, you seem to be out of breath," she responded.

"You would too if you had just run a mile and climbed three flights of stairs to take your last ride," I said. "The only thing I would hijack right now is an oxygen mask."

After three more security guards had a few laughs checking out the photo on my driver's license, I was the first passenger ushered aboard the plane. I made the mistake of bringing along a *Newsweek* magazine and began to read an account of how an American Air Lines jet crashed in New York when its tail snapped off. No matter how I twisted in my seat, I couldn't see if our plane had a tail, but I resolved to keep an eye on the wing. If it fell off, I would rush to the front to inform the pilot—then I remembered that cockpits have been converted into fortresses with padlocked doors.

My nerves were really ragged after the engines roared to life and a recorded message gave instructions about what to do in case of a crash. We had to find the exit doors and help little old ladies out first. I double-checked to make sure there was a life jacket under my seat in case we went down in the Apalache Pond, the largest body of water between Orlando and Greer.

Eventually, the plane taxied out to the runway and bolted forward, pinning me back in my seat. It was the same terrifying sensation that

I had the night before while shooting up toward the roof inside Space Mountain. That roller coaster ride had me doubting that the $75 Magic Kingdom spaghetti dinner that I had just consumed would arrive at the end of the ride at the same time I did.

The white-knuckle trip on the big jet was even more traumatic, causing my fingers to make permanent impressions on the arm rests. I mentally kicked myself for not packing a change of underwear.

When the plane finally leveled out a few minutes later, I observed a man roaming the aisles and thought for a second that we had been hijacked. Turns out, the man was a male stewardess. Of course they are no longer called stewardesses. Now they are known as flight attendants. The airlines are saving money by not having to employ ex-beauty queens to comfort passengers.

A flight attendant soon came along pushing a cart filled with soft drinks. She packed a small cup to the brim with ice, like those served at the Bi-Lo 'Rena, and proceeded to fill it with one-quarter of a can of Diet Coke. She handed me the cup and put the nearly full can back into the cart. When the woman trundled by again, I asked, "What are you going to do with the rest of my can of Diet Coke?"

"Oh that," she replied. "This plane is going on to Cleveland from Atlanta. I'm sure someone on that flight will get the rest of it."

With that, she grabbed my half-empty cup and stuffed it into a trash bag. "Fasten your seat belt," she commanded. "We are starting our approach to Atlanta."

The Joys of Timesharing

Locked Out (Part 1)--Apr. 17, 2008

It took a huge leap of faith to purchase a time-share in a Neon Sandbox condo eight months ago, especially for someone—me—who religiously avoids buying green bananas.

My hopes of getting to spend a week at the beach were finally rewarded when our turn came last week, and for only the third time in 47 years of marriage, my wife and I set out for an uninterrupted week-long vacation.

"I can't believe we are actually going to get a real vacation," I declared as we wedged into my "Exploder." We didn't know how to act. We certainly didn't know how to pack. So we just packed it all: coolers and baskets of food, suitcases and hanging bags of clothes, a small library of books and puzzles—even washing machine detergent in case we had to reuse some of our outfits.

We had planned for everything. Well, almost.

After five hours and 30 minutes of fighting the wheel in bumper-to-bumper traffic, not to mention numerous pit stops, we pulled up to the semi-posh Walrus Way in picturesque Pearl's Outlet.

"Why is that black cloud still following us?" my wife wanted to know. "Do you think it is going to pour down rain?"

"No," I countered. "That black cloud follows me everywhere."

We jumped out of the car, grabbed armloads of stuff and hit the elevator button for the fourth floor. After an agonizingly slow ride, we arrived to an incredible surprise! When we attempted to open the door to the condo, the key would not fit into the lock.

"I don't understand," I said, even more befuddled than usual. "Raoul gave me this key when we handed him the check for the condo. He's an airplane pilot. He should know what he is doing."

This was the first time I really appreciated my cell phone. I hurriedly made an emergency call to Buddy Dillard—after all, he had persuaded us to buy the time-share.

"We are here at the Walrus Way, it's dark outside, and the key to the condo doesn't fit," I blurted out when Buddy answered.

"What a wonderful coincidence to hear from you," Buddy gushed. "I thought about loaning you one of my three dozen keys, but I simply forgot," he chirped, adding helpfully, "Sometimes, the door is hard to open."

"No, the key won't even go into the lock. When Raoul gave me the key, I made a copy the same day. Now I have two keys that don't fit anything," I babbled on.

"Oh, don't you worry," Buddy advised. "I'll call Nancy Welch. She knows everything. She can get you in the condo!"

While grabbing a burger at the Halibut Hangout next door, I made mental contingency plans for sleeping on the sand under the stars. "What a turn of events," I observed to my wife. "Retiring to start a new life as a pair of beach bums."

A half hour later, the phone rang. It was Welch. "Keep your chins up. I have called everybody in Greer, including Jackie Atkins, and they all are trying to figure how to get you into the condo," she said.

Shortly after the TV set on the bar wall piped up "it's 11 o'clock. Do you know where your parents are?", Buddy called back. "I've got a plan," he said. "I finally made contact with my niece who lives at

Pawley's Island. She has a key to the condo. All you have to do is drive down there and get it," he said ticking off the directions.

"After driving 300 miles, another 50 is no problem," I replied.

At 6 a.m., an hour after we had gotten into the condo and collapsed on the bed, there was a loud knock at the door. "We are resurfacing the parking lot this morning," a voice informed. "You must move your vehicle immediately, and you cannot walk outside until the work is completed."

"How did you happen to select this week to pave the parking lot?" I asked.

"We checked the list of timeshare owners and determined that the least important folks are here this week," the voice explained.

So we spent the next five days trapped in the condo, albeit with a beautiful view—the rooftops of other condos where vacationers were able to enjoy walks on the beach and soak up the sun.

Locked Out (Part 2)--Apr. 24, 2008

When my diary left off last week, my wife and I were prisoners in our semi-posh Walrus Way timeshare at the Kmart-by-the-Sea while crews were resurfacing the parking lot with used motor oil. That did not mean we were isolated from the outside world, however.

On Tuesday morning I got a call from Richard Howell. "Guess what," Howell said. "I was knocking around with our buddy John on Sunday, and we had nothing to do, so we decided to haul your old golf cart up to the trailer park in the mountains."

"Why, that's very kind of you, Richard," I replied. "I was dreading having to walk up and down those hills, so I owe you big time for taking my ride."

"Well, a funny thing happened during the trip," Howell continued. "When we got up to the park, we pushed your cart off my trailer, and I told John to go around to the other side and help me roll down the cover. When we reached up to grab the cover, it wasn't there," Howell said. "It had disappeared. We just stood there laughing."

"No kidding," I gulped.

"Your cover must have blown off coming up the mountain," Howell continued. "So we drove real slow going home and looked in all the ditches. But we didn't see your cover anywhere."

"That's okay, Richard," I said. "I don't mind riding round topless, letting my belly hang out and flop around, especially on hot summer days."

"Oh, I've already bought you a new cover because your cart looked kinda naked without one," Howell hurried on. "You would never have known anything about it, except that John is planning to tell everyone at the annual July 4th barbecue at the trailer park."

"You've got to find out how much the new cover cost and repay Richard!" my wife exclaimed when I related our conversation. "Only a cad would leave him holding the bag."

"I think I saw a cad in the mirror this morning when I was shaving," I replied. "Besides, Richard has learned a valuable lesson for life—no good deed goes unpunished."

Mr. Home Handyman — Nov. 18, 2009

Thousands? of subscribers say they enjoy reading about my vacation experiences. Since being "put out to pasture" with the rest of the over-the-hill studs, I seem to be taking more vacation trips—not necessarily a good thing.

When our kids were young, we went to the beach in the middle of the summer and spent every day in the ocean or the swimming pool. Now we go in the fall to avoid the crowds, but the water is too cold for swimming. That's fortunate for other vacationers who are not subjected to the visual pollution we would create by waddling outside in our bathing suits.

During our most recent 'vacation,' I found myself complaining about being bored on our second day at the Grand Strand. I was sitting by the window looking at the ocean—if you've seen one ocean, you've seen them all—and wondering exactly what someone afflicted with attention deficit disorder, me, is supposed to do all day at the beach.

We had visited Brookgreen Gardens so many times they gave us a personalized parking place, and we couldn't afford to go to the outlet mall where the prices are three times as high as TJ Maxx. "The only thing we haven't done is visit the Tomb of the Unknown Terrorist," I grumped.

"Well, you can always go out on the beach and pick up shells," my wife suggested. "Not again!" I exclaimed. "I cleaned off the beach last year, and when I checked yesterday, all the shells were back just like before."

"Why don't you make a list of all the things in the condo that are broken down," suggested my brother-in-law, "First Class George" Camp, who needs no prodding to point out any and every thing that should be improved upon or done differently.

"No way!" I screeched. "Fixing things is not our problem. It's not anybody's problem. That's just the way it is. Besides," I continued, "haven't you noticed the little signs taped on the things that are broken. Like the message that says 'please don't put garbage in the garbage disposal. We are working on fixing the problem.' So we put garbage in the garbage can. It's that simple."

"But George's suggestion is wonderful!" my wife exclaimed, hinting that it would give us an excuse to visit Bed, Bath and Broomsticks.

I pointed out there are no hand tools in the condo. "That means no one is supposed to try to fix anything. It's like we would have been given wings if God meant for us to fly. We aren't meant to fix anything," I insisted, while hoping no one would remember that I am the recipient of the Home Depot Lifetime Customer Appreciation Award for having started the most unfinished projects in Greer, S.C.

"But a spring is broken in the sofa," George injected.

"I know, I know," I said. "I spotted that yesterday when I was looking under the cushions for loose change."

My wife, who doesn't give up easily, connected to the Internet and entered us among millions of candidates hoping desperately for an Extreme Home Makeover.

About that time, the bathroom ceiling light went out. "Maybe it's an answer to prayers," I suggested. "At least I can change the light bulb." Wrong! I could not remove the globe from the fixture to get at the bulb. The fixture had no screws and it simply would not twist or turn.

"This is like the old joke about how many Poles are required to change a light bulb. There are four of us, and we don't know what to do," I explained to Buddy Dillard during a long distance phone call for help. "It's just about impossible to shave in the dark without that light," I added.

"Try pulling the globe straight down," he advised.

Overcoming fears that I might be ripping out the ceiling, I yanked at the fixture, and it flopped down.

Changing the bulb did not make up for what happened a few hours later when we were returning from dinner, and I was unable to unlock the door. Ten frustrating minutes later, I handed the key to George who opened it on the first try. "You just have to pull on it a little bit," he explained.

Which prompted my wife to tell the story of the time she brought home a power strip, one of those gadgets with dozens of sockets that will enable you to overload an electrical outlet to the point of burning down the house. I could not get the gadget to work until the next day when I discovered that I had plugged the strip back into itself instead the wall outlet.

Long Waits Always

The DMV-- Where Time Stands Still

"Are you going to write about us?" one of the clerks asked as I was leaving the highway department office. I had spent a good part of the day getting a vehicle title transferred to my son's ownership. I really don't want to write about the Department of Motor Vehicles (DMV), but readers expect the newspaper to investigate everything, report what's wrong and state how it should be fixed—just in case anyone out there could do anything about a situation.

The new Greer DMV office attracted so much use when it opened that folks were telling horror stories of waiting four hours and longer for service. It's the only place in town where the wait is longer than the time needed to get a hair cut at Bullock's Barber Shop.

The DMV has taken waiting to the next level with a high tech computerized system that can form a line of 26,000 people by spitting out tickets, numbered 1-1,000, for each letter of the alphabet. Ticket numbers are flashed on huge digital message boards on the walls of waiting rooms.

Waiting Room is not an adequate name, by the way. It should be an Expectation Room because you can expect that your number will be called—eventually.

I don't know if visiting the DMV adds or subtracts from your lifespan. But I can attest that on Friday afternoon the wait was down to one hour and 15 minutes, and that was with four clerks away on vacation.

When our number was finally called, we stepped up to a window to be greeted by a large sign that stated: "New employee in training, please be patient." Patience—what would be more necessary in a place where time stands still?

I slid into my super patient mode and was informed that taxes would have to be paid on the car before the title could be transferred and a new tag issued. I was genuinely disappointed, not because we had to drive 15 miles to County Square in Greenville to pay the taxes, but because I hated to miss seeing how a huge female, who had come in behind us, would cope with a tight situation. She had wedged her 400-plus pound frame into a one-size-fits-all chair, and I didn't think she would be able to remove the chair when she had to stand up after her number was called.

An hour later at County Square, we got another taste of government downsizing—a term that really means it no longer employs enough people to do the job. We had to wait in a long line at the auditor's office for someone to figure out the amount of taxes owed on the car. Then we had to wait in another line at the treasurer's office to pay the taxes so we could get a receipt and return to the DMV office where the crowd had been together so long that they were like family. By the time we got back, the fat lady was gone. I'm pretty sure her chair was missing too.

During all that time, my mind was constantly working, and I figured out how to fix the DMV short of using it as test site for a nuclear bomb. The very obvious solution is to simply hire more clerks. But in an election year, I'm sure politicians will favor solutions like taking appointments—reserve a time on Monday and come back on Friday. Or giving rebates by mail, like a reverse sales tax. For example if you bought a $10 license plate for $15, you would get 50 cents back; get $300 cash back for titling a $40,000 car as a $60,000 BMW, etc.

Campaigners habitually propose the same economic approach: give rebates to stimulate consumers to spend ourselves into prosperity.

Failing that, waiting could be made more comfortable. The DMV could put in tanning booths and palm trees so we could take our summer vacations there.

My favorite idea, though, is for the DMV to hire stewardesses like the airlines employ to pamper customers. Of course I would want them to dress a little more like the waitresses at Hooters. They could show you to a recliner with a pillow, fasten your seat belt so you wouldn't fall out of your chair after dozing off, even give you a pill for nausea in case you get dizzy from watching people whirl though the doors. The stewardesses could serve something cool to drink and give you bingo cards with a chance to win a prize by keeping up with the numbers as they are called.

They could even fit you with eyeglasses—while you are getting your license renewed. The eye chart and the wait are about the same length of time that eyewear shops need to make a pair of glasses at the big malls.

When the DMV adds stewardesses, people will be buying tickets on line just to get in the door.

Old Folks Don't Have Time to Wait--Nov. 15, 1995

Between Bullock's Barbershop and the Post Office, you can spend the better part of an entire day just waiting in lines in Greer, S.C. My biggest pet peeve is waiting because old people don't have much time left to wait.

So believe me when I advise you to avoid the Post Office—unless you are doing research on the Law of Probability. In that case, you will discover that the Greer Post Office has established its own version of Murphy's Law: *The more people waiting in line, the fewer the number of clerks will be working at the window stations.* And conversely: *the fewer customers waiting, the more clerks will be on duty.*

Whenever I visit the post office, I always become trapped behind someone who is lugging a postage meter machine. I've witnessed workers assemble a BMW Z-3 faster than a post office clerk can re-set a postage meter. It takes longer than licking a roll of 500 stamps, one-at-a-time.

The last time I visited the post office, one postage meter locked down the entire operation. Instead of saving time, this infernal machine caused five hours of lost time by forcing 20 customers in the lobby line to wait 20 minutes apiece while it was being reloaded.

Not only was the postage meter blocking traffic, there also was a woman who wanted to return a Book-of-the-Month Club selection without buying a stamp. The clerk refused to accept the package, contending that the book club would not pay for the postage at the receiving end. The woman insisted that she had returned books before without using postage. The clerk argued that this was impossible because it goes against regulations. Then the woman demanded to see the supervisor who was out back feeding the snail.

When the supervisor finally arrived, he also refused to accept the stampless book. He explained there is no space left on the book truck. Like being lost in the Twilight Zone, this truck is in constant motion hauling books back and forth between the publisher and post offices because no one will pay the postage.

Next came a woman who wanted to pick up the mail for a certain street address, but she did not know to whom the mail was addressed. In a real life game of charades, she kept a clerk running back and forth to the dead letter closet looking for names and other clues.

Then a man plopped a box on the counter and asked for two-day delivery. The clerk said the Post Office no longer offers two-day delivery. "We can get it there in three or four days," he promised, adding a qualified maybe. "But we have overnight delivery for $10.75."

Then it hit me. If only the Post Office would think big, it could become a profit making enterprise. They could offer same-day delivery for $99.95! Come to think of it, the post office could auction spots in the window service line to the highest bidder, like $10 for first; $5 for fifth place, etc.

The Rev. Jimmy Skinner snapped me out of my daydream by suggesting, "if you stand in this line long enough, you will have plenty of material for a column."

Seeing the mote in his eye, I suggested, "This is a golden opportunity for you to preach to a captive audience. I will be glad to take up a collection."

I also saw the silver lining: the Post Office is a great alternative to Weight Watchers. Just get in line during your lunch hour, and you won't have time to eat.

Don't get me wrong, I really appreciate the Greer Post Office. If not for it, we would have to stand in line in Greenville or Spartanburg to buy a stamp.

Always Long Waits, Always

I was minding my own business enjoying a peaceful Sunday afternoon of golf in front of the TV when my wife rushed in and announced, "I have found just the thing for the windows in the den!"

I instinctively knew this was bad news, but my number one rule is *don't argue with the Missus*. So I asked, "What did you find?"

She replied "I found two beautiful palms at Wal-Mart." There went rule number two: *stay out of Wal-Mart, no matter what.*

As you guessed, a few minutes later I was on the way to Wal-Mart. "It's Palm Sunday after all," I told myself. Sure enough, there were towering palms in the garden department, and the size seemed okay, although we overlooked the fact that the store's ceiling is 40 feet high. Somehow we wrestled the palms into my Exploder and lugged them home with the branches hanging out the tailgate window.

Once we got the palms inside, they completely covered the den windows, reaching the ceiling. We no longer could see outside, but the tradeoff was that no one could look through the windows and spy on us.

The good news is that one of the trees began to turn brown a few days later. "I think we should take the palms back," my wife declared (see rule #1, above).

So I gladly phoned our son John David, and he agreed to carry the palms back to the store in his pickup truck. Thinking it would take only a minute to unload them for a refund (wrong!), we parked at the Garden Shop entrance.

"I have two palm trees to return," I explained to the Greeter at the gate.

"You have to go to the next door for garden shop returns," she instructed.

We went to the next door, and it was locked. So was the door after that, even a third door. Finally, we returned to the Greeter for better directions.

"She informed us that we had to go to the GM Entrance. "It's about half a mile, way down there at the flower displays."

When we arrived at the GM Entrance it turned out to be the main entrance to the store. "We have some palm trees to return," I announced to another Greeter as we entered.

Go that way to Customer Service," she said, pointing another two blocks to the east.

We arrived at Customer Service to find 20 people waiting in line and only one clerk on duty behind the counter. "This must be the line to buy postage stamps," I remarked.

"No, Dad," John David shot back. "Look at the sign on the wall, it says 'Always Long Waits, Always.'"

Eventually we arrived at the counter, and I announced, "We have two palm trees to return."

"Are they dead?" the clerk inquired.

"No. But they're on advanced life support," I answered.

"In that case you must return them to the garden shop," she said.

"But we just came from there," I huffed.

"Then go back up there and tell them to phone me when you have taken the trees inside. Then come back here for a refund," the clerk instructed.

That very instant, the PA system blared an announcement threatening to tow away a red pickup truck parked in the fire lane at the garden shop. John David and I ran the half-mile back to the truck to discover that it was blocking the path of a huge 18-wheeler loaded with more palm trees.

We wrestled the big palms onto buggies and pushed them up to the gate. "I have two palms to return," I said for the umpteenth time to anyone willing to listen.

"I know," the Greeter said. "Go on in to the cash register."

We could not get that far because the palms exceeded the height of the doorway by a good three feet. I eventually persuaded a cashier to come out and look at the palms. She agreed to call Customer Service.

All's well that ends well, I suppose. Once home with the refund in my wallet, I could again see out the windows of what had become known as the Safari Room. Now we will have to find another name for the room.

The Sporting Life

How Do You Shoot a Fish?--Sept. 21, 1994

I've been forced to give up playing golf for an entire month just so I can get ready for National Hunting and Fishing Day this Saturday.

The problem is I don't know how to go about shooting a fish. Furthermore the Great White Hunter, Don Wall, is out of town as usual, so I can't ask him for advice. It's quite a job to prepare for this big event by myself.

There are some things I don't like about hunting. One is the requirement to buy a license for the right to shoot an animal. Although some people think a driver's license gives them the right to bag another car on the road, I agree with the NRA that all Americans have a constitutional right to shoot at anything that moves.

Besides, I wouldn't want to insult a deer by throwing a rock at it. The only problem is that I don't own a gun. The sound of loud banging noises near my ears jangles my nerves.

Don't get me wrong. I've always fought for the right to arm bears. They can have all the forest to themselves as far as I'm concerned. My idea of a good hunting trip would be to fly over the forest in a helicopter and drop water balloons on the animals.

I don't have the proper hunting clothes, either. My excuse is that Greer doesn't have an Army-Navy store where I could shop for a hunting outfit. The truth (I hate to admit) is that I don't understand the reasoning behind dressing up in camouflage and then sticking a silly orange hat on your head. That's like turning on the porch light for a burglar.

I can imagine a deer spotting such a spectacle, and saying to his buddy, "Look...there's a Clemson fan tiptoeing through the bushes with a shotgun."

I also don't know why it's necessary to get up at 2 a.m. to go deer hunting, either. Unless, of course, the object is to surprise a buck weaving his way home in the wee hours after a stag party. It would be much more civilized if hunters made appointments, like golfers reserve tee times.

If I were to drill a deer, I wouldn't know what to do with it. I don't care for eating venison, and I couldn't give it away. Too many other hunters can't give their kills away. I might end up having to buy a lot in the pet cemetery for my deer.

I might enjoy a turkey shoot, except I would probably become the hunted.

If I must go hunting on Saturday, I would prefer to hunt something more edible, like a cow.

I think the grocery stores have really missed a good thing when it comes to hunting. They should install a shooting gallery in the meat market. You could fire away until something that was already cleaned, sliced and wrapped for the freezer fell into your grocery cart. I could get turned on by shooting at T-bone steaks and picnic hams.

So I think I'll go fishing Saturday instead. With a semi-automatic rifle, of course. That seems like the clean, quick method of snaring a bass, rather than with a hook stuck through the intestines of an unsanitary worm. Which reminds me why I don't like fishing...

Wake Me Up When It's Over--June 30, 2010

I had never considered the possibility that anything worse than a kidney stone could spoil a day of my life. My outlook changed when the World Cup Soccer tournament took over my favorite television channels, ESPN One and Two. One soccer match after another amounted to wall-to-wall, non-stop boredom that ranks alongside watching paint dry.

The World Cup is the only televised sporting event, other than the Super Bowl, with commercials that are far more entertaining than the show. Actually, monitoring the BP oil eruption spewing into a camera at the bottom of the gulf was more interesting than watching a soccer match.

A number of people asked me, "did you see the Clemson-Carolina baseball game in the College World Series last night?" But not single person inquired, "Did you watch that great World Cup soccer match on ESPN?"

I have never been at Hardee's or Bojangle's or Southern Thymes for breakfast with the old timers gathered around when someone asked, "how do you think the high school soccer team will do this year?" My answer to that would be that the quality of soccer seems to be in decline nowadays because so many guest workers have departed to find work south of the border. Instead, the talk around restaurant breakfast tables is always about football, fishing and politics, with a sprinkling of baseball and basketball thrown in.

I don't recall ever attending a high school soccer match when the stadium was even half full of spectators. Almost no one ever anxiously awaited the announcement of which college would sign a local soccer star recruit, assuming such a specimen could be found in these parts.

Some sports writers are lamenting that soccer, an ongoing threat to put Nyquil out of business as a low cost cure for insomnia, has never caught on in America. But what is there to like about watching a bunch of folks in short pants running up and down a field like they are trying to avoid stepping in a cow patty? The object of soccer is to kick a ball into a net as big as the side of a barn with your hands tied behind your back. Soccer is the only game in which players cannot use their hands and arms except to gesture at the referees, so I will concede that it could provide a recreation outlet for double amputees.

Soccer is the only sport that people in third world countries can afford to play. All you need is a ball and colorful underwear.

Obviously biased soccer referees give color-coded cards to players who break the rules or misbehave. There is no bite to such punishment like the 15-yard penalty in football or getting ejected from a baseball game. After the matches, soccer players can exchange their cards for a smoothie at the local Dairy Queen.

Amazingly, tens of thousands of spectators packed into stadiums to watch the World Cup matches. Even more amazing is the noise that sounds like the world's largest beehive. That sound apparently prevents fans from falling asleep during waits of 60 minutes and longer for anything to occur on the field. When a goal is scored, often seemingly by accident, the ESPN announcer adds 38 syllables when screaming the word "sssssccccccooooooooooooorreeeee" because he won't get to say it again for another hour.

Each soccer goal sets off a 10-minue celebration while the players form a human pyramid in the center of the field. I would find it much more interesting if the entire team revived the 1960s escapade of attempting to pile into a Volkswagen beetle.

Cured of Braves Fever - May 13, 1992

After nearly winning the World Series in 1991, the Atlanta Braves got off to a great start the following spring. Why was I not overjoyed? Because I have been cured of Braves Fever. Ted Lindsay cured me years ago, when the Braves were lousy.

Don't get me wrong. I love baseball. I love the Braves. I just don't love going to Atlanta to see them play. Such trips bring back bad memories.

Back in May, 1985 I was chomping at the bit to see the Braves play. Our youngest son was a member of the Greer Rec youth baseball team that sold the most boxes of candy and won the trip to Atlanta to see a Braves game. This outing was a pet project of Lindsay's, the City Recreation Director at the time.

Lindsay had done quite a bit of planning, even to the extent of sending the city's old bus to the shop for a tune-up. Yes, the bus was old, and its seats were slightly harder than the concrete benches dotted around Mountain View Cemetery.

The bus did not deter me, although it should have. I gladly volunteered to help chaperone the kids (because it was an all-expense-paid trip).

I should have suspected the worst when Lindsay decided we must be on board the bus at 12 noon for an 8 p.m. game. The trip to Atlanta takes three hours max, but I figured we would arrive early to watch hours of pre-game activities like mowing the playing field.

All went well until it was too late to turn back. We had traveled less than 25 miles when the air conditioning quit. After toiling for a half hour on the side of the road, Lindsay finally got the air working. Only 10 miles later, it quit again. So Lindsay stopped and worked on it again.

Several more repair stops and four hours later, we arrived at Commerce, Ga., (normally less than a two-hour jaunt). Although it was only 4 p.m., Lindsay decided it was time for supper and handed out meal tickets for Hardee's 59-cents hamburgers.

After the meal, we were moving again at 5 p.m., and it dawned on me that we were going to miss the pre-game activities. We made Lindsay promise not to work on the bus when the air conditioning went out again. That meant we rode the rest of the way with the windows down, hoping none of the kids would jump out.

Somehow we reached the outskirts of Atlanta at 7 p.m. No problem getting to the park for the opening pitch, I thought. Wrong again! Less than a minute later, the bus became ensnarled in one of those traffic gridlocks that only a big city dweller could love. I've gotten a haircut at Bullock's Barber Shop in less time than we sat stalled on the highway.

It took another two hours to get to the stadium. By then, the game was in the third inning. We had missed a bench clearing brawl and a home run that landed in the seats where we should have been sitting.

The homer must have been an amazing blast because Lindsay had gotten us fire-sale tickets, two miles from home plate on the back row of the upper deck in right field. From that vantage point, the game resembled a bunch of ants crawling around on a patch of green the size of a postage stamp.

No matter how much of the game was left, it was interrupted by 47 trips to the concession stand. I could have bought a week's supply of groceries for what I spent on junk food and soft drinks for the kids.

And, did I ever regret drinking all those Cokes when Lindsay refused to stop for a restroom visit, even once, on the long ride home. His cure for Braves fever was far worse than the disease, and it worked. My kidneys have not let me leave for Atlanta since then.

Blimps Deserve Equal Time--Sept. 13, 1989

I am urging all of you folks out there in TV land to write to your favorite sports channel and demand that the networks stop ignoring blimps. In fact, I think blimps should have a TV show of their own.

Did you realize that every time you turn on a big college football game, the World Series, Super Bowl, or the Masters golf tournament a blimp is there? Quite often, the blimp is totally ignored. If viewers are lucky, however, the announcer will point to the sky and remark: "there overhead is the Goodyear Blimp, piloted by Joe Blow from Hot Springs, Alaska."

But that's as good as it gets. The pictures of the beautiful blimp are immediately interrupted by the game.

TV executives do not realize that millions of us viewers are tuning in just to see the blimp. Even the blimp's own TV camera is looking away, trained on a stadium overrun with fans and players in scenes that bear a striking resemblance to ant hills.

I think blimps deserve equal time. If television can offer programs (even re-runs in the summer) about a super helicopter and a car that talks, then why can't we have a show about a super blimp? If there aren't enough blimps to go around, the new series could star large people (like me) dressed in blimp costumes. I would encourage department stores to offer this latest fashion trend in their big & tall departments.

But if television refuses to give us a show about blimps, the least the producers could do is to set the blimps down on the playing fields to make sporting events more exciting. Wouldn't it be wonderful to watch the Atlanta Falcons offensive line trying to block a blimp? It would be great to see Albert Pujols trying to hit a baseball over a blimp parked in the outfield. And wouldn't a blimp make a fantastic hazard on a golf course. A golf ball that hit the side of a blimp would ricochet back over your head, leaving minus yardage on your tee shot.

Why am I hung up on blimps? Well, after fretting all weekend about how to solve the Greer Commission of Public Works' challenge of removing a seaplane that is squatting on Lake Cunningham, I finally arrived at a solution. The seaplane owner could trade it for a blimp. The blimp would become a tourist attraction that would put Greer on the map, and the owner could sell tickets and amass enough money to buy his own lake.

The Easter Bunny

What I Like About Easter is ...--March 31, 1999

The countdown to Easter is on. Only three more days, and I am scrambling to get ready.

Since my social blunder of wearing mismatched shoes to the Economic Development Banquet—and nobody noticed, I have had to rethink my approach to Easter. I've decided no one would notice if I'm wearing a new suit this Sunday, so it was an easy decision not to buy one. The tough choice was whether or not to have my old suit cleaned. Maybe nobody will notice the stain on the lapel or the missing buttons on one sleeve.

All right. I confess to planning a Greer Relief Easter—meaning I'll even accept a handout. My Dad always got a new pair of shoestrings for Easter, but everyone else in the family got a new outfit. I even remember when women wore Easter bonnets, a custom that I hope is never revived.

It's hard enough just to get to church in time to find a seat on Easter Sunday morning without having to look like you stepped out of a page in a fashion magazine. The people who need religion just once a year will show up this Sunday and put the squeeze on the rest of us who must get a sermon every week to stay on the straight and narrow.

My one concession to Easter is to get a haircut, which means spending most of Thursday enduring Greer's version of ethnic cleansing: waiting in Bullock's Barber Shop. The reward is that you come out looking like a new man.

Next on my to-do list is a dash to the grocery store. We must have an Easter ham for Sunday dinner. Why a turkey won't do, I don't know, unless turkey tastes like rabbit. We wouldn't want the grandchildren to think we were serving the Easter Bunny, would we?

We also need Easter Eggs, a project guaranteed to keep us in the kitchen on Saturday night. My wife's an expert at boiling water, so no problem getting them cooked. I always get stuck with the tedious job of cutting out those little paper decals in the box of dye and sticking them on the eggs.

If there is enough time, I must shine my shoes (with something other than a brick or the back of my pants leg).

And then we have to go to bed early because daylight savings time starts Sunday, which means getting up at 2 a.m. to turn the clocks back. After that, it's nearly time for the Easter Sunrise service, and I might as well go since I'll already be awake.

Hiding eggs is the one thing about Easter I really don't like, because the kids never find all of the eggs, and they turn up unexpectedly throughout the summer.

I have planned for every eventuality except if a chocolate rabbit shows up in someone's Easter basket. That would cause a real dilemma. If I eat the candy in self defense, it will wipe out all of my Weight Watchers points for the entire week. If the grandkids get to the rabbit first, they will be bouncing off the walls like ping pong balls.

The Easter Bunny--April 14, 2004

Yes, Virginia, there is an Easter Bunny. I made this belated discovery on Saturday night, about the same time we finally understood why God never intended for old people to have children.

I had just bribed our grandchildren, who were visiting during spring break from the big city of Gilbert, into bed with a huge dish of ice cream. "Pssst," my wife whispered, summoning me out of my recliner. "I just remembered asking the grandchildren this morning if they believe in the Easter Bunny, and they do," she informed me.

"So?" I replied.

"So we can't disappoint them. We don't have Easter baskets for them," she explained.

I looked at my watch. It was nearly the midnight hour when I turn into a pumpkin. "You don't want me to go to the store at this time of night, do you?" I asked hopefully.

"Yes!" she exclaimed, reasoning "besides, the Easter stuff is probably on sale now, like gift wrap the day before Christmas. Anyway, we are out of mayonnaise. And we need Easter egg dye, too. I will have the eggs boiled by the time you get back."

"What do you want?" demanded the supermarket clerk who was obviously not excited about working the third shift.

"I was on my way to get a good seat at the Easter Sunrise service, and I need a pair of sunglasses in case the weatherman is wrong about the rain," I mumbled.

When she reached for the phone to dial 911, I added hastily, "Actually I'm the Easter Bunny, and I need a couple of baskets."

"In that case, the Easter stuff is over near the windows, next to the back-to-school stuff they just put out," she pointed out.

The Easter display was nearly as bare as our cupboard. I found a couple of cellophane wrapped baskets filled with trinkets and lugged them back to the cashier, asking "How much?"

"$9.95 each," she answered.

"What?!" I screeched. "Why aren't they on sale. It's only a few minutes until Easter."

"Because of people like you who always wait until the last minute. You have to pay the full price too," she shot back.

So back to the shelves went the shiny baskets. I fished out two plain baskets and filled them with candy. Which wound up costing $10 since name brand candy wrapped in pink, blue and gold tinfoil commands a premium price.

"Where's the grass for the Easter baskets?" my wife asked the minute I arrived home.

"I didn't see any grass," I responded. "You didn't see any mayonnaise, either," she remarked.

I headed back to the store, knowing full well that I wouldn't need to set the alarm clock for the Sunrise Service. As luck would have it, there was not a single blade of plastic grass anywhere in the store. "We sold out of grass weeks ago," the clerk explained. "I think people must be smoking it."

I bought two jars of mayonnaise and braced myself to deliver the bad news about the grass shortage.

"Okay," my wife grumped. "I'll go up in the attic and see what I can find." A few minutes later she came down with three baskets in one hand and a bale of plastic grass in the other.

"After piling up all this candy in the baskets, I can't even see the grass," I fumed.

"Are you trying to pick a fight?" she asked.

"No," I said. "I don't have time. I have to dye the eggs."

I went to work carefully filling six cups with white vinegar, according to the directions on the box of egg dye. That's when I discovered we were short of white vinegar.

"Where are you going?" my wife asked, as I headed out the door again. "Back to the store for vinegar," I said.

"Just use the regular vinegar," she suggested. I did, and the eggs came out covered with splotches.

"These eggs look like they have the measles," I said. "Maybe I should drop them off at the emergency room on the way to the Sunrise Service."

"Don't be silly," my wife said. "Besides, you don't have time. You have to get cleaned up."

For the first time I noticed I had more dye on my hands and clothes than I had applied to the eggs. "Heck, I'll just go to the service dressed as a Madras suit. It's time they came back in style anyway," I said.

But first, I decided to sit down and rest my eyes. Three hours later, I awoke to the sounds of wrappers being torn from candy bars. "No need asking the grandchildren if they want bacon and eggs for breakfast," I told my wife. "And after eating all that chocolate and sugar, they will never sit still in church, either."

"Look on the bright side," she remarked. "At least they didn't touch the grass. We can save it for next year."

Happy New Year

Year of the Oops!--Dec. 29, 2010

My New Year's resolution is to avoid getting sentimental about the departure of 2010. I will not shed a tear, not even when they prop up 105-year-old Dick Clark under the big ball on Times Square in New York City to welcome in the New Year. I, along with millions of others, am more anxious to find out if Clark is still alive.

Another big unanswered question is "why do such odd things happen in even-numbered years?"

I won't miss 2010, which will always be remembered as the year of the "Oops." The BP Oil Spill wiped out the gulf coast vacation season, shrimping season, etc. Then BP attempted to compensate by giving everyone a free tank of gas—the only catch was that you had to suck it up off the beach.

Good old Allen Bennett Memorial Hospital, where many folks entered and exited the planet, delivered a parting Oops by leaking 1,500 gallons of heating oil into Frohawk Creek at Christmas.

The newspaper got in on the Oops when the lead story on the December 8th front page boldly proclaimed that it would not snow this Christmas. Naturally, snow blanketed Greer the first time in 47 Christmases. The weather Oops came on the heels of the November 2nd elections when four of the five candidates the newspaper endorsed managed to lose.

Equally forgettable were my personal embarrassing moments. I lost the battle of the bulge and put on 10 pounds during the holiday season weight loss competition at SSI (Salvaging Super-size Senior Indulgers). I had to exchange my T-shirt, which each participant receives, for a larger size. The new shirt proclaims: "I found the cure for anorexia."

Don't ask how it happened, but I dropped my cell phone in the toilet. Luckily I was able to rescue the phone before I pulled the handle. My phone didn't work very well after getting soaked, but the really hard part was explaining what had happened to the Horizon Store clerk. She exchanged my phone for a rebuilt dry one that some other idiot had dropped in a toilet.

In May, my wife went to two NASCAR races, her first and her last. Prior to the race, we were recognized as the oldest couple ever to visit the Charlotte Motor Speedway. We didn't even need earplugs for the noise because our hearing is so bad we can't hear it thunder.

Another inexplicable brain dead decision was getting a 15-pound attack dog. Gabby needed only two days to remake the household schedule so it revolves entirely around him.

The hospital put my wallet through an MRI when I hatched a kidney stone in June.

Then the transmission fell out of my Exploder as it was returning from Greer High's football rip-off in Rock Hill, and GEICO sent out a lizard to tow it in.

Our bank account continued to shrink when my wife and granddaughter Emery sold a dollhouse at Big Thursday for considerably less than the $500 we had invested in it.

Personal recollections aside, who can forget that Buddy Clayton made a hole in one at the Greer County Club after he had given up playing golf. A star rose in the East the last time a miracle of such magnitude occurred.

I don't remember anything from the time ESPN anesthetized America by televising every World Cup soccer match until the DOT got around to issuing a Georgia Bulldog license plate. That was in September, after the Dawgs had staggered off to a 1-3 start, and my pal Bill Hardman refused to buy the new tag for his Toyota.

Scrooge events came in spades in 2010. Public school teachers bought their own classroom supplies so the Greenville County School District could build a $50 million reserve fund. And city residents were double taxed so Greenville County could build a $50 million reserve fund.

The military went from "Don't Ask, Don't Tell" to "Go Tell It On The Mountain." Sen. Jim DeMint refused to sign on for a federal grant to dredge the Charleston port, which means cruise ships can no longer dock at Pelham.

The hit song of the year, "Grandma Got Molested by TSA at the Airport," arrived in December. The same month proved that Global Warming is a hoax by freezing us solid. That was confirmed when the CPW heating bill was twice the size of our house payment.

Better Resolutions--Jan. 2, 2002
(for the coming year)

You know that 2001 was a bummer of a year when the only thing worth celebrating was the return of the blue light specials at Kmart. I have no one to blame but myself for a less than memorable year since I failed to make adequate New Year's resolutions last January 1st. I am turning over a new leaf today by making better resolutions for 2002. I hope to avoid such pitfalls as flying 500 miles to stand for three hours in a drenching rain to watch a football game.

To get my priorities in proper order, I resolve never to do anything today that can be put off until tomorrow.

I resolve not to gulp down a huge meal of collards, cabbage, sweet potatoes and black-eyed peas on New Year's Day—or any other day for that matter. This deadly combination would be useful only if you were trying to blast a terrorist out of a mountainside cave. Besides, I've eaten that sort of stuff for years in hopes of good fortune, and the only things it has brought me is nickels and dimes. From now on, I'm going to take out a loan and dine on steak and caviar to start the New Year.

There is no point in resolving to go on a diet. Been there, done that. Didn't work. Therefore, I resolve not to stand in front of mirrors in 2002.

I resolve not to buy any new clothes until I stop growing. Instead, I will visit the Goodwill store to get all the things Santa failed to deliver at Christmas—bigger shirts, bigger pants, longer belt, larger jacket etc.

I resolve to be more health conscious in 2002. I have already made an appointment to visit the Mental Health Center.

I resolve to relax more. I will no longer wait an hour after supper before climbing into the recliner to start snoozing.

I resolve to be more patriotic. I have started by responding to President George W. Bush's call to help end the recession by spending more money. I am applying for a dozen more VISA cards.

I resolve to put more effort into conservation. I will wash the aging family car instead of replacing it with a new one.

I resolve to get a new pet to keep up with my neighbor, Thomas Grady. The long awaited goat did not arrive this Christmas, but Grady is now the proud owner of a battery-operated alley cat. No messy litter boxes or expensive chow to contend with. Grady's plastic pet keeps you from falling asleep at the dinner table. It purrs at a flick of a switch, and then it unexpectedly pops up and meows a variety of familiar tunes. It won't even take a catnap until you turn the lights off.

After freezing all winter, I resolve not to complain when the temperature hits 95 degrees in the shade this summer.

I resolve to hire a full time investigator to aid in our quest for rewards by finding missing people and lost causes. These include GARP, GCDC, GGDC, AC-DC, the downtown pigeon flock, a pair

305

of Als—Gore and Tomkins, the Strategic Planning Committee, Greer Business Assn., etc.

I resolve to buy a skateboard so I can ride the scenic roller coaster sidewalks from Five Points to the Depot.

I resolve not to watch another football game played on a blue carpet.

Jan. 21, 2020: Lorena Bobbitt Day--written Jan. 19, 1994

(A look at the somewhat distant future; Lorena Bobbitt had slightly more than 15 minutes of fame after slicing off her husband's penis, but had vanished from the national spotlight years before 2000)

As fast as things are changing, many readers are wondering, "What will Greer be like in the year 2020?" To find the answer, I borrowed Errik Bridwell's crystal ball (a Blue Light special at Kmart), and programmed it with the date Jan. 21, 2020. This is what it said:

"Today is Monday, Lorena Bobbitt Day. It is a national holiday, so the banks and schools are closed for the fourth time (thus far) in 2020.

"I climb into my all-electric BMW, which I bought at the outlet store on I-85, and head toward downtown Greer. The two mile drive takes 30 minutes because of heavy traffic, the 10 mph speed limit, and 28 red lights.

"When I arrive downtown, I pay the $2 toll to enter the historic preservation district that is now a tourist attraction. I plug my car into the curbside meter and immediately head toward City Hall.

"Because of the delay, I must skip Denise Riddle's autograph session for her autobiography, *Memoirs of a Redneck Housewife*. I am late for an appointment to interview Mayor Shirlee Rollins.

"That's right. In one of the remarkable political comebacks of the ages, Rollins defeated incumbent David Goley who had quite a comeback himself. But I digress.

"Mayor Rollins is in the throes of a new crisis. The Bradford Pear Trees she planted in 1988 have become so large they occupy most of Trade Street and obstruct vehicle traffic. Furthermore, walking is virtually impossible because the pigeon population, which numbers 50,000 now, continually dive bombs pedestrians.

"And a federal grant to install moving sidewalks enclosed in plexi-glass tunnels has been stalled in a Senate committee for six weeks because the chairman, Strom Thurmond, has lapsed into another coma.

"At age 118, Sen. Thurmond recently won a bitter reelection campaign over challenger Bob Inglis who wanted to impose a 10-term limitation on Senators. During the campaign, Attorney General Shannon Faulkner, who went on to a distinguished career in jurisprudence after graduating from The Citadel, ruled that a coma has no distinguishable effect on any Washington office holder.

"As I arrived at City Hall, Ken Westmoreland was taking off in his personal hovercraft to inspect the city's 200-mile perimeter. He will check for illegal aliens who might have crashed through the city limit wall during the night.

"At that precise moment, Rollins received the first message ever heard from outer space. It came through on the mobile phone in her flower pot hat. It commanded: Go therefore and plant a Yard of the Week in every nation."

Index

Allen, Dr. Kyle, 53, 91, 92, 94, 105, 108-109

Alverson, Dr. Bill, 227

Anthony, Susan B., 263

Applegate, Marshall, 40

Ashmore, Mark, 136

Atkins, Dr. Robert, 75

Atkins, Jackie, 272

Baker, Robert Hammond, 46-48

Beck, Glenn, 220

Beckham, Mickey, 317

Belk, Bill, 167

Bell, Alexander Graham, 56

Bobbitt, Lorena, 307

Bridwell, Errik, 307

Bright, Larry, 218

Bruce, Ronnie, 19, 38, 62, 257

Bullock, Mike, 36-37

Burch, Cameron, 66-67

Burch, Eddie, 317

Burch, Eli, 79-80

Burch, Emery, 302

Burch, Joey, 150

Burch, John David, 252-253, 284-285

Burch, Margaret Griffin, v, 315

Burch, Preston, 151

Burch, Sarah, 28-29

Burch, Susan, 178

Burch, Walter, 15-16, 132, 134, 138, 178, 267, 317

Burns, Bobbi, 317

Bush, President George W., 12, 72, 305

Camp, George, 88-90, 276-278
Campbell, Carroll A., vi, 145
Carlisle, John, 64-65, 84
Carlisle, Margaret, 62, 64
Clark, Dick, 301
Clayton, Brad, 104
Clayton, Buddy, 302
Clayton, Elizabeth, 106-107
Clayton, Sam, 105-106, 111
Clinton, Bill, 203, 221
Clooney, George, 147, 172
Cole, Susie, 99
Cole, Wayne, 98-100, 231
Coleman, Carolyn, 20
Collins, Javan, 38
Crisp, Dean, 110
Davenport, Denby, 31-32, 148, 160-163, 165-166
Day, Doris 92
DeMint, Sen. Jim, 12, 303
Dill, Cory, 11
Dill, Joe, 2
Dill, Pam, 10, 11
Driggers, Christy, 94-95
Driggers, Edward, 111-112
Duckson, Hazel Austin, 120
Einstein, Albert, 252
Emory, Ken, 38
Fair, Gloria, 317
Fair, Jim, 224
Faulkner, Shannon, 4, 49-50, 308
Freeman, Eddis, 148
Frick, B.L., 148

Gibson, Carl, 80

Gibson, Drayton, 80

Glover, Lucas, 206

Godfrey, Bunchy, 88

Goley, David, 307

Gore, Al, 306

Grady, Thomas, 305

Gravley, Robbie, 234, 267

Greene, Alvin, 219

Greer, Manning, 38

Griffin, Elsie, 61, 83-84

Griffin, Gary, 15, 88

Griffin, Hayne, 84

Griffin, Ruth, 72

Hannon, Robert, 216-217

Hardman, Bill, 303

Harrill, Bill, 15

Harrison, Bob, 21, 199

Henderson, Christy, 73

Hendrickson, Rob, 103

Hendrix, Bill, 12-14

Hendrix, Marilyn, 12-14, 317

Hiatt, Joada, 44

Hilfiger, Tommy, 245

Hitler, Adolph, 75

Hodges, Jim, 244

Holcombe, Julie, 317

Howard, Alison, 216-217

Howell, Richard, 134-136, 274-275

Hughes, Rob, 158, 160, 163, 165

Hussein, Saddam, 12, 43

Inglis, Bob, 308

Jackson, Gary, 9

Jackson, Stonewall, 47

James, Larry, 241-242

Johnson, Glenn, 103

Johnson, Ron, 67

Jones, Dr. L.P., 168

Jones, Hal, 157-158, 160-162, 165

Keller, Kim, 59

Kiemle, Fred, 103-104

Klein, Calvin, 159, 245

Lindsay, Ted, 291-292

Lister, Paul, 49

Mathis, Dr. Tony, 223-224

McCain, John, 22, 141

McCall, Duke, 3

McCord, Peter, 4

McKinney, Ron, 22

McLeod, Ed, 103, 110

McWilliams, John, 106, 111

Mickle, Gala, 123-124

Miller, Johnny, 206

Milliken, Roger, 124

Millwood, Bill, 258

Nader, Ralph, 195

Nicholson, Linda, 88

Piergiovanni, Bill, 317

Pujols, Albert, 293

Rather, Dan, 43

Reynolds, Chief Dan, 36, 111

Riddle, Denise, 307

Ridge, Tom, 44

Rollins, Shirlee, 307-308

Sagan, Carl, 252

Scott, Fred, 62, 65

Sherman, General Tecumseh, 47

Shi, Dr. David, 4, 5

Siddens, Dr. John, 229-231

Skinner, Rev. Jimmy, 283

Smith, Jean M., 101-103

Smith, Sen. Verne, 49

Snoddy, Dr. Warren, 30

Sondov, Lori, 135

Stewart, Buzzy, 73

Stewart, Martha, 157

Thurmond, Strom, 308

Tomkins, Al, 306

Tompkins, Scott, 209

Tompkins, Susan, 104

Truby, Dr. Roy, 1

Wall, Don, 287

Washington, George, 141

Waters, Marion, 256, 267

Welch, Nancy, 13, 20-21, 106, 111, 198-200, 272

Westmoreland, Ken, 308

White, Rev. Ray, 96

Williams, Theresa "Granny", 124-125, 137

Williams, Tommy, 38

Wilson, Larry, 6

Younts, Melvin, 3

About the Author

Leland E. Burch, Sr. grew up in Greer, South Carolina where he attended public schools, graduating from Greer High School in 1957.

After graduating from Wofford College in 1961, Burch married his high school sweetheart, Margaret Janice Griffin, and returned to his hometown to begin a lifelong career in journalism with the family's weekly newspaper, *The Greer Citizen*. The Burches are parents of four sons, Eddie, Joey, Preston and John David.

Since retiring as editor of *The Greer Citizen*, Burch has been compiling the best of his award-winning newspaper columns into a series of three books. The first, "Greer, the Center of the Universe," is devoted to Greer people, places, events and history, and was published in December 2013. The second book, "What Could Possibly Go Wrong," features a variety of topics as will the third book, scheduled for late 2015.

Active in community affairs, Burch has served as a Greenville-Spartanburg Airport Commissioner since 1985. He is an Elder in the First Presbyterian Church of Greer, past President of the Greer Lions Club, a founding board member of the Greer Heritage Museum, a director of the Greer Christian Learning Center, co-founder of The Greer Rose Society and past President of the South Carolina Rose Society.